THE NUDE BEACH

SOCIOLOGICAL OBSERVATIONS

series editor: JOHN M. JOHNSON, *Arizona State University*

"This new series seeks its inspiration primarily from its subject matter and the nature of its observational setting. It draws on all academic disciplines and a wide variety of theoretical and methodological perspectives. The series has a commitment to substantive problems and issues and favors research and analysis which seek to blend actual observations of human actions in daily life with broader theoretical, comparative, and historical perspectives. SOCIOLOGICAL OBSERVATIONS aims to use all of our available intellectual resources to better understand all facets of human experience and the nature of our society."

—John M. Johnson

Volumes in this series:

The Nude Beach

Jack D. Douglas
and Paul K. Rasmussen
with Carol Ann Flanagan

SAGE Publications   Beverly Hills / London

For information address:

SAGE PUBLICATIONS, INC.
275 South Beverly Drive
Beverly Hills, California 90212

SAGE PUBLICATIONS LTD
28 Banner Street
London EC1Y 8QE

Printed in the United States of America

Library of Congress Cataloging in Publication Data

Douglas, Jack D
    The nude beach.

    (Sociological observations ; 1)
    1. Nudism. 2. Beaches—California. I. Rasmussen,
Paul K., joint author. II. Flanagan, Carol Ann,
joint author. III. Title.
GV450.D6   301.5'7   77-22287
ISBN 0-8039-0813-X
ISBN 0-8039-0814-8 pbk.

FIRST PRINTING

Contents

Acknowledgments

This book is dedicated to the many up-front people who so willingly opened up about their lives on the beach—once they saw we were "into the scene," and to the few up-front straights who willingly helped us, but often without knowing we were part of the nude beachers. We also want to extend a special vote of thanks to some of our colleagues who went to considerable trouble to help us find out what was going on from all social perspectives on the nude beach. Steve Phillips and David Altheide were invaluable in helping us to determine what the police were into on the beach; Robert Gilmore in seeing how the beach nudity compared with more traditional forms of nudity; Kathy, Karla and Linda in seeing it from the standpoints of the novices and the never-to-be-initiated; and many others in getting at specialized parts of the whole complex picture, such as Charles Freeman in getting at the legal angle. We hope this depth-probe into one segment at our tumultuous American life has contributed to all of their understandings of themselves and their world and to everyone's understandings of where we're at and where we're headed. Maybe it will help us put it all together again.

THE VOICE OF EDEN BEACH

by Robert Garner

I am the nude beach
cliffs
pocked by the sea
rising up to touch
the blue sky

Surf crash
hot sunshine
unclothed people
pursuing happiness
experiencing liberty
enjoying life
wondering about the future

With Navy battleships on the horizon
loud reports
    exploding shells
ghostly silhouette
of the immoral sword

World of contrasts
where nudity is lewd
but armaments are proper
that which creates new life
is obscene
while that which destroys life
is sanctioned

And yet I go on
oblivious to man's twisted vision
lending my sand body
to the feet and torsos
of those who seek my harmony

A miraculous many colored wonder
I am a part of life
I soothe refugees from the
concrete plastic world above
I welcome you to join me
in the sun
before your time winds out
and you drift away
never having known the feel of flight
of those naked to the wind

Keep me open to choice
let me stay free
or else call God immoral
for having you born in nudity. . . .

(Printed with permission of author.)

Preface

To join the nude beach is to cross the great divide between the clothed-world of respectable civilization and the unknown. It is also normally a time of joyful excitement, confusion, shame and shaming, self-deceptions and lies.

That may sound overdramatic, perhaps slapdash. It is neither. It is a cautious, systematic conclusion about the experience of almost all people joining the nude beach or any other public nude scene. In fact, we have come to see it as the common experience of anyone taking the first small steps into the knowing violation of a basic social rule that has up to that point governed his or her behavior. The only people who do not feel and do those things when crossing the divide into nude living are those who have previously been into some form of very casual sex or group nudity (such as the people from our burgeoning sex industry).

The iron social rule against public nudity is one of the most basic, most important rules in our society. It is so important, so rigidly adhered to that, once it is learned at approximately the age of three, it is almost never spoken of again. (The age varies slightly from one Western society to another and from one social group to another within each society.)

What social rules are more important, more iron-clad and rigid? The rules against incest and murder are two, of course. But what else? Treason? I doubt it. I've known plenty of people who would shamelessly commit treason, if they knew anything worth giving to an enemy. Violence? I've seen a good bit of violence in our society. Theft? I've known lots of thieves. Though public nude displays occur in our society, they are quite rare. Before the nude beach, I do not remember seeing anyone nude in a public situation. Until recently, intentional public nudity has been seen in our society as an act of madness, extreme immorality, and criminality. That is a severe combination.

All of our Western societies have strong laws against most public genital nudity. (We should always remember that the human breast is a secondary sex object. It is not a genetically inherited sign triggering sex feelings or acts. Thus, it is much more subject to social variation.) But laws are only of peripheral importance in matters of passion, as they are almost entirely the product of the deep feelings of threat almost all members of our societies have felt from any *possible* revelation of a

9

nude body in a public situation—and, commonly, though to much less degree, in any private situation where others can see us.

The most important rules governing the display and hiding of the sex organs, of sexual acts, and, in our more repressive Northern European societies, of all other basic bodily functions, have grown spontaneously—that is, with almost no rational intention—out of our deepest feelings in concrete social situations over many centuries. As with almost everything else in our vastly complex human life, there have been significant social and individual variations in the feelings, the interpretations and uses of these rules over the centuries. But the range of these variations has not been great since the fourth to sixth century A.D., when the social catastrophe of Rome triggered the profound feelings of threat, anxiety, and dread that created the basic ambivalence of Western people toward worldly, physical behavior and desires.

Most of the foundation stones, the basic rules, of our society are spontaneous growths that are spontaneously ordered, all arising from our basic feelings in concrete situations. This is still true, though decreasingly so, in our age of big government. But, precisely because they are so basic, the spontaneous rules are largely out of sight and out of consciousness. It is a great tragedy of the social sciences, and a greater tragedy for all of us now affected by social laws built on the myths of social science theories, that these basic rules of social life have also been largely invisible to social scientists.

Social scientists, and especially sociologists, have come increasingly under the spell of the Rousseauian Myth of Rational Man, a belief that human beings are governed primarily, if not entirely, by conscious (symbolic) thought and rationally intended goals. For the past few decades, the sociology of deviance, or of conflicts over rules and rule violations, has been concerned primarily with rules (and consequent labels) which have been "rationally" legislated to govern other people's behavior. This has led them to focus on very recent kinds of social rules, such as those against marijuana use. Such rules are socially superficial. They come and go; they are subject to extremely wide variation in interpretations, uses, and effects; they are not widely shared and often are imposed by a power élite on a weaker minority or even a weaker majority; and they reveal little directly about the basic nature of human beings, human rules, human interaction, or any basic aspect of human society. They have occasionally turned their attention to what they call "social stigmas," but these are almost always *defined* as "symbolic discrepancies" of social selves and self-images, which eliminates all of the *basic* aspects of stigmas. But one only stigmatizes in situations that arouse feelings of profound threat. Symbols and most rational cognition are mere fripperies with which the threatened try to control the unknown.

Our study of the nude beach is, first of all, a search for the foundations of human life. This is a study of primal feelings and primal communications of those feelings—body signs that make up the universal body-code and that predate, underlie, and contextualize all language. We are obviously making a study of sexual feelings and signs in American society today, but that must never obscure the fact that this is always a study of the foundations of the individual and social life of human beings in the most general sense. Having discovered the primal feelings and signs involved, we try to show how these reveal the fundamental properties of human rules, the uses of those rules, their effects and relations to social orders. Of course, we do that only briefly throughout the work and at the end. We reserve much of that kind of analysis for other, more theoretical works (especially for *Creative Deviance and Social Change*, which I expect to publish soon). Here we are more concerned with descriptions of the basic phenomena—human bodies feeling, communicating, and acting on the nude beach.

Why would we choose to study the foundations of society on a nude beach? We did not choose to do so, nor, indeed, choose to have anything to do with the nude beach, at least initially. Our study of the nude beach has grown spontaneously, often threatening to overwhelm us. Almost all social research, including everything from sociology to journalism, is consciously chosen and planned in some way. Moreover, almost all social research has reasonably clear boundaries, a beginning and an end, spanning relatively brief periods, which are almost never more than a year. This research has none of those properties. Indeed, it is probably best not to call it research. I myself have looked at it almost entirely in the way Leonardo da Vinci looked at his "scientific work" (a term he would not use). This has been first and foremost raw (natural) experience, direct experience. Most thinking about the meaning of the experience has come after the experience, and all theoretical ideas about its significance have come years later.

My experience began over nine years ago when I went for a walk on the beach one day. At that time, the beach was only a short distance from where we lived, within easy walking and running distance. After about a half-hour, I came to some rocks at the foot of the 300-foot cliffs near the water's edge and cautiously crossed them. After several hundred yards of rocks, I made a slight turn and there was Eden Beach—beautiful, about 50 yards across at its widest, stretching as far as one could see, lying beneath the towering sandstone and clay cliffs. (The name is, like all other names in the book, a social fiction to protect privacy. It is a bit "corny," but it is primal.) There was almost no one on the beach, though about half a mile further on I came upon some surfers riding in on the blue-green Pacific breakers.

I started walking, and later running, on the beach almost every afternoon, and I have now done so almost every day, summer or winter. My afternoon trips along the beach had nothing to do with nudity, especially since it was quite some months before I noted any or thought about it. (I have little doubt that, had the choice been put to me in such a conscious and rationally manageable way, I would have refused to have anything to do with it. In fact, I had long had an excellent opportunity to study a nudist camp, which I believed would be of great sociological value, but refused to do so because I feared being labeled a "nudist creep.")

I do not remember the first nudes I saw at the beach. They were undoubtedly just skinny-dippers doing the kind of thing I had done at least once as a child. I know from succeeding years that they must have quickly covered themselves with towels, so that any passerby like me would not see their nudity, though it could be inferred from their actions. On such an extremely "lonely" beach, as Eden was in those days, this did not seem strange and, thus, made little impression.

The first clear memory I have of nudity in those early years of my beach experience was accompanied by a feeling of shock. I had become aware that at the far north end of the beach, just in front of some other rocks, were often a small number of young men in the tall grasses and bushes that grew near the cliffs. I no doubt suspected some were nude, but thought little of it. Then one day, as I walked along the water's edge, I looked toward the cliff and saw a young man standing in a statuesque pose on a low rock, and he was nude. Even in such an isolated place, it seemed shocking—tremendously different. Public nudity just is not part of our world, so when we first encounter it it comes like a lightning bolt. I also thought from his posing that he must be gay, which made it the more anomalous. (I would eventually come to call this pattern of behavior a "gay display," but at that time I had no words for it.)

Having been shocked into awareness of the realities of the situation, I became more observant of my surroundings in succeeding months. Being perceptually sensitized to the nudity, I saw more of it intermit-tently, though still infrequently. For the next few years I saw only an occasional gay nude, and a few skinny-dipping couples who made a dash for cover as soon as they spotted me. By 1970 or 1971, I realized that both types were becoming more common and seemed less furtive, more open to public view. Over these past seven years, the number has grown steadily, slowly at first and then very rapidly; and the nude beachers became more and more open, more and more public in their nudity. Today, a bright summer's day will entice as many as ten to twenty thousand people of all varieties to expose their bodies to the California sun—and to public view—on this beach alone.

The slow emergence of the nude scene before my sometimes startled eyes in the early years did not seem terribly significant. I did not care about the gay nudity and, as the nude women became more visible, I felt the "natural" pleasure and excitement of looking at them. It was only when I began to see small groups of nude people at the beach, a few of whom I knew from the nearby university at which I taught, that I began to see it as socially significant—something to think about and try to figure out, to determine and, perhaps eventually, explain what they were up to. Most importantly, though I did not realize it at the time, I had begun to wander, to drift, beyond the "natural" shame-enforced rule-bounds of clothed civilization. As I saw more of the nudity, it became more natural to me, though the nude women remained exciting. I still did not talk to anyone. (I tried to avoid the few people I recognized. A few times they waved, and I waved back and ran on.) I knew very well that this behavior was still highly illegal and socially stigmatized, and I must have suspected, without knowing very much about it, that it was some form of "indecent exposure," therefore a SEX CRIME. I had no desire to join "sex criminals" in prison, and I had seen the police at various times speeding by in a white van and suspected they were looking for nudes. But as the small groups began to coalesce into small public scenes of nude strangers (not more than twenty or thirty people), it did become tempting to go nude. Very importantly, at some unknown time, I began to feel vaguely uneasy about wearing a bathing suit when the nude people looked at me.

Then one morning in June 1972, I saw a small paragraph in the newspaper which announced that the State Supreme Court had unanimously overturned the conviction of a young man for indecent exposure on Eden Beach. I have a vivid memory of that, and I think it was then I first realized clearly that something important was happening. Very soon after that, I noticed the number of nudes was growing very rapidly—and the police were doing nothing. I felt more uneasy than ever at being clothed as I walked or ran past the nudes; and I was more tempted to join the nude scene. But I was very afraid of being shamed by being observed by students or faculty members who might come by and know me, though in those early years I could hardly admit this consciously.

Eventually I did what I now know a high percentage of beginners do, but which then seemed like a "discovery." I gently *eased into* the scene, one toe at a time, with abrupt jumps back and forth, like someone entering the cold Pacific. I started far from the other people—out of sight—and only slowly worked my way into public view over quite some time. And I watched intently for any possible shamer, staying away from situations in which I could not tell who might be looking at me. Some time during this painful but exciting process, I began to think of the value of trying to find out what was going on—what was this "revolution" all about? But it remained only a thought on the dim edges of consciousness until I was more comfortable in the scene. Then I thought more about it, and eventually asked Paul Rasmussen to join me in a study of the nude beach. He did so with seeming ease, though I later discovered that he had experienced the same inner fear and trembling. I later discovered Carol Ann Flanagan on the beach and quickly saw that she was a brazen "sociability gadfly," liked and trusted by most of the nude beachers. She was a *natural researcher* who had been into the scene for a few years, and we enticed her into joining our team.

A crucial and relatively unique aspect of our "research" into the nude beach scene was our decision at the beginning to "go native." We would immerse ourselves in the total nude scene and, only after thoroughly grasping the whole body experience the way any nonscientist is likely to do, would we resurface to think analytically about the whole thing. We wanted to feel the things others feel but do not talk about largely because they cannot. All of our experience up to that point, and far more since we became involved in the nude world, had convinced us that human experience is vastly more complex, more passionate, deeper than our conscious experience normally allows us to know and than our social science experience allows us to feel. If we approached the nude experience only with our minds, we would get only the surface, only the abstract symbols that people use to deal with strangers who do not have the common fund of *felt experience* to go on—and who may have to be lied to because they are aliens. We wanted the total experience so that we could use our minds, and above all the vast profusion of emotional and cognitive experience in the deeper layers of the human brain, to reveal the vast complexity of everyday emotions. Our study of the beach would be a depth-probe into the foundations of human life. We knew full well the dangers of bias in this approach. (I have previously dealt with the vastly complex research methods and issues in *Investigative Social Research*.) We shall see that we have discovered that some of those dangers came true—there were some important ways in which the deep emotions of real life experience led our bodies to deceive us, to suppress threatening emotions for years. But one of the most remarkable rewards of this approach was that our bodies relaxed those defenses as we stayed in the situation longer, so we could glimpse these vital parts of life at work in ourselves and, once we glimpsed them, begin to more fully understand how they operated and why.

An important part of this "going natural" was learning the body-code and the situated body language of the nude beach. The situated language, the subcultural dialect of a universal body-code, is being created slowly to deal with the scene as people come increasingly to grasp and understand it. Much of the communication on the beach, especially the most important kinds about sex, is done almost entirely in terms of the body-code—facial expressions, the way one walks, autonomic responses (from erections to quavering voices), and so on. But the people involved did have a lot of "casual verbal language" which they brought from the young or "hip" outside subworld when they created the nude beach scene. The more specific, more situational verbal language of the beach has emerged only slowly over the years.

One of the unusual aspects of this work—and one that many social scientists and students who are used to immediately translating natural experience into scientific terms (jargon) may find grating at first—is that we have tried to use this natural language as much as possible. The intention is not at all to be hip or casual, but to communicate as much as possible in terms of the emotional, meaning-laden words people on the beach *use*. The meanings of words, especially the all-important emotional meanings, are, like the foundations of society, a spontaneous growth of vast complexity and richness, partially embedded (situated) in the concrete experience in which they are created. We want to allow the ordinary reader to grasp their meaning without having the beach experience.

Another aspect that might be even more shocking to traditionalists who believe scientific truth is born of immaculate conception in the white purity of the lab is that *we* have created some of that language. We have used terms which are in common usage whenever possible, but we ourselves are part of the scene and we, like everyone else in this emerging situation, are constantly looking for word combinations that communicate our inner feelings and evanescent thoughts. When we use such words with other scene-members or they with us, people will accept or reject the words, generally very spontaneously and quickly, only to the degree that they *fit* and communicate their own experience (and to the degree they are willing to admit this publicly). Just as feelings are the ultimate wellsprings of our actions, so are they of words—words, especially those of the beach scene, communicate *feeling-idea complexes*. The words we have felt forced to create in writing this book in order to communicate the feelings and thoughts of the beach to outsiders (since we cannot show you by our body communications) are ones which we have tested on ourselves and other members— they fit even when they are not yet in common use, and so we are using them here. We have no fear that our words will "pollute" the things we are trying to study. We know from experience that the words are given meanings in terms of what our internal states are in such an emerging situation, and they are rejected to the extent they do not—or to the extent in some instances to which they reveal what people want to keep secret.

In the beginning of our depth-probe into the nude scene, we thought only of finding out what was going on in that scene itself. But over the years, especially these last few years (since I first wrote a totally descriptive account of our nude experience), I have come to see the beach as a scene in which primal feelings and body communications are more exposed than in most life—at least more exposed to us, after carefully analyzing it comparatively. Thus it is that the study grew on us, or happened to us, emerged around and within us, rather than being something we rationally intended and planned to do. And thus it is that it became a focus of our quest to determine the foundations of human life—of human nature in society.

Since I still run down to the beach for at least a few hours almost every day, the nude beach scene is still emerging around me, and my experience and understanding are still emerging, seemingly with increasing volatility and, I hope, creativity. It has already been of great importance in carrying me far beyond the normal confines of the social sciences and certainly beyond the normal confines of everyday (clothed) life. My journey into this unknown world of new experience has helped me to "suspend the natural attitude" of clothed life and, thus, to more easily plumb the depths of that life, to see it more starkly. I cannot yet decide in my own mind whether it has been worth it. I think of it in roughly the way I think of life itself—it exists; it's exciting; it has its own truth, beauty, and other joys in spite of all its problems and pains; and so we get on with it—painfully and joyfully. While I shall never be so presumptuous as to try to convince others that this journey is either "good" or "bad" in itself, I think many others will find it an interesting experience to read about and, hopefully, a source of greater truth about us all.

La Jolla, 1977   *Jack D. Douglas*

Note: *Although there are three authors credited on the title pages of this book, the major work in the writing was done by the senior author, Jack D. Douglas. Therefore, when the language is first-person singular, "I," it can be taken to refer to Douglas. When the language is first-person plural, "we," it can be taken to refer to Douglas and one of the two coauthors.*

1

The Emergence
of the Bareass Beach

We first met Janine on a beautiful summer morning as she waded in the shallow water at Eden Beach. It was early, and the sun's rays had just streamed across the tall cliffs, lighting up the foam on the breakers. Janine was nude except for an unbuttoned navy-surplus shirt for warding off some of the chill. Her delicate facial bones, pinned-up hair and granny glasses made her look like an elementary school librarian, but one with a "sexy all-over tan." Her appearance inspired us to say, "Hey, you've gotta be a student!" She laughed and said, "Not any more! I graduated from UC last year." She was one of the regulars on the beach and really into the nude scene, working nights in a local Mexican restaurant as a waitress to make enough to stay alive. Her days were free so she could do her own thing, which often meant coming down to the nude beach to lie in the sun, read, ride the waves, and meet new people. She was really "up-front" and loved the nude scene, so she relished the chance to talk with us abut it. She would go on for hours about what she was into and what she thought everyone else was into:

"Yeah, I'd heard a lot about the nude beach before I came down to try it myself. A lot of my friends said they'd been down . . . . It sounded super-neat. It sounded like one of those things I'd like to try, you know, and see what it's like. And the thought of getting a sexy all-over tan really appealed to me—you know, I thought how it'd really turn a guy on when we got in bed . . . . I don't know why, but it's *really* sexy. . . .

"I wasn't up to going alone, so I got this girl friend of mine to go with me. She'd been before and was glad to go again. Well, we came down the steep road and as soon as we got to the beach my friend started stripping off her clothes—she just took 'em all off and carried them in her hand. Wow . . . . She seemed really cool about being nude. I think I kept my cool outside, but inside I was really up-tight. People had told me it was legal and all, and there were a lot of people running around nude, but I could hardly believe I wouldn't get arrested if I took my clothes off in public like that—right on a beach! I just kept looking over my shoulder.

"The only time I'd ever seen a guy nude on a beach before was when I was a freshman. I was walking along this lonely beach when a surfer came out of the water—and I was really shocked to see he was completely nude . . . so I just turned my head and looked at the cliffs. And now here were all these nude guys on the beach— most of the nudes were guys. There were very few nude women right then and I didn't know what to make of it . . . so as we walked along I kept my bikini on, but there was my girl friend just looking at all the nude guys real casually.

"We found a spot away from all the people where we could sunbathe. Then I took off my top, but left my bikini bottom on. It was during my period and I was kind of embarassed, I guess. My friend started reading her book and I did some embroidery. All the time we were looking around at the nude people and soaking up the hot sun. I was feeling more cool, but was still up-tight about the whole thing. Then these three Chicano guys came walking along the beach, all with their bathing suits on.

"One of the guys came right up to us, looking down at us, and said, 'Hey, do either of you girls want to fuck?' Wow! That blew my mind. All I could say was 'No.' But my friend just said really casually, 'Not today.' Well, the guys left and that was it, but I was awfully glad my friend was with me. And then she turned to me and said, 'Hmm, they were kind of cute. Maybe we should have said yes.'

"The three guys kind of blew my mind all right, but it didn't last for long and nothing else like that happened. By the end of the day I was beginning to feel more casual about the nude thing. I was beginning to see it's a really beautiful and mellow scene. It's really sexy, no matter what people tell you, and I don't think anyone would bother to come down here if they didn't really

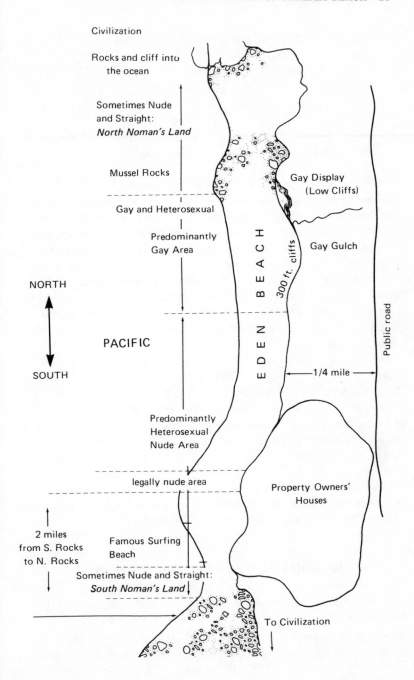

enjoy seeing others' bodies and showing their own body. I've met some guys here that I really liked and sometimes we'd get it on together after we left. This one guy, Matt, is still a good friend, and I keep seeing him down here—he's always picking up on some cute chick—he's just super-horny! Not everybody's that nice. Sure, there are bound to be some creeps running around, but that doesn't bother me, generally . . . that's their thing. But it's also really beautiful. The nude beach is a cool scene."

Janine is one of many thousands of Californians who now flock every warm, sunny day, summer or winter, to the growing number of nude beaches stretching between San Diego and San Francisco, or beyond. Though they don't think of themselves as such, they are the spearhead of one of America's fastest-growing social movements—that of body and sexual freedom. It's a complex social movement, one with many cross-currents, and one that has already generated counter-revolutionary movements, but it has been gaining strength all over the country for more than a decade. Its future is necessarily uncertain, but its importance to contemporary society and to our knowledge of human nature *in* society is already clear.

The 1960s and 1970s have been decades of great change in American society. From the riots of the 1960s to the Watergate scandals of the 1970s, our way of life seems to have been challenged by one "revolt" or "counter-revolt" after another. We have been confronted repeatedly with new visions of the "good life," from drugs to women's liberation. Most of us have felt liberated by some of these and threatened by others. Whichever we feel, few of us would doubt that our lives have been changed by these new ways of life. One of the most basic changes—and certainly one which has aroused the deepest feelings of liberation and anxiety, joy and dread, often within the same people—has been the explosion of body and sexual freedom.

THE BODY AND SEX IN CIVILIZATION

Unfortunately, there do not seem to be any historical works on the freedom or constraint of the human body in general, presumably because in our civilization there has been so little freedom and such obvious constraint that it did not occur to historians to study them. There is, however, a vast literature on clothing, especially on fashion, and a valuable, if limited, literature on the history of morality in civilization. Both reveal a simple picture concerning body freedom throughout the history of civilization.

Nudity is, of course, reasonably common among noncivilized people in warm climates, though even there a great majority of cultures prescribe some forms of clothing. Most have moderately strong norms against exposing the genitals in public situations, though one of the most frequent exceptions is in bathing or swimming. But all civilizations have been clothed cultures. In fact, the general arguments of historians, especially those of two of the experts in this field, Haesaert and Elias, have been that civilizations have become more and more moralistic in the suppression of such "primitive" or "animalistic" forms of behavior as nudity or sex in public.

Public nudity in certain situations was reasonably widespread, at least among the upper classes (about whom we have good information) in Greece and Rome (for details and theory relating to the background and theoretical perspective of this study, see the Appendix). But the intense asceticism of Christianity by the fourth and fifth centuries led over the centuries to an almost complete ban of nudity and sex from public life. As W.E.H. Lecky has pointed out in *History of Western Morals*, "In the latter days of the Pagan Empire some measures were taken to repress the profligacy that was so prevalent . . . . A practice of men and women bathing together was condemned by Hadrian, and afterward by Alexander Severus, but was only finally suppressed by Constantine." (Constantine was the emperor who made Christianity the official religion of the Empire.) This was true more among the upper than the lower classes, because they were more directly affected (and watched) by the ascetic clergy than were the "earthier" peasants or, centuries later, the more "debauched" urban craftsmen. The rising prosperity and courtly leisure of the feudal classes in the medieval period led by the twelfth century to an increase in the erotic arts of the troubadours and in the sexual fashions of the gentlemen and ladies of the courts, especially in Southern France. There were, for a brief period, extreme "plunges" in the female neckline and evidence of some limited nudity in baths (probably rather restricted to private groups of friends).

Some historians and analysts of love and sex in the Western World, such as Denis de Rougemont, have argued that we have had a demi-monde, or largely hidden, subculture of ("bohemian") erotic arts and wiles in the Western World since that time. But, of course, the amount of body and sex freedom has varied greatly from one place to another and from one time to another.

A brilliant general theory of fashion and style has been developed by Rene König out of this mass of evidence. Drawing on the earlier work of psychoanalysts, especially of Edmund Burgler and J. C. Flügel, he has been able to show why clothes have been such an important part of human life, especially in civilizations. We know from the nudity of noncivilized peoples, who share the same general genetic inheritance we do, that there is no genetic—and, thus, no human nature—basis for "sexual modesty"—or that feeling of shame about exposing the parts of the body defined as sexual. Rather, even the experience of modesty is vastly variable from one culture to another. Modesty does seem to exist in all societies, but the forms and degrees are extremely variable. Nude societies have feelings of shame only about certain forms of body displays in public situations. (We shall deal with this later, especially in discussing the leg positions of women on the nude beach.) Some civilizations train women to feel shame at exposing their faces (Arabian), others their toes (Chinese), while Western civilization has allowed women to fully expose their faces in public, but often not their toes. (Again, of course, the poor had more latitude, especially when they had no shoes.)

But there seem to be at least two basic fashion "reasons" why clothes were adopted and vastly elaborated very early in all civilizations. All civilizations were born in ferocious struggles by military leaders to dominate other people. Dominance, a much more general motive than Adler's "power drive," but including it as one of the most important parts, is a basic (genetic) part of human nature, just as it is in all primates and most higher animals. One of the most basic things clothes do is symbolize dominance and submission relations. Though I doubt there is sufficient evidence available to be sure, we must suspect that the early conquerors always used clothes in public situations where inferiors were present and dominance had to be shown by *clothes-displays*. Indeed, there were probably "sumptuary laws" (laws against luxurious living), which forbade the inferiors, especially slaves, to make clothes-displays. In any event, clothes' crucial property is that they are not initially cover-ups, or something intended to end one's shame (in the Adam and Eve sense), but are the exact opposite—displays of dominance, which is a display of sexual power and desirability, since dominance is also a vital social aphrodisiac and provider of access to sex for the male clothes-displayers. Indeed, clothes initially may not have covered genitalia very well—and are often used to accentuate genital power by exaggerating size, as in the well-known codpiece of Renaissance Europe. There is an even better reason why clothes would be developed to cover the genitals.

One of the basic rules of thumb of the pornography industry in America today, and probably of all porn-industrialists of all ages, is that lust (eroticism) is titillated (triggered and heightened) by partially revealing and partially concealing sexual organs at the same time. Clothes produce a perceptual and consummatory ambivalence—you see it and you don't. (As we shall argue later, this rule must be slightly modified to take into account that when people have not often seen other nude bodies, or sex organs, their initial exposure can be extremely exciting.) Even when the body is fully exposed, a slow (teasing) unveiling of it in little steps is the most titillating—hence, the long success of striptease.

The unknown titillates and focuses the attention of the human animal (and of all primates and, though to a much lesser degree, of most animals). It arouses us in and of itself—hence, the excitement of secrecy and of all secret knowledge—the power of gossip and the allure of investigative social research—the power of curiosity! (All highly motivated social researchers are probably best described as *research voyeurs*.) This is one good reason why any hint of the great unknown, God, is so exciting, even in a sexual way; and why all religious cults guard the secrecy of their knowledge, frequently hiding it in an inner sanctum. It can also explain why modern social scientists short on real knowledge always hide their ignorance in the power of obscurantistic jargon. Everyone, especially those who are too frightened by repressive inhibitions to give in to the desire, is by nature a voyeur of whatever is new—especially of the powerful and beautiful human body that has been covered for millenia. Modern Western peoples are the world's most total sexual voyeurs, as we can see in the veritable explosion of erotic films—and nude beaches—both because they are still ambivalent about sex, which titillates the lust, and because they have been titillated by millenia of clothes which only hinted at genitalia-secrets.

This seems to be the basic motive for clothes and for variations in clothes—that is, the search for something that will further titillate once we have been habituated to a given fashion. (Everything that is new eventually becomes old, sometimes even boring, and we must find *new* newness to arouse attention and excitement.) This, in itself, especially in conjunction with the other aspects of fashion (which need not concern us here), would have been enough to lead to the vast elaboration of clothes we see in the history of civilization. We can even see that the need for fresh titillation would lead to partial clothes-displays by the lower-class groups because they would want to catch up symbolically and sexually with the higher classes, as Herbert Spencer and Georg Simmel long ago argued.

But this motive would not have led to the degree of clothes-repression of nudity, the cover-up that "hides our shame," which we see in all civilizations, especially in our body-repressing Western civilization. Here I think we have to invoke the explanation I explore in greater length in the Appendix—the threats experienced at certain times by civilized man, especially because of ferocious military struggles that have always been part of civilization, and also because of the steady work necessary for our earlier, poorer civilization. These two factors have produced an other-worldly orientation in all the great religions of civilization and a concomitant stigmatization of the worldly (natural) functions of the body. In turning to religion to survive the chaos of empires rising and falling, Western man tried to please God by magical ceremonies and the purification ritual of sacrifice of his own beloved body instincts.

The Western World seemed to be coming out of its repressive shell from the twelfth century to the beginning of the sixteenth century in Italy (the seventeenth century in England and most of Northern Europe). During the Renaissance in Italy in the fifteenth century, there was an almost steady growth in body and sex freedom. As with all eras of transition, including our own, which is far more revolutionary, it was a time of immense ambivalence, of profound feelings in conflict, driving individuals from one extreme to the other, from soaring optimism to the deepest depressions. The vast creativity and productivity of the era surely sprang from the unstable balancing of opposites involved. Anyone who looked only at the most secularized—and, thus, sexualized and body-freed—parts of Italy in 1490, would have thought it would become a totally secularized society with vast body and sexual freedom. But that kind of simple projection into the future never works. As Pitirim A. Sorokin argued long ago, there is always a *principle of limits* at work in human society. Trends go only so far and then are changed or reversed, at least temporarily. This is most especially true wherever there is ambivalence at work. And the Italians did indeed swing back from total worldliness to total repression—and one of the first things they did was to cover bodies, even those in paintings. It has only been in the last 50 to 100 years that we have slowly been working our way once again back into public displays of the body, first through a vast profusion of fashionable clothes-displays at all levels of society and, more recently, through actual sex and body-displays in some limited public situations.

THE BEGINNINGS OF AMERICA'S
NUDE "REVOLUTION"

No modern Western nation has been more Puritanical than America in its public attitudes toward the human body and sex. As early as seventeenth-century colonial America, there were a few recorded instances in Quaker communities, of so-called "insane" people who used nudity as an attack on the community. Court records from Essex County, Massachusetts, show how the community counter-attacked against this "unnatural" behavior: "The wife of Robert Wilson, for her barbarous and inhuman going naked through the town, is sentenced to be tied at a cart's tail with her body naked downward to her waist, and whipped from Mr. Gidney's gate till she come to her own house, not exceeding thirty stripes." Even 40 years ago, women commonly wore bathing suits that covered everything from their shoulders down to their knees. The indiscreet public revelation of a dimpled knee was commonly seen as shocking, and the "flapper" bathing suits of the 1920s, which still covered the thighs, were seen as erotic and scandalous. Fifteen years ago, the maxi-bikini, which gave a woman a lot more camouflage than today's band-aid bikinis, aroused widespread sexual anxiety and prurient hopes on America's beaches. Only a few years ago air-brushed nudity was the order of the day in popular men's magazines like *Playboy*. And it is still the custom among most American women to shave any errant hairs on their thighs or stomachs.

Little wonder, then, that nudists have always been highly stigmatized in America. In contrast, Europeans, especially Southern Europeans, have been more relaxed. Americans are often perplexed and sometimes shocked by the Southern European's relatively more relaxed attitude toward the natural necessities of the body. A sociological colleague, who frequently spent periods living in politically repressive Spain, happened to say something at home about the authoritarian use of repression to make people obey the strict rules of the government. His son, who knew little about politics but much about everyday life in the streets of America and Spain, was perplexed and asked, "They're really repressive, huh? Then how come people pee in the streets?" Such body-function freedom is not generally associated with much body-display freedom and is in some degree a social response to urgent body demands in the absence of public toilets. But Americans are once in a while shocked that even in affluent parts of Paris men are using partly screened "pissoirs" in the middle of the sidewalk.

In France and Yugoslavia, nudism has existed for years in a few public vacation resorts, like St. Tropez. Few Frenchmen consider their

fellow countrymen to be "weirdos" and "perverts" because they sometimes prefer to sunbathe, gamble, or dine in their natural state. And
even fewer consider the more widespread toplessness on the beaches to
be a sure sign of immorality and cultural decadence. But in America,
social or public nudism has been kept beyond the pale of civilized
society. Civil order has been defended against the "naked ape" by
pushing nudists into remote corners of the mountains or the isolated
canyons of California and surrounding them with peek-proof fences.
These nudist camps are so remote that most Americans have never seen
one, and many literate adults probably don't even know they exist. In
fact, in spite of our years of involvement in the nude beaches, we
ourselves have never even seen one of those tall fences that guard our
sensibilities.

Most Americans continue to view public nudity as weird, creepy,
incomprehensible, senseless, and immoral—stigmatized. As a colleague's
wife said when he tried unsuccessfully to get her to go to a camp to
help him with a study of nudism, "I just can't understand why anyone
would want to run around naked in front of a bunch of other people."
Because of this incomprehensibility, and because we link sex and public
nudity together in all situations involving both men and women, except
perhaps medical examinations, we tend to think of nudists as somehow
sexually perverted. If they are no longer seen by educated people as
leering sex maniacs, they are at least seen as "kinky" exhibitionists with
whom few respectable people care to publicly associate. Our colleague
studying nudism found that some people still literally shrink from
association with nudism. While helping at a state fair to pass out some
pamphlets extolling the healthfulness of all-over sunbathing, he found
that some people looked shocked when they realized what they had in
their hands and rushed to thrust the pamphlets back upon him. He
knew by the looks some gave him that he had suddenly changed into a
"creep." It's easy to see why our traditional nudists are generally
people with a certain religious fervor about "the movement" and why
they continue to put out implausible public relations manifestos asserting that sexual feelings normally aroused by sight of the nude body are
somehow extinguished in the bright sunshine of the "health camps."

Given this background of the social repression of public nudity, the
explosion of nudity in magazines, in movies, and on the stage struck in
the 1960s like a revolution. The stage musical "Hair," with its vibrantly
publicized nude scenes, was seen by many as a cultural apocalypse. In a
few short years, the revolution has made nude bodies, including some
bodies engaged in sex acts, a reasonably common sight in staged and
photographed events. Like political revolutions, this one generated

intense controversy on all sides, from exhaltation to screams of agony, from demands for total freedom to demands for total repression. And yet these feelings and this controversy have centered on framed nudity and framed sex—nudity and sex which are not as real as live bodies. These bodies are merely cellulose images on a screen or a sheet of paper, though they may certainly trigger erotic excitement. In those few instances in which nude bodies are real, they are generally carefully removed from the touch of the audience by stages or go-go cages, and only the self-deluded see those real bodies as inspired by genuine sexual feelings. What most people consider to be a nude revolution has really been a revolution in celluloid images, in posed pictures and make-believe—a plastic revolution. These images and the controversies over "porn" swirling about them are important in some ways. Certainly they have served as a psychic wedge to pry open our repression of the human body. But they must be seen for what they are—largely plastic images and battles over make-believe.

America's real nude revolution, if there is such a thing, is happening on the beaches, where real nude bodies are doing real-life things. It is on the beaches that for the first time Americans are displaying their bodies in massive numbers in public situations.

California is the center of this social movement, but, as in so many other things, it already seems to have set the pattern which other areas are following, especially the beaches of Cape Cod, in Massachusetts. In the past several years, more and more Californians have been baring themselves all-over to the golden sun on what were first popularly called Bareass Beaches. The process began long ago with small groups on isolated beaches who were willing to brave the terror of civiliza-tion's law and the impact of social stigmatization for "indecent expo-sure." But in recent years, beach nudity has been progressively accepted and even provisionally legalized in a few places like Eden Beach. On a sunny weekend day, many thousands of nude beachers swarm on the shores and play in the waves from San Diego to San Francisco. This is the real challenge to our traditional feelings about public nudity and the sex associated with it. The challenge has been met by a serious counter-attack from those who feel threatened by live nude bodies. As the public has become more aware of what was happening, the inevi-table political controversy has progressively polarized people into those who see the nude beaches as mass orgies and those who see them as the fulfillment of a dream of the free and "natural life." We shall see much of these political conflicts in this book, but, unlike the stark simplicity of the nude body, the realities of the nude beaches are more complex and less obvious than the conflicting partisans seem to think.

SKINNY-DIPPING AND OPEN-AIR SEX

Skinny-dipping has been traditional for farm boys from frontier days to the present. However much they might present it as simply a matter of practical necessity because they didn't have bathing suits and didn't want to get their clothes wet, jumping into the old mud hole was also an adventure because of its sense of body freedom and its naughty aspect, the public nudity. It was also something done almost entirely by boys, only in the presence of other boys who were friends, and commonly only with co-conspirators who could be trusted not to tell your parents or the preacher. Those who were discovered were apt to be denounced by the local moralists, such as the author of an item in the Santa Barbara *New Press* of 1873: "Bitter complaints still reach us regarding the disgraceful conduct of the fellows and boys who congregate about the Bennett Bath Houses. It is a shame and a disgrace that such hoodlums disport in the waves or recline on the sand arrayed in nature's costume." This form of surreptitious nudity, skinny-dipping, became a widespread pleasure in recent decades.

While there are no facts on how many people have been involved, it's obvious from personal accounts that most people have gone skinny-dipping at some time in their lives. It's also obvious that a large percentage of adults have made love under the stars at some time. Lots of people simply make love in the back yard on a summer evening after the kids have gone to sleep. Others seek out a lonely mountain path by a stream, but even more find the beaches an especially beautiful and romantic place. They find a sense of freedom and beauty in the sound of the waves, the smell of the salt, the feel of the soft sand under their bodies, and the feeling of the breeze on their bare flesh.

Some people seek isolated beaches for their love-making. But this often involves an arduous trek that is inconsistent with the spontaneous feelings and immediate needs of lovers, so most people simply use the public beaches. As any California policeman who's worked the beach patrol can tell you, the most crowded urban beach by day becomes a lovers' haunt by night. One of the regulars on the beach described earlier experiences on straight beaches:

"My wife and I love the ocean and the beach, so it seems natural, and really beautiful, to make love there. You just feel freer, more excited, more intimate, I guess. The first time we did it was down South on the East Coast, maybe ten years ago. We were at a beach where there weren't many people that day. We made love in the water first. The ocean there is so warm, not like the Pacific.

It's not real easy, but it's exciting because it's so different . . . and that was in the sunshine. We also made love under some pine trees by the water. We've made love on several of the beaches at night in San Diego . . . . The time I remember most was on Coronado. It was a big public beach, with a lot of people in the daytime and even at night there were a few people walking around on the beach, and there were lights not far back on the street. There were even all these navy planes that went right over us to land at the navy base . . . they made a hell of a noise and you had to watch for people every now and then . . . but there are some small sand dunes . . . and hardly anyone would come near if they saw someone lying on the beach . . . almost everyone knows that people like to make love on the beach and no one except cops wants to bother people. It'd be even better if you didn't have to watch for the cops, or someone stumbling over you . . . but it's still a beautiful thing."

Tod told me of his adventures on the clothed beaches in earlier days:

"I've knocked off several pieces of ass down on the [clothed] beach. These mini-orgies generally turn out to be really beautiful, I guess, because there are none of the hangups that frustrate sexual relationships with people you know better. It's a one night stand, you'll never see each other again, so all you have to worry about is the here and now. It's super-casual. I guess one of the nicest times I had was with this girl Joanie. She was a lovely nineteen-year-old blond visiting the beach from Utah. I've seen a lot of flesh in my life, but she was one of the greatest. There wasn't a bulge or an ounce of flesh that didn't belong. We met on one of those hot summer days down on the beach where the bodies are stacked basting in the warm summer sun. We sat on the sea-wall and talked about all sorts of things for at least two hours and then arranged to meet that night back down on the beach. I don't know exactly what turned her on, possibly the romantic fantasy of making it with a West Coast surfer or simply the mystique of the 'all together' Californian. Whatever, I was glad to fill the bill. Our timing was just right. She seemed to know just what turned me on and I also seemed to do just the right things. We spent the whole night rapping and making love until the sun rose, then each of us went our own ways. No games, no hang-ups, no worries. Real casual, man. If love-making could always be that good, there'd be a lot more of it."

Private nude bathing and love in the open air form the background for the development of nude beaches. The motivations, at least in the beginning, are much the same. Freedom, the sense of naturalness, of being one with nature, of being open, of a tingling feeling of skin caressed by the air, of romance, of natural beauty, of a certain delightful sense of naughtiness and abandon. All of these and, no doubt, other feelings lead individuals to seek out isolated forests and beaches for private acts. They are also found as an almost constant background motivation of the nude beachers. In this limited sense, the nude beaches are simply an extension of a long-developing trend toward private acts of skinny-dipping and making love under the open skies. But it would be a complete mistake to conclude that nude beaches are *simply* an extension or expansion of these private acts.

Anyone who has ever *joined up* at a nude beach—that is, taken his suit off in front of a sexually mixed crowd of *strangers*—knows there's a big difference between furtive private acts and that act of public exposure. As we shall see in more detail later, all reliable accounts indicate that most people experience tumultuous and often conflicting emotions at the point of taking their clothes off in public for the first time. Even those who think of themselves as uninhibited and liberated feel some of the weight of those "centuries of repression" as they reach that moment of commitment. This has always been true even in nudist camps, which are closed off from the smirking of the voyeurs and where there are no realistic fears of the law. As one nudist described his first experience,

"We went out, found the place, drove in, parked and walked across the lawn and up to the pool. Now this was a Wednesday afternoon . . . probably about June. School was out, there were . . . eight women around the pool playing cards and there were a whole bunch of kids in the pool swimming. They were the children of the women playing cards around the pool. We walked over and shook hands with a guy, and he asked us if we'd like to stay a while and go for a swim.

"Well, we said, 'What do we do with our clothes?' He said, 'Just leave them in the car.' We walked back across the lawn . . . it seemed like four miles . . . and we yawned and stretched and took off our clothes. It must have taken us fifteen or twenty minutes to get undressed . . . and it seemed like 400 miles back across that lawn. This was the first time ever in public that I'd taken off my clothes in the company of women and children. I'd been involved in my particular type of sex orgies as a teenager with maybe two couples—one in the front seat, one in the back seat—but this was really a new experience for me. I got up on the diving board and did a gainer. I landed on my stomach and splashed water all over the card game."

The secret panic reaction so often felt by the initiate is well understood by nudists. They sometimes even play upon it in practical jokes. A sociologist, Robert Gilmore, studying a nudist camp in San Diego was congratulating himself on how well he'd handled these emotional problems his first day when, about to head back to civilization, he discovered that the camper in which he'd left all his clothes, with his keys in them, was locked. His immediate sense of panic reminded him of the delicate position of public nudity in our society.

That sense of crossing the great divide is even more common and intense on the beach, where there are often many smirking voyeurs, where the legal situation is often felt to be precarious, and where one cannot be sure whether his co-workers will hear of his new "perversion." Given these great differences between surreptitious acts of private nudity and the public commitment of the nude beach, it is little wonder that our bareass beaches emerged slowly and in small stages over the years. That they emerged at all is testimony to the strong motives involved and the creative, deviant courage of some people, since all the original nude beachers faced the grave danger of arrest for "indecent exposure."

THE NUDE SCENE AND WILDCAT BEACHES

All of California's nude beaches started out as favorite haunts of skinny-dippers and open sky lovers. Though to greatly varying degrees, all are "isolated" beaches—that is, beaches that are in some way less accessible to the general public than are the normal public beaches. This isolation was crucial in the beginning because of the danger of arrest. Indecent exposure in California is to this day a very serious offense, a "sex crime" (under Penal Code Section no. 314). A first offense normally led only to a period of probation and maybe a fine, but as of 1969 mere arrest, *before* conviction, led to mandatory filing as a sex offender of one's description and fingerprints with the State Bureau of Criminal Identification and Investigation (Penal Code Section no. 11112). If convicted, the criminal was required (by Penal Code Section no. 290) to register as a sex offender with the chief of police of his city and to file with him fingerprints, photographs, and other personal information. Thereafter, the sex criminal is required to register any change of address with the police chief for his entire life, unless a court releases him from this penalty. Conviction for a second offense was punishable by not less than one year in prison and subsequent convictions sometimes led to imprisonment for life. Few people realized how serious their nude bathing could be, but everyone knew that the police could and did arrest people for it. Many people were aware that the charge could be "indecent exposure" and that this would stigmatize one as a sex criminal for the rest of his life. This is certainly why one almost never hears of anyone going nude at one of the big public beaches, at least in the daytime. We've been to beaches thousands of times all over the country and have never seen anyone nude on beaches used by the general public.

But many of the beautiful beaches that stretch the length of California are reasonably isolated and uninhabited. Sometimes they are isolated only by their distance from population centers or by the social customs that lead most people to other beaches. But they are often cut off from civilization by rocks that are difficult to cross, especially to those with tender feet or weak legs, and by golden cliffs that can be several hundred feet high and that have been carved sheer by eons of wind and pounding waves. The access routes to some of these beaches can be treacherous, especially at high tide. I've seen many injuries suffered by people trying to get to Eden Beach—two broken backs, a broken shoulder and concussion, a broken leg, a broken ankle, and numerous lesser ones. Over the years, I myself have suffered numerous shin wounds from underwater rocks, a bad shin splint from jumping off a rock to avoid big waves, and many scrapes and bruises from sliding on slippery rocks or sheer trails. The first time we visited Cliff Beach, which is a small cove below some precipitous cliffs near San Diego, I lost my glasses when a giant wave hit me in the face as I was trying to crawl along a narrow ledge at the base of the cliffs. (As one old man viewing Eden from the 300-foot cliffs above put it, "Some people will go to any extremes to get their pants off.") Because of these access problems, until they officially went nude, these isolated beaches were normally used only by diehards willing to make an arduous journey across the rocks or the sometimes dangerous descent down the cliffs, by hearty surfers who will go anywhere to find the perfect wave, and by those in search of the pleasures of skinny-dipping.

For many years, anyone strolling along one of these isolated beaches might suddenly come across a lone nude bather or maybe a couple. They would almost always dash into the water, put a towel over themselves, or hide behind a sand dune. They knew that anyone seeing them might lodge a complaint with the police, and they were generally aware that even isolated beaches are commonly patrolled by the city or county police, sometimes with special vans. For these reasons, skinny-dippers generally chose spots where they could see strangers or the police coming from a long distance away. This made beaches like Eden ideal for surreptitious nudity. It is a long beach with difficult access at either end. Nude bathers would stay away from the entrances and keep a lookout for the police. If they saw them coming, they would quickly put on their suits, which they kept handy for such emergencies. One nude beacher at Eden reported having been skinny-dipping there for thirty years before it became a legal nude beach and taking precautions against the especially vigilant police force by carrying around a skin-colored bathing suit. If they said they'd spotted him nude from the cliffs two hundred feet above, he could then argue that he was wearing the suit the whole time. Skinny-dippers also sometimes wore caps and sunglasses which they could discard before the police arrived, thus preventing the police from photographing or identifying them in the nude from the cliffs above.

Until several years ago, skinny-dipping was relatively infrequent even on most of these isolated beaches. However, for many years, several beaches have been the sites of the progressive development of *nude scenes*. Nude scenes are distinct from skinny-dipping or open-sky sex in that they are socially recognized patterns of *public nude behavior* that occur in specific places. These places are commonly the subject of myths in their local area, of "big yarns" about sex orgies or "homo-sexual musclemen flashing their nude bodies in the sun," or hushed or joking comments by high school students. But there has generally been some truth to them, at least to the extent that there were a relatively few people who went to the same place to do nude sunbathing, swimming, or furtive sexual cruising.

Nude scenes have not been restricted to the beaches. In fact, some of the most developed early scenes were in forests or mountains, especially in those few areas where there are hot springs for bathing and sunning. For example, one of the most beautiful nude scenes developed at a hot springs in the mountains of central California. The hot springs themselves have been the site of some mixed nude bathing at night, but the main nude scene developed a short distance along the stream. Here, on a warm summer's day, one can now see as many as fifty people, mainly couples, sunning on the surrounding rocks and bathing nude in the pools of warm water. The same thing has been reported about hot springs in some of the forest preserves and in isolated canyons. (One of the biggest nonbeach nude scenes is in the hills near Santa Barbara.) These nude scenes, however, seem to have developed later than those on the beaches and none has become very large. They seem to have been largely a product of the hippie interest in nudity and the development of communes in the forests of California in the late 1960s.

The beach nude scenes all began as *wildcat beaches*. That is, all of them were started by people knowingly taking big risks with their social respectability and freedom. (That is, they were originally all illegal nude scenes.) While there are no very reliable records or memories of their earliest days, it is most likely that male homosexuals ("gays") were the most active group in trying to "liberate" the beaches from clothes and from the traditional laws. The gay males are still a very active group on all the beaches that have been liberated. Moreover, they are still trying to liberate new beaches. Today wildcat beaches are springing up all over the state and wherever they do you can generally count on finding a lot of gays involved. A gay doctor told us about one of the most remarkable of these recent gay wildcat beaches. We found it remarkable because it sprang up in a highly urban setting, right near an international airport, and because it illustrates the great risks the gays will take in their attempts to liberate a new beach.

"The one by the airport is strictly illegal, but again I presume that the police let it go on at one time . . . . They just call it bareass beach. I stumbled upon it accidentally driving by. I was looking for an isolated area and that was when I first came out here. I saw a couple of guys swimming nude and figured that it· was O.K. There must have been as many people there as there are at [a well-known nude area] on a warm day and all nude. But that was in 1970 and since then they've put in a parking lot. They bulldozed out a lot of the sand dunes and the guards came by and if they saw someone nude they would just say, 'Get your trunks on.' Then one day there were four of us swimming nude. One of them was this guy that was a professional dancer and he had known the area for a long time. We were swimming out in the waves. It wasn't that crowded. There was only this young kid and he had just taken his trunks off, and I saw this cop put handcuffs on him right there on the beach. He walked down to the water's edge where we were swimming and so we just went out there further, knowing that he wouldn't shoot at us and that he wasn't going to get himself wet. We always carry our trunks with us wrapped around our necks. We didn't want to get arrested . . .

but they hauled him off. Don't know what they did to him. Usually you just end up paying a fine."

The gays had created and maintained partially liberated beachheads at places like Eden at least a quarter-century before they were much used by other nude bathers. There were also some organized groups involved in the early attempts to liberate the beaches. The sexual freedom league near San Francisco was crucial in liberating Northern beaches, and traditional nudists were very active at some Southern nude beaches.

But these three early groups had only limited impacts on the liberation of the beaches. By themselves, they would never have produced the nude population explosion that has occurred. Moreover, none of them directly contributed much to the *nude beach ethos* that is dominant in the public statements of the nude beachers (though we shall see that this ethos is similar in some important respects to the traditional nudist ideology). The crucial early development of rhetoric in the nude beach scene was the *hippie vision of the free beach.*

THE FREE BEACH VISION

In the late 1960s, one sometimes saw on the isolated beaches a group of four to ten nude hippies (as they called themselves) sitting around a fire, passing around a joint of marijuana, romping in the surf, playing with their children, or listening to one playing a recorder or a guitar. Couples, or, more rarely, groups, would sometimes camp out on the beaches for days, roaming the shores from dawn into the night. Sometimes the groups were made up simply of friends, but they were often communal families. Probably the first sizable group of nude bathers I ever saw on Eden Beach was a communal group of six adults and four children. I was jogging along the beach on one of those warm fall evenings when the California sunset fills the beach with intense golden light. They came running out of the cold Pacific surf and were standing around laughing and talking as they dried off. The golden light made their wet bodies shine. I was impressed with how peaceful, unconcerned, and natural they seemed. In the next few years, we saw many such hippie beach scenes, including some in which we knew some of the members, which gave us some small insight into what was happening.

Most people are vaguely aware of hippie nudity. They may have seen some pictures of a hippie wandering nude along the rows of a communal farm or read of Don Juan's dismay over finding a nude hippie wandering among the cactus and popping peyote with no proper sense of ceremonial form. But it's more likely they associate hippie nudity with movies or accounts of "nude-ins" at peace demonstrations or maybe at Woodstock. Regardless of the source, most people have come to think of hippie nudity as part of the "nude rebellion," and a large part of the public has subsequently come to associate all of beach nudity with the nude rebellion. This image has been reinforced by a few well publicized happenings such as a "nude-in" on the beach at Santa Barbara, carefully staged for the media by some of the sexual freedom groups. All of this publicized background has led most people to think of the nude beaches as places where, as one dentist told us, "People run around waving their suits in the air and thumbing their noses at the police." This image of hippie nudity and of beach nudity in general as part of a nude rebellion is true in the sense that both involve a conscious rejection of traditional cultural standards, but it is very misleading in that it makes these forms of nudity appear to be purposefully political. Today they are in no way political acts for 98% of nude beachers, unless the police or other agencies intervene with force to stop nudity. Official force commonly causes political rebellion.

It is certainly true that in the early years nude beachers shared a general sense of rebelliousness and that the great majority were liberal to radical in their national politics. The older habituées were rebels, not radicals. They did not know or care much about radical politics. The younger, "hipper" ones were different. In their national politics, they commonly saw themselves as "radical," or at least jokingly as "radiclibs." Some of the beaches had a rock or wall somewhere with their political slogans chiselled or painted on them. At one beach in Santa Barbara, for example, there was an elaborate painted sign proclaiming:

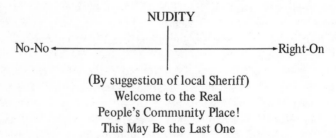

NUDITY

No-No ◄─────────────── │ ───────────────► Right-On

(By suggestion of local Sheriff)
Welcome to the Real
People's Community Place!
This May Be the Last One

On the wall of a box canyon above Eden Beach is enshrined one of the now historic rallying cries of college radicals—"The People's Park." But these slogans are fading. The winds and tides have worn most of them away and the people on the beach will forget them, unless police power is invoked. The proportion of "radical types" has shrunk rapidly as the nude beach population increased and encompassed a broader spectrum of the American population, and as college students moved in new directions. Many of the older nude beachers today are staid conservatives in economic politics; but rarely in cultural standards.

This rebelliousness and radicalism in political orientation was important only in determining who was willing to take the initial social risks involved in pioneering the nude beach or who was interested enough to experiment with new lifestyles. Politics and the nude-ins of the mass media now have little or nothing to do with why people join the nude beaches (as we shall see further in Chapter 2). Most radicals—and certainly most liberals—know little or nothing about nude beach pioneering and wouldn't go to the beach if they did. The people who liberate the beaches do so for feelings and reasons that largely transcend politics. One of these is the hip vision of the free beach.

Almost everyone in our society shares some feeling that the oceans and the beaches, like the mountains and the deserts, are escapes from the worries and dullness of everyday life. We go to the beaches to "get away from it all," for a vacation, for a day free from cares and worries that plague us on the job or at home. At the beach, we relax and forget it all. For many of us, this escape from civilization takes the specific form of not taking a watch to the beach. Time is the great constrainer, organizer, scheduler, and rationalizer in our world. It is Time, and its elaborate pieces of technology, which we carry on our bodies that tie us "cogs" into the great formal structures of society. Time is a cornerstone of the whole of modern civilization. When you wish to escape society's structure for a spell, so you can once again commune with your inner self or the deeper, eternal forces of nature, one of the first things you do is escape Time. The escape from everyday tensions and certainly from Time has always been a basic motive in our own visits to the isolated beaches. We found the same to be true of most other people.

Escape is the negative side of motives that lead so many millions of us to love the seashore and the surging sea. Freedom, a feeling of openness, and naturalness are the positive side. When we are not constrained by the press of everyday obligations, we are free. To be free, we must escape from those constraints. When we are free, we feel expansive, open to the world, at one with ourselves and nature, a welling up of joyful emotions, of exaltation at the moment when we realize we are away from all those constraints we have come to take for granted. These feelings are often intensified manyfold for the nude beachers because they are also shucking off one of the most basic and pervasive symbols of civilization and its massive constraints—clothing. The basic reason why most people find skinny-dipping and open sky love so exhilarating is not because it is some feeble and secret rebellion against the traditional values of a Puritanical society.

The nude beachers, then, feel all of these same emotions, only more intensely than do most other people. Yet, while they are important aspects of the nude beach scene, they are only background factors, and are not responsible for most people being on the nude beach. For all of these motivations might be best satisfied for the vast majority of people in private, by skinny-dipping and furtive open sky loving. The nude beach scene is a *social* scene, and that is a crucial difference. It is very likely that most people love being nude out in nature, but dislike being nude *in public*—which is equivalent to being exposed.

There are two big motivations that separate the nude beach scene from skinny-dipping. The overriding motive for involvement in the nude beach scene is a secret one, all the more carefully guarded from the general public because it is so obvious. That motive is sex, and we will minutely examine it later in this book. The second distinguishing motive is less important in leading to actual participation on the beach, but it is crucial in the thoughts and feelings of those on the nude beach. And, while it is not the most important motive for participation, it is important to some people, especially to the casual young, who are still the largest group of nude beachers. This is the motive of *being up-front,* free, and natural.

One of the basic messages of all the youthful counter-cultures, but especially of the hippie movement, was that we live in a world of lies, of cunning, and deceit. Everybody is hiding from everyone else, pretending to be what they are not, presenting themselves as better than others by circumstance of their social status and wealth, presenting fronts to the world instead of their real selves. Probably most Americans, regardless of age, feel that there is too much insincerity and too many outright lies in the world. (In an important sense, Watergate was a national purgatory for our sins of deceit.) Sincerity and honesty have become cherished and sought-after personal characteristics in our private relations with others. But among the young, this desire became *a rage for sincerity,* a hunger for being the "real" or "natural" you, a refusal to put up with any of the white lies or shams or fronts that most older people take as a natural part of their lives, and which protect our private selves from conflict and shaming in the harsh realm of public life in our pluralistic society. Being "up-front" in life became a basic goal with the casual young. Nudity, like casual sex, was an important way of being up-front, of being your "real self," of shucking off the deceitful façades of civilization, the dominance or status symbols of clothes. Casual sex (or situated sex) with friends, or being open to friends sexually without the traditional emotional and moral con-straints, became an obligation for many in the casual life, since it was assumed that sex is a natural drive and any lack of sexual expression must be an instance of social repression. Nudity did not become an obligation, but it did become one of many forms of being open, up-front. If nudity was an individual's thing, then he should do it. If not, who cares? It was, however, an obligation not to get up-tight about anybody's nudity. You do your thing, they do theirs. For the casual young, then, nudity was *ideally* aimed at being truly casual—you do it if you want, when you want; you don't otherwise. In fulfillment of this, it was common to see hippies and later the casual young, who no longer use a word like "hip," on the beach in all states of clothing and nudity.

The hard-core hippies, with all their ideas of the psychedelic drug trip and communal living, have largely disappeared. But their vision of the nude body remains in the fragmented form commonly called "being casual" (or cool, mellow, etc.). The hippies are gone, but the casual young are more common than ever. This is true in general and certainly true on the nude beaches. The hip ideas of being open, up-front, free, unconstrained, and natural constitute the core of what we might call the *nude* or the *naturalistic ethos:* everyone does his own thing with his own body, takes his own trip, without interfering with the things others are doing. If it feels good, do it—but don't hurt others in the process. That's the supreme law of individual freedom, as propounded by John Stuart Mill and most nude beachers.

On the beach, the nude ethos takes the specific form of the *nude beach ethos.* The nude beach ethos pictures the clothed beach, the straight beach, as a scene of repression of the natural urges in the human animal, while the nude beach is the scene of freedom from constraint, of being up-front, being natural. Those on the straight beaches are often depicted as the prisoners of their repressive and immoral culture, of civilization. Consequently, when someone first joins the nude beach scene, the white rings caused by bathing suits, which stand out so starkly on California's tanned bodies, are sometimes referred to as "Prisoner of War (POW) bracelets." Nude beachers see wearing a bathing suit as not only constraining and submitting to repression, but downright unnatural. Once they get used to going without a suit, this feeling gets even more intense. As one young man said, "Man, I couldn't even think of wearing a bathing suit now. It just wouldn't feel natural." The nude beach is the only form of natural

beach-going. The nude beachers don't have a common name for themselves yet, and one of the first things they are apt to tell outsiders who
ask their motivations is: "I'm not a nudist." By this, they mean they
are not like traditional nudists and have not been part of the nudist
movement. If they had a name, it would probably be something like
body naturalists or just *naturalists.* And that's how they see themselves:
free, open, natural.

The naturalist ethos of nude bathing has been rung clear and sharp
many times, but nowhere has the note been more beautifully struck
than in a Berkeley *Barb* article by Gina Shepard back in the beginning
of the movement. It was her first day on a nude beach, and her
experience was almost sheer joy:

> "Full nakedness; all joys are due to thee!" Nudity on a beach,
> meadow or forest is an experience that is very much apart from
> sexuality. It is a communion with all of the gods' creations. It is a
> pure animal delight in the freedom of the body wildly playing in
> the elements. It is an aesthetic joy in the beauty of the human
> form. It is one of life's richest and most pleasureable experi-
> ences . . . . My first reaction was the realization of how natural it
> all was. I didn't feel any sexual arousement [sic] from all the
> nude male bodies, nor did I feel any particular aesthetic apprecia-
> tion. It was just the way things were meant to be. Nothing seems
> to be more superfluous and ridiculous now than wearing clothes
> on a beach . . . Nudity makes one free of hang-ups. One becomes
> a part of the wind and water, and once this is experienced one
> can never wear a bathing suit again.

Her only discordant note was struck when a group of young voyeurs
encircled her for a close-up, but even that did not faze her long, as she
decided, "If it's their thing, just let 'em leer."

A young man, now a graduate student, told us of the hip vision of
the free beach he had one day in the late 1960s while returning from
the beach to civilization.

> "I'd walked way out into the dunes. I took my clothes off and
> dropped some acid . . . then I just sat there for hours in the sun
> tripping out. . . . You know, it just felt really free, natural and
> beautiful, being nude on the beach. . . . It got late so I put on my
> clothes and started back down the beach. . . . I guess I was
> coming down from the acid trip, but, anyhow, as I walked down
> the beach there were more and more clothed types . . . and the
> more clothed people there were, the more I could feel the
> constraints of civilization descending on me like some big

weight. . . . I just felt more and more oppressed, kind of weighted down by it all."

A sixteen-year-old athlete, a very straight-looking young man with short hair, summed it all up as he was putting his suit back on to cross the rocks that would return him to the POW beach: "Well, back to the horrible society!"

THE LEGAL REVOLUTION AND THE PUBLIC INVASION

In the middle and late 1960s many college students in California became hippie types and many more became casual, sharing some of the key ideas of the hippies about freedom and being natural and up-front, without going all the way into the movement and dropping out of straight society. The percentage of the student body who were really hard-core hippies was always extremely small, probably no more than a few percent anywhere, because of their strong tendency to drop or flunk out. But the casual students on some campuses, such as the University of California at Berkeley, Santa Cruz, Santa Barbara, and San Diego, constituted a much larger percentage of students, probably running as high as one-fourth or more. (There were no precise ideas of membership. Some extremists contend that just about all the students at the University of California at Santa Cruz were of the casual type because Santa Cruz's reputation as *the* "hip" school led high school students to choose or reject it on that basis.)

Given a total college student population running into the hundreds of thousands, there were many tens of thousands of students alone who were quite casual. Many thousands of nonstudents swelled their ranks, commonly hanging around the campuses along Telegraph Street in Berkeley, living in Isla Vista at Santa Barbara, in Del Mar north of the San Diego campus, and in every conceivable abode and non-abode around Santa Cruz and the nearby Monterey area.

A sizable but undeterminable segment of this large group was vaguely inspired by the hippie vision of nudity. Some of them even temporarily liberated college swimming pools. A provost of one of these famous colleges said he couldn't see what was so important about nudity to them, but it was better not to notice what was going on in the pool at certain hours than to risk a confrontation. Far more sought out the hot springs in the forests and, above all, the isolated beaches. They almost always did so generally in small groups, as a couple, or even alone. But in the San Francisco area, this vision was picked up by the more organized sex groups, especially by a sexual liberty league. The nude beach ethos fit very well with their generally casual lifestyle and their more specific sexual motivations.

It's likely that the male gays were already doing their furtive nude scene on the northern beaches in the same way they had been doing on southern beaches such as Eden Beach, where they had been for decades. But, as we said before, the gays would probably never have succeeded in liberating the beaches. Their small number and the social stigma they bear would have continued to prevent any governing body from making their beach nudity legal. Only when the casual young joined them in nude sunbathing and swimming did the political and legal situation begin to change.

In the late 1960s, the casual young were appearing on the isolated northern beaches in rapidly growing numbers, and were wildcatting beaches just north of San Francisco. The sexual liberty league was very active and open north of Monterey, but south of San Francisco, where they concentrated their efforts to liberate several beaches. The hetero-sexual nude beach scene developed, complete with children, dogs, garbage, and trash. It's always hard to know what to believe about what the officials say are the reasons for their actions on the nude beaches. It appears, however, that the rapid development of an open sexual scene on the beach was a key reason in local officials' decision to permit the opening of a private nude beach, charging fees, excluding "lewdness" from the beach, and, perhaps incidentally, putting the beaches partly beyond their political responsibility or liability. They allowed a private party to open a private, so-called *Victorian* nude beach—one with more rules. At about the same time, smaller private beaches were opened nearby.

To the south, at Big Sur, mid-way between Monterey and Santa Barbara, the hip psychology of encounter groups had led psychologists at Esalen Institute to develop nude therapy. Nude therapy has generally been done in encounter group situations, but at Esalen the hot springs provided it an early open-air site. Nearby Pfeiffer Beach was also opened up to the public as a private nude beach. Similar groups later developed the now well-known "nude tubs," which were big enough for mixed groups of about six to bathe nude.

At the same time, other casual young people were joining the gays in wildcatting far to the south, especially near the University of California at Santa Barbara. Students and the hip street people who lived with them in Isla Vista liberated a long beach with sand dunes just north of the university community. The police rarely bothered anyone in this area, probably because the dunes afforded people considerable cover for their nudity and sex. The bigger nude scenes further south seem to have opened up only later because of their greater proximity to the straight beaches and to houses.

Even in Los Angeles County, one of the best-known nude beaches was opening up. This very small cove, about an eighth of a mile of narrow beach, was highly isolated by the precipitous cliffs and by rocks extending out into the water. Casual young people were joined by some traditional nudists in liberating the beach. Conflicts with the property owners near the access route led to a ban on nudity and a small mass arrest in the summer of 1972. It was soon liberated once again, but the conflict continues.

Further to the south, the most conservative part of the state and one of the most conservative areas in the nation, the liberation of the beaches had progressed more slowly. But it was here that the greatest nude beach thus far, Eden Beach, was soon to explode. In the late 1960s both Eden and another major nude beach, Cliff Beach, were still simply the sites of skinny-dipping, though the number of nudes was growing rapidly. The gays were most active, especially on a beautiful half-mile stretch. The police were unrelenting in their attempts to root the nudes out of their windbreaks (made of piled-up stones or just sand) and canyons. Using telephoto lenses, they would spot and photograph nude beachers from the 300-foot cliffs from as much as three-quarters of a mile away, then send a beach van speeding along the beach to arrest the offenders. One such offender was Chad Merrill Smith, whose name became famous among California's nude beachers.

The facts of the Chad Merrill Smith case are starkly stipulated in a published decision of the California State Supreme Court (Crim. No. 15986. In Bank, June 13, 1972: In re Chad Merrill Smith on Habeas Corpus, pg. 364):

> The facts are undisputed. On the morning of August 7, 1970, petitioner and a male friend went to a beach for the purpose of sunbathing. Although the beach was open to the public, it was not in a residential area and was apparently used by relatively few people. Petitioner removed all his clothes, lay down on his back on a towel and fell asleep.

> Some hours later the police appeared on the scene and arrested petitioner on a charge of indecent exposure. By that time several other persons were present on the beach. It was stipulated, however, that petitioner at no time had an erection or engaged in any activity directing attention to his genitals.

> Petitioner was found guilty as charged; the imposition of sentence was suspended for three years, and he was placed on informal

probation to the court on the condition he pay a fine of $100. He subsequently learned he was also required to register as a sex offender pursuant to Penal Code Section 290.

The unanimous decision of the Supreme Court noted that there were two basic conditions required by law for conviction on a charge of indecent exposure, "willfullness" and "lewdness" of exposure of sex organs. Smith and everyone agreed that he did willfully expose himself. His case hinged on the charge of his having done so "lewdly." After reviewing the relevant precedents of convictions for indecent exposure, the unanimous decision of the Court was that (pp. 366-368):

> From the foregoing definitions and cases the rule clearly emerges that a person does not expose his private parts 'lewdly' within the meaning of Section 314 unless his conduct is sexually motivated. Accordingly, a conviction of that offense requires proof beyond a reasonable doubt that the actor not only meant to expose himself, but intended by his conduct to direct public attention to his genitals for purposes of sexual arousal, gratification, or affront. . . . It follows that on the undisputed facts of this case petitioner's conduct was not prohibited by the statute under which he was convicted. In such circumstances, he is entitled to the relief of habeas corpus. . . . The writ is granted. The judgment is vacated, and the petitioner is discharged from the restraints thereof.

The decision at Eden Beach was one of those little noticed, but sometimes crucial turning points in social developments. The court decision was publicly noted only by a small AP article in the local papers and in the Los Angeles *Times*, and to this day most people, including the vast majority of nude beachers, have at best a vague understanding that something happened to change the legal status of nudity on isolated beaches. Its full implications are not yet known and will not be known until further cases are tried using this as a precedent or until we know better just what directions legislation and public behavior will take, whether toward more or less nudity. But some of its short-run implications were very clear.

Because most people who used the beach were only vaguely aware of the decision, there was no immediate significant change on the beach. The same individuals and small groups of surreptitious naturalists continued to appear. It is not even clear whether the police immediately stopped arresting people for indecent exposure. Our memory of events at that time is that the police mysteriously stopped patrolling for some time, or else came so much less often and less speedily that we did not notice them. What we did notice was a slow increase in the number of naturalists. There were scores and even a few hundred in the more isolated parts of the beach in late summer. The police patrols resumed on a more regular but infrequent schedule. Instead of running for cover, most nudes now merely ducked or cowered in the sand as the police van wended its way slowly along the beach. The clothed people began going up to the van to ask about the legal status of nudity on the beach; then the naturalists began approaching and inquiring in respectful tones.

One day in the fall I was jogging along the water's edge when we noticed the police van coming toward us. As the van drew nearer, two beautiful teenage girls, completely nude, walked slowly into the path where the van would soon arrive. They smiled at each other and lay face upward in the middle of the path. The police van circled around their still bodies and slowed almost to a stop. The two officers peered out the window, then almost seemed to show a flicker of appreciation. The van moved inexorably on. The two girls got up and ran down the beach laughing, probably exulting in their newly proven freedom. I jogged on, knowing that a "revolution" had surely come to the beach I had been visiting almost every day for several years.

By the summer of 1973, it was clear that a revolution, at least a local one, was indeed in progress. Probably as many as three to five thousand people came to Eden Beach on several hot weekend days (though that summer was unusually cloudy and the tourist business was near disaster), either to cavort in the nude or ogle those who did. By 1977, that many came on a few warm weekends even in the winter, and in the summer there were many thousands more. Additional thousands were hitting the northern public and private nude beaches whenever the coastal clouds cleared long enough to offer hope of warmth and suntan—and when the police left them alone. Very importantly, nude beaching was spreading to new social groups. The casual young remained the most numerous group, and it was largely a body-beautiful scene. But now all groups of society were joining up. Short-haired marines and sailors who once came only on the "voyeur trip" were staying to take off their suits, play frisbee, and loll around on the sand drinking wine and looking at the women. Groups of very young teenage girls were coming down and slowly working their way into the scene. Some older people were also coming. Young families became a common sight, with nude children running amid the adolescent frisbee players. The skinny and the chubby were joining the lithe and the muscular. Every day there were more bright-white POW bracelets flashing in the sunlight. The sight of all these *nude beach virgins* was enough to delight even the aging veterans, those with the deepest all-over tans.

Most significant of all, wildcat beaches were springing up all over the state. Wherever a small cliff, tidal pool, cove indentation in the coast, or long walk afforded any protection from the offended stares of that dwindling portion of the public still shocked by nudity, and from the police, there were likely to appear a number of nude sunbathers on any warm day. It was also clear that the nude beach revolution was spreading along the East Coast. California nude beachers were returning from Cape Cod and other points east to compare the different scenes.

It was an exciting scene of natural beauty and free expression. But with the vast increase in the number of beach naturalists came those who preyed upon them—the heavy voyeurs, exhibitionists and sexual hunters.

The numbers also brought publicity, which brought an additional horde of predators and the rapidly growing forces of the counter-revolution, the property owners and, far more, those who felt threatened by the nude body. The nude beach vision was progressively embattled by the conflicting groups. Repressors charged in from all directions to put down the revolution. The inevitable conflicts and deceits of politics had come to the nude beach and threatened its future. Yet those on the beach believed the new struggles could not turn back the rising tide of body freedom.

2

Joining the Nude Beach

The best studies of nudists (especially those by Weinberg, Ilfeld, and Lauer) found that for almost all of them becoming a nudist was a fateful process pervaded by powerful emotional conflicts. For most people, joining the nude beach is equally momentous. It may not be as exciting as the first step off a towering cliff dangling from a hang-glider, or as portentous for one's physical existence, but it has potentially far more lasting impact on one's social life.

Anyone who doubts this can test it out by casually mentioning at his next dinner party that he spent Sunday down at the local nude beach. I once forgot our cautionary rule on such an occasion and mentioned that some colleagues and I had been doing research on the nude beaches. The response was an immediate gasp of shock from our gracious hostess, "You mean you take your pants off!?" I simply muttered that I didn't feel any urgent need to discuss the "vastly complex" research methods involved and made a vow to stay underground with Dostoivsky's possessed souls and Kafka's cockroaches.

Since then, we've found that any casual mention of a nude beach, especially among older people or young teenagers, will commonly elicit giggles or guffaws, except among those few from whom it elicits yelps of outrage. (We shall look at them more closely later.) With today's more relaxed attitude toward the body and sex, the nude beach is not threatening enough to most people to elicit stigmatizing yelps of denunciation, but it causes enough uneasiness or vague anxiety to call forth a derisive laugh which marks the nudes down as "creeps." This conspiracy of laughter seems aimed at keeping them in their quasi-stigmatized place, and thus at great social distance where they compose no serious threat. The so-called sexual revolution, which has been primarily a revolution in talk rather than behavior, has gone far enough to relieve nudes of the stigma of insanity ("nuts"), but not enough to normalize them. To most people, they are no longer nuts, only creeps.

There are no clearly stated social rules against nudity, like "Thou shalt not go to a nude beach." Who needs a clearly stated social rule? Nudity is so closely linked in our basic social feelings and thoughts with sex—and public nudity with evil sex—that almost everyone who feels threatened by sex acts "feels in his bones" that there's something "wrong" with it. This feeling of wickedness and the shame that is potentially inspired by it are so ingrown in our society that there are people who will go to great trouble and expense to spy on the nude beachers from the cliffs with binoculars when they could easily come down and join them. (We called them the *cliff-dweller voyeurs.*)

Even more striking are the vast numbers of people who, generally without any realistic fear of being recognized, but inspired by the paranoid thinking that springs from anxiety, will take the *voyeur-tour* along the beach in "CIA disguise." Some of these voyeurs walk among the nude bodies in street clothes, with tennis hats down over their ears and eyes. Anyone must have feelings of guilt or anxiety before he will take a walk on a hot, sunny beach looking like an Eskimo protecting himself from arctic glare and cold. His emotions must be so great as to disrupt his reason before he can imagine that such incongruous regalia will make him inconspicuous on a beach full of nudes.

Sociologists, psychologists, psychiatrists, criminologists, and other social scientists have been analyzing violations of basic social rules for about two centuries now to try to explain why people do such things. The potential penalties for such violations are severe—shame, guilt, stigmatization, ostracism, possibly institutionalization, or worse. The great majority of people must surely see such actions as very risky, so what powerful forces lead them to do such things? Social scientists have almost always taken the rules for granted—that is, they assume the rules exist and are what they appear to be on the surface. They have also almost always taken *conformity* to the rules by a majority of people for granted: Social scientists do not tend to study the conformers, the rule users, or, until recently, the enforcers. In this work, we are not taking such things for granted at all. On the contrary, one of the most important things we have tried to do is to get to the roots of the rules, to see what the rules are, to see how they originate, what causes rules to be created and used—what powerful forces lead human beings to do something as extreme and painful as suppressing—or even repressing— the genetically inherited aesthetic and sensual enjoyment of the human body and of sexual action? By studying the conformers and rule enforcers, as well as the rule evaders and violators, we are trying to show the powerful feelings that lead people to create and enforce such rules—and to evade and violate them.

Theories of deviant behavior have almost all shared two general properties—arrogant "simplificationism" and "reactionaryism." The simplificationism has grown largely out of the modern scientists' self-imposed professional myopia, the insistence of each specialist on seeing everything as caused by the few particular variables he happens to "own" professionally. In the theories of deviance, sociologists almost always look at other rules (or symbols) as the basic cause of the violations of rules. For example, sociologists like Robert Merton have argued that the rule on success leads those with few legitimate opportunities to achieve the success they crave by illegitimate means. Psychologists have been a bit more complex and generally look at deviance in terms of a conflict between super-ego rules and libidinal or emotional forces normally repressed by those rules. For example, psychoanalysts like Flügel have explained the great cover-up, clothing and fashions, in terms of the theory of ambivalence, drawing on Freud's basic idea that behind every taboo (or stigma) there is also a desire. Most of these theories are right to some degree about some part of the things they are studying, but they almost all deal with small parts—as if the parts were the whole thing—and the theories wind up being distortions of the vastly complex realm of human life. As we have found in our holistic study of the nude beach, our study of all the groups and kinds of individuals involved in this basic conflict over rules and ways of living from the many perspectives involved, there are no simple explanations of such vastly complex natural phenomena. Simple theories that purport to explain such highly complex natural processes are myths, not science.

The reactionaryism of most of the theories is seen first of all in their taking the status-quo rules for granted, as if those rules were God-given realities. The historical fact is that all rules are at some time created, and they change, other than the relatively few that seem to be directly derived from genetic programming (such as the parent-child incest rules and a few other parent-child rules), and even these few are normally elaborated in various ways at different times. We must see what forces in a given concrete situation lead to the creation, specific construction of the meaning of, and use or nonuse of those rules before we can understand such things as deviance and conformity.

But the reactionaryism of the theories is seen even more, and more importantly, in their general presumption that people violate rules, especially basic rules, primarily as a *reaction against* something that has gone wrong in their lives. People supposedly steal, fight, or go nude because they have failed by legitimate means or because someone subjected them to repression when they were children. Only a few social scientists and psychologists have seriously considered the possibility that people also violate rules for many other reasons, including nonreasoned and creative ones—searching for something more, something better, not out of unhappiness, but out of a craving for richer pleasure, more happiness.

We shall see in this work that the people who are enforcing the rules seem to be largely reacting against something, especially reacting against a feeling of threat from nudity and sex or just the threat of being stigmatized. It is the rule-enforcers who are "suffering" from something, from fear, even at times from dread, not the rule violators. (Of course, we shall also see that their feelings, thought, and actions are neither simple nor easy to determine.) We shall see that there are some people evading and violating this basic rule who are reacting against something, but far more importantly we shall see that the great majority of them are *creative deviants,* not reactive deviants. As we will argue in the Appendix, nudity and sex, especially more casual sex, are outgrowths of affluence and success, not of poverty and failure. It is precisely because people have leisure and wealth, almost a surfeit of satisfaction of the basic drives in life (such as hunger) that they are yearning, craving, searching for something more, something better. They are trying to fulfill themselves, to grow, to create.

But I do not intend to say that nude beachers are all nude artists. Creativity, especially the active or conscious creativity I have just stressed, is only one of many motives involved and leads to only some of the many paths to this form of deviance. We shall see that many who try strenuously to be creative in this way are not able to overcome their feelings of shame or dread of stigmatization, and that many others are partly seduced into it before they can begin to feel the creative urges—some even wander into nudity or casual sex almost blindly, a few by accident. Let us begin our explorations of how and why people join the nude scene by studying how and why people do not join it and, instead, sometimes strive furiously to repress it.

THE MOTIVES OF THE NON-JOINERS

Those who oppose the nude beaches and those who simply will not go, but do not oppose the right of others to go, have different motives. Most of those who simply do not go are older people for whom the idea of a nude beach (or a nude anything) is a revolution in feelings, ideas, and lifestyles. Nudity is not their custom and seems totally "unnatural" in the same way it is seen as "natural" by those who *do* join the beach. To people who take this uncomprehending but libertarian point of view, the nude beach just isn't their thing. It's simply beyond reality—out of sight and out of their world. Since the nude beachers are commonly libertarian in their own views, they understand and accept this point of view, though they reserve the right to work strenuously to convince you to strip once you get to the beach. What they object to with counter-moralism and counter-shaming are the people who oppose the nude beachers, sneer at them, and try to shame and stigmatize them by police power, in the name of a higher morality.

Some of the moralism of the enemies of the nude beach is clearly just rhetoric for public consumption, window dressing to take in an unsuspecting public. We shall see later (Chapter 6) that this is the case with some, but by no means all, of the property owners who are leading the legal counter-revolution. Some of these people have fought for years to prevent public access to the beaches because they saw it as *their* property, but have now suddenly discovered the virtues of democratic participation and Christian moralism on the beach.

They are really just trying to do anything to get rid of the people and traffic. Such economic motives are clear. Property owners face some potential loss in property value if they no longer control a private beach (except that no California beaches today are legally private beyond the mean high tide line). The serious bother of a great influx of traffic and of pedestrians because of the nudity is also clear. Some of the property owners who launch moral barbs against the bare flesh on the beach do so as political rhetoric, to arouse the opposition of more fundamentalist groups. Their moralistic pronouncements are not expressions for their own motivations, either for not going to the nude beaches or for wanting to keep others from going.

At the other extreme from this cynical position there does appear to be an unknown percentage of people who are opposed to the nude beaches out of sincere feelings of the fundamentalist morality of the Judeo-Christian civilization. They are people who are in direct communication with a sterner God than that known to most of us today. Their reasons for opposing the beach nudity—and *all* other forms of public nudity and sex—are simple: God banned nudity for Adam and Eve after the fall, forced them into exile from Eden, and this ban is still in effect for all of their descendents.

One woman, a national vice president of a women's league, stated it resoundingly in a public hearing:

"I'm a Christian wife and mother of three daughters and a son and I
feel that everyone has the right to enjoy our public parks and
beaches paid for by our tax dollars without being offended and
embarrassed by other people running naked in public. I feel that,
if nudity is allowed at Eden Beach, it will pave the way to our
realization of total public nudity. America is supposed to be a
civilized nation, yet we are becoming one of the most immodest
nations in the world. Even in Africa where women have less cloth,
as soon as they can get a piece of material, they wrap it around
themselves. We live in a Judeo-Christian society of rules and we
must not forget that the Bible is God's rule book and that many
rules against nudity are found in his work. Public nudity is an
invasion of privacy as well as being immoral and indecent, and I
ask you to rule against this additional moral decay here in our
city. And if I'm accused of being old fashioned, then I agree with
that. I'm as old fashioned as the word of God and I would like to
say that where today I heard a man speak for nudity in the name
of God and when he finished the audience respond with oral
applause [sic], I also heard a man speak against nudity in the
name of God Almighty and was laughed at by those same people.
And I would like to remind those people that many years ago
Jesus was laughed at and ridiculed too, and I stand before our
Lord ashamed of what our society has become."

These religious types almost universally deny having been to the
nude beaches. To go would be to sin against God. They oppose them
out of absolute moral feelings, in the abstract, regardless of what may
or may not be going on down there, regardless of how it may or may
not feel to be nude in public. (There is one moralist, Jerry, who used to
visit Eden Beach almost every day, fully clothed, Bible in hand, to
preach to the nude beachers on "the evils of nudity and fornication."
We shall later see that there were some doubts about his sincerity.)

But most people who oppose the nude beaches and refuse to go are
found, upon closer examination, to have more situationally or person-
ally emotional "reasons" for not going and for opposing the beaches.
When nude beachers hear that someone is opposed to the beaches for
this or that reason, they commonly brush it aside with "Yeah, that's
just their hang-ups." As we shall see, this is an oversimplification of
counter-moralism, but for most opponents it is not such a big one. As
far as I have been able to determine (by all the methods explored in my
book entitled *Investigative Social Research*), most of the expressed

reasons really are cover-ups for real, unexpressable emotions—feelings of being threatened.

The emotional "reasons" for not going are often not people's own feelings of "not measuring up" (see below). Rather, they are often the fears and resentments about others, about loved ones, or the general public. A large percentage of people won't go to the beach because parents, lovers, spouses, or friends would think badly of them, or worse, if they did go. We came across the ultimate example of this one beautiful fall day when we were visiting a wildcat scene north of Eden.

A muscular young man, no more than twenty, came up to us. He was looking uneasily in the direction of a uniformed government maintenance worker, who worked for a state park down the beach and who had just admitted to us that he was doing the voyeur trip (after first stating *very officially* that he was "checking for slides since the tides were so high last night"). The young man asked in hushed tones, "Hey, man, what are the pigs doing down here?" I assured him the boy in the uniform was really a very sympathetic non-pig in disguise as an official, and would probably love to get his own pants off. (Our bet was that it would take about a week for him to fearfully cross the great divide.) The young man looked surprised, asked for a light, and said, more with awe than dread, "Man, if my wife knew I was down here, she'd kill me." We laughed knowingly, strangers temporarily bound together in our conspiracy, and I reassured him that I couldn't believe she'd go that far. Unlaughing, he mumbled, "Man, you just don't know—she don't mess around."

Most of these pressures and threats to keep loved ones off the beach are done without explanation and without any serious attempt at explanation. The loved one simply insists absolutely that you not go down there at all. They issue orders and unconditional demands, not value judgments or tightly reasoned disquisitions in jurisprudence. (Jaweh speaks from the whirlwind, not from the code books.)

The ones forbidden the evil fruit often profess not to know why. We suspect they sometimes know very well, at least by intuition, the deep feelings and fears that produce these absolute "moral" injunctions. But we also know from experience that it is common for both the repressor and the repressed to be unclear about *why* they feel so deeply against the nude scene. One good example of this confusion was given by a young woman living with a couple:

"I'd been going to the beach for quite a while and had a pretty good all-over tan. It looked real nice and my roommate Ellen decided that she too wanted a good tan to excite her boy friend. Chuck had been sort of living with Ellen and me for a few months. Ellen was pretty free-spirited; but Chuck was almost a prude. I found out later that he objected to my occasionally answering a late night phone call nude or not bothering to cover up to come into the kitchen for a minute or two. That shocked me! There I was—naked on the beach all day in front of God and everybody—then to come home and have to put clothes on. In my own house! It was, to say the least, a bummer.

"Well, Ellen wanted to go to the nude beach with me and told Chuck so. He said absolutely and unconditionally, 'No!' Ellen and I talked to him later about it. We wanted to find out his objection and get around it if we could. Ellen and I told him two girls would be safe—we could protect each other. Ellen said she would even keep on her bathing suit. But Chuck still said, 'No.' Then we asked Chuck if he would go down with us—clothed or unclothed. Ellen for sure would be safe then. Ellen and I were puzzled. We really couldn't figure out Chuck's hang-up. He wouldn't even let her go down clothed, with two clothed chaperones. Ellen's last try was to promise not to look at any naked guys. Chuck looked embarrassed at this but still said, 'No.'

"I moved out soon after all this happened. I doubt that Ellen ever did get to the free beach. Last I heard she was doing a furtive topless trip on an isolated part of a beach, near where we lived. Ellen and I never really did figure out Chuck's objection. The only thing we came up with was that Chuck was a true-blue prude and was embarrassed at the thought of anyone looking at 'his girl' or, worse yet, of his girl digging looking at any naked bodies. Ellen and I desperately wanted to prove to him that the beach was really a mild sort of scene—nothing to get up-tight about—but Chuck's mind is closed and he'll most likely never know the freedom of a free nude beach."

The problem of understanding such injunctions seems to arise from the fact that the feelings leading to them are so deep and so contrary to some of our most cherished public values about freedom and equality that people don't want to talk about them, or may be all confused about them. The conscious experience of those making the injunctions often seems to be I-don't-know-why-and-don't-give-a-damn-why-but-you-goddamn-well-better-not-go.

Feelings like jealousy or envy are of basic importance in understanding the creation and invocation of such repressive rules, but they are not only in bad repute today, they are also almost always kept secret. Hardly anyone will admit even to him- or herself that he or she feels jealous or envious. How many times have you heard anyone say, "The reason I say nasty things about him is because I envy him (or feel jealous of him)"? To say such a thing would, of course, be an admission to ourselves and others that we feel inferior to another person, which is exactly the thing we don't want to be. So when we do feel inferior, or feel that others might think we are inferior, we feel the powerful and corrosive emotions of envy or jealousy, but we try desperately to deceive ourselves and others by making our feelings seem rational invocations of absolute morality.

The jealous husband is always a great moralist, a veritable reincarnation of Moses. The little girl who says, "I'd hate to have an ugly doll like hers," may in fact be feeling deep envy for the other girl having the doll, but she is saying exactly the opposite. In the same way, the voyeur whose smirk is ridiculing (shaming as ridicule) the nude beacher is actually either envious of the other's body or, even more likely, jealous—but that's the exact opposite of what he's *saying*. Only by knowing the very complex and fleeting emotional code of the body, the so-called body language, can we determine what a person is really feeling, and thus how he is most apt to really act. In conflictful or ambivalent situations, especially those involving feelings of threat and dread, his overt activity is largely a protective shield, a deceiver of himself and others to protect him from powerful emotions and reactions. (This was an extremely important conclusion from our experience in the nude scene and has contributed greatly to our other, more theoretical works, especially *Investigative Social Research, Existential Sociology,* and *Creative Deviance and Social Change.*)

There are, of course, other feelings of threat that lead to invoking the ancient rule against nudity. For example, many parents wouldn't think of letting their children go to a nude beach, especially their teenage daughters, because they've heard the atrocity stories about heavy sex on the beach (which we shall discuss later) or because they fear, more realistically, that their children will give way to the temptations of sex. There definitely are many teenagers who don't want to go, and many girls are scared off by some first experiences with heavy sexual overtures on the beach. But the worst we've heard any teenagers say about the beach is that "it's really dumb" or, as one surfer anxious to rid the beach of everyone, said, "Get the creeps and gonads off the beach!" With almost no exceptions, all the atrocity stories about how "frightening" the beach experience is to teenagers come from the middle-aged parents. On the contrary, it is common to find teenagers telling unconvincing stories about how willing their parents are to let them come.

Many other people won't go because they are afraid of being seen by friends or associates and branded a weirdo or a sexual pervert. Some of these people go anyhow, but to distant beaches. Thus, it is quite common to find people on the beach from a hundred miles away, both because there are not yet any nude beaches or other public nude scenes close to them and because of the fear of public stigmatization. Those who go nearer home often begin as CIA types. Those who have discovered that this kind of disguise merely makes them more conspicuous among hundreds or thousands of nude people develop a more sophisticated beach early warning system, which mainly consists of being constantly alert. It is not unheard of to find a surfer wearing a tennis hat and sunglasses (which are the mark of the tourist and are absolutely forbidden by all rules of surfing) sitting back against a cliff observing intensely.

You develop your visual perception to an acute degree, peering down the miles of beach for any familiar figure or watching the border regions separating the nude scene from civilization for a friend who has decided to take the voyeur trip. You soon learn that a person's walk or body motion gives them away long before anyone can make out a familiar face, so you watch for body motion. This state of anxious vigilance also involves periodic surveillance over your shoulder for anyone who might be jogging behind you. Joggers pose a real threat to the undercover types because they can come up on you so fast you have little time for flight or cover-up.

When a familiar form or motion is spotted far enough in advance, you can execute any number of evasionary tactics. These must be executed at the slightest suspicion and with the speed warranted by the dire emergency facing you—better overly cautious than a reputation destroyed by one voyeuristic glance. You can turn and run the other way, but your body motion might betray you, or you might run out of breath before you got far enough to avoid identification. You can also rush into the water, but, unless you can hold your breath a long time, you can still get spotted. The most effective evasionary tactic is to throw yourself face down on the sand near the cliff.

Some voyeurs might approach, but none of them would dare say, "Hey aren't you Joe Schmidt?" because voyeurs almost never make direct human contact. Besides, this would blow their own cover. In fact, the desire of your friends also not to be seen on the beach is your greatest protection, if you play it right. The worst things you can do are to panic and try to scale the cliff, because then everyone can see your mad flight, or to try to pretend you didn't know this was a nude beach. No one on the beach ever believes a plea of innocence, least of all a voyeur. He may pretend to believe you to avoid breaking your relationship, but he now knows the "real you"—a wierdo.

If the CIA types play it cool, they can commonly avoid detection for a long time. Their undercover life is actually abetted by certain crucial aspects of the casual style intended to communicate up-frontness, but easily used as well by the most lying predators. The casual nude beacher uses only first names (Joe and Sue) because the trappings of one's past life and present social identity are not supposed to count—except, of course, the vital identity of "being casual." Nothing counts but the immediate situation, being "real selves," letting it all hang out, right here and now. (This *ethos of situatedness* is allied with the *ethos of equalitarianism*. Both are quite absolutist, as are all moralistic stances. Absolutism violates both ethoses—but contradiction and dishonesty are common to moralisms born of the feeling of threat.) On the beach, the use of first names becomes a fetish, especially to those too old to be honestly casual, precisely because it prevents up-frontness. If other people don't know someone's last name or other identifying criteria, they can't follow that person back into civilization. If anyone with an all-over tan reveals his last name on the beach, you can figure that he is either so distrusting that he's creating a false identity, or that he is so trusting that he's willing to be found off the beach.

But even the best early warning system, evasionary tactics, and dishonesty often fail. The main reason people get discovered is the intense California sun. Nude beach virgins commonly get sunburn on their buttocks or sex organs because they don't realize how fast a burn can happen, sometimes even when the skies are overcast in the summer. Sunburn can destroy their cover at home almost every time, unless they suddenly develop extreme modesty. If they manage to avoid discovery that way, they will probably eventually be unmasked by the all-over tan. Everyone knows that even the intense California sun will not tan a penis or buttocks through a bathing suit. The consequences of such discovery by friends or mates can be just as severe as the undercover agent fears, because they unleash deep sexual fears, jealousies, and resentment.

Undoubtedly lying behind many of these emotions is the uncontrollable fear of organ inferiority, of not measuring up in your loved one's eyes when everything you have is revealed to the world and can thus be compared with what others have. A sense of organ inferiority comes in all shapes and sizes. Some people may feel confident about their sex organs, but be deeply ashamed of their obese bodies, or their skinny bodies, or whatever they have and think they shouldn't have. This kind of body embarrassment is moderate, so people are much more willing to open up about it. As one of my middle-aged colleagues admitted wistfully, "I went once, but I decided it just isn't for someone my age." Art Seidenbaum, columnist for the Los Angeles *Times,* has seen fit to expose his body embarrassment in the pages of the *Times.* When he first discovered the nude beach scene in 1972, Seidenbaum wrote a column attacking beach nudity for the "reason" that it infringed the "rights" of those who, like himself, did not find the nude scene natural and wanted, supposedly as a consequence, to keep it all covered up. But, after numerous attacks from his liberal friends, he decided to get up-front about the whole thing, and wrote in the *Times* of September 7, 1973:

> From San Francisco to San Diego, however, nude beaching is becoming more and more fashionable. There are strands in Santa Barbara, Malibu and La Jolla where strap marks are seldom seen and both sexes bathe without suits. . . . Form, alas, is important to this issue. The majority of nude sunbathers are young and usually well shaped. There are few esthetic questions about the beauty of such bodies. And then youth becomes an art form, which tends to bury most moral arguments in the sand. The first time I saw some skinny dippers was at Big Sur, a few years ago. They were attractive and they made me uncomfortable. Uncomfortable because I wondered whether my dressed presence made them uncomfortable. Uncomfortable because they had disturbed my peace. And maybe I was jealous of their youth. I wrote about them and their rights versus mine, only to discover that a majority of readers decided my sunburned nose was blue, not tan. Older but cooler now, I've learned that nude bathers are not bothered about their nakedness unless somebody, some outside body, deliberately bothers them. . . . I'm now ready for a new coastal initiative that says suit yourself, or unsuit yourself. The way to preserve the rights of all bodies is to provide separate facilities for both kinds of beachers. Southern California already reserves areas for surfers apart from swimmers. Establishing some secluded, legal sanctuaries for skinny dippers by the summer of '74 is a logical response to a healthy trend. . . . A dirty mind invented indecent exposure, as the cover story for a sense of shame. While I continue to carry my trunks to the beach, I have no further objections to a younger spirit who travels lighter. The

Pacific is big enough for both of us, the skinny dipper and the not
so skinny one who finally peeled a few prejudices for fall.

But the more intense feelings of organ inferiority are those associated with the sex organs themselves. Those are the feelings that really
count, that seem to hide shamefully behind so much of the rhetoric
about the evils of the nude scene. It is precisely because these feelings
are so intense, so important, and so in conflict with some of our public
morality, especially that of liberals and radicals, that they are the ones
almost never mentioned. In fact, while we heard people joke about this
sort of thing a great deal, and while we could make sense of some things
they did say only by understanding that these emotions lay behind
what they were saying, we almost never heard anyone *say* that they
were afraid of not "measuring up." Most of the time, in fact, people
would only joke about other people, since they didn't want anyone to
think that they might have fears that they themselves didn't measure
up. ("It's him, not me!")

Typical of this was the conversation reported by one of the regulars
on the beach:

> "There were the four of us waiting to meet one of our friends down
> on the beach. Linda and Jim were new to the scene so we all
> decided to keep our suits on. (Hell, we were too nervous to do
> anything else!) But the guy we were waiting for was like a regular
> on the beach and would be nude for sure and we really didn't
> know how to handle it. We figured it might be funny if we could
> get one of the women folk to comment 'My, you're so big, we
> never knew before' or to really get at him 'Gee, Pete, you really
> let us down . . . kind of disappointed us.' But that sort of humor
> didn't seem quite fair because he couldn't joke back about it. We
> had our suits on. We were all laughing about it when this guy
> came by that was hung down to his knees. Christ, with studs
> walking around like that . . . it's no joking matter. Nobody, but
> nobody could measure up to that! We all decided that we'd better
> joke about something else."

But we did find one guy who was up-front enough to joke about
himself. As one of the researchers reported it,

> "There were a whole bunch of us sitting around drinking beer and
> smoking. . . . All of us were nude except this one dude so we
> started to get on him about being dressed. The other three guys
> that were with him had gotten nude right off. None of us could

figure out why he was holding back. Finally, half-jokingly, he said, 'Man, I can't take this suit off. If I did, you'd see I'm so small I'd blow my whole image as The Big Stud.' But he also said that he had scars that looked pretty bad. He never did get nude, so we'll never know."

Probably the one totally up-front expression of this fear I have found came from a colleague of mine who visited me from England. He had read a descriptive account I had written of the beach and was anxious to see it, so he accompanied me down onto the beach one very crowded day. He looked normal, if a bit frozen. But after he had flown back to "civilized" England, he wrote me his impressions:

> The visit to Eden Beach was my introduction to nudism actually. Because of my reading of the manuscript for *The Nude Beach* and all the discussions, I was not at all apprehensive, and even anticipated my initiation to the scene. I did, however, experience some strange thoughts and feelings while on the beach—ones that I 'knew about rationally,' but weren't precisely what I expected. For example, by this point in my life I know, rationally, that I've reached the point where I've come to accept my body for what it is, and isn't, and all that crap about feelings of "organ inferiority" is essentially for those who haven't achieved my transcendent position. And then, as we were walking along, I saw that big, muscular guy with an enormous whang, and I thought, Holyshit! I've really got a dinky one! I wonder if he can do it better with his big one than I can do it with my normally sized one?

We found that people were more willing to talk seriously about *other* people's hang-ups without often having been told directly that the others *had* these hang-ups. Rather, they themselves were indirectly inferring the hang-ups from behavior and, presumably, to a greater or lesser degree, from their own feelings. After all, almost everyone is willing to admit feeling some doubt about their personal attractiveness, especially in comparison to a nebulous standard, "the beautiful." Considering how vital sex is in our lives, how could they possibly not feel the doubt and fear of "not measuring up."

One of the most common behavioral syndromes is found among women. Even beautiful and terrifically well-endowed women sometimes have deep anxieties about showing their sex organs, for fear that people will think they are repulsive. Typical of this syndrome is the case reported to us by a regular.

> "My girl friend and I go to the nude beach all the time but she never ever has gotten nude. . . . She hasn't even taken off her top. Even

when we're alone, she changes in the bathroom behind a closed
and locked door. The only time she gets nude is when we make
love and then only with the lights out. Shit, she even spends her
working hours in a clinic that teaches women to examine themselves so they wouldn't have to be exposed to a male doctor! She
told me that there is something about clothes that kind of teases
people and she may be right; everyone down on the beach is
always trying to get her out of hers . . . to see what she is really
like. She has a nice body, for sure nothing to hide. She's just
up-tight about letting anyone see it."

The fear of organ inferiority is one of those great secrets of human
life which is understood by everyone but almost never admitted. It is
vital to understand that the fear of feeling inferior exists and deter-
mines a large part of what people are doing or not doing; without an
understanding of that fear, people cannot be dealt with successfully.

Most of the time, one comes to realize such secret feelings exist
by initially observing them in oneself. This is the same way we
discover other secret feelings in human life—for example, envy and
jealousy. We all feel envy and jealousy, certainly to different degrees
and from different causes, but we know what they feel like, when they
are apt to occur, and how they affect our actions. It is remarkable that
these deep emotions, which determine so much of what happens (from
national warfare to personal debates), are not only kept secret by those
who feel them but also by rules of etiquette and kindness. It is both
unkind and ill-mannered—downright nasty—to attribute envy or jealousy as the motive for someone's actions. In fact, telling someone
"You're just envious (or jealous)" generally makes them angry. Presumably, they feel, first, that it implies they have a basis for feeling envious
(meaning that they are inferior) and second, because it is an insult to
them in itself.

But we do observe individuals talking about others' secret feelings in
a very interesting way on the nude beach, a quasi-mocking way that
does not directly insult the person. We have noted a number of times
that people will look at someone with his suit on, or someone nude but
"accidentally" hiding his sex organs by holding something in front of
them, and say in a lilting, squeaky voice, "Oh, I just don't dare show
my thing to the world because I'm scared it isn't as big as the others
and no woman (man) could ever enjoy my little thing."

Because everyone on the nude beaches is aware of the fears of
inferiority, and take it for granted that straights will have such fears and
will probably stay away because of them rather than for all the fancy

reasons they usually give, a little booklet put out by some nude beachers in Santa Barbara starts out by trying to lay such fears to rest:

> Anyone can find something to his liking on California's nude beaches. He may not find it to keep, but he can find something to see, and certainly to fantasize about. Body-watchers of either sex have a ball. What is supposed to be the epitome of the all American male stud may not exist in all that great a number, but there are enough around to make it interesting. Most of the men are pretty much average and there is nothing wrong with that! Many of them are slightly below the norm, a few are above. Actually, the biggest bulges are often beer bellies which is unfortunate since most of the men are comparatively young. Women seem to be about as blessed as are the men. Super-development is no more abundant with them than it is with the men, averages remaining about the same for all endowments. Penile penury and minimal mammalia exist, but not to an extent to discourage or minimize the general interest.

Regardless of such blandishments, the fears probably remain intense, and it seems unlikely that people will soon overcome them. This haunting fear of inferiority, this anxiety over body-shame, and the intense *anticipatory jealousy* aroused by the image of your loved one ogling or lusting after someone better endowed and, thus, discounting your own "meager showing" is the primary source of the feeling of sexual threat posed by public nudity.

The feeling of threat is basic to understanding the whole gamut of social responses to body and sexual freedom. But its secrecy, reinforced by the knowledge that its very admission implies there is reason to feel inferior and seems to invite *others* to agree, makes it extremely difficult to assess. We believe it is the course of this and similar secret feelings that will determine the future of body and sexual freedom. Much of the threat feeling is inspired by shared social myths, which spring largely from paranoid anxiety and are supported by the secrecy surrounding them. The most obvious myth is that the size of the penis in its unexcited state indicates its size and effect in an excited state. Medical research gives no support for such beliefs (or such fears or hopes). In fact, our years of observation indicate that the male organ is highly flexible and nervous in the social setting of the nude beach, waxing and waning in direct response to feelings of shame, pride, lust, and even the warmth or coldness of the air or water. New arrivals are apt to go to one extreme of the other. A few have erections at first, but far more "shrink in embarrassment" as the men "clamp down on their feelings" to avoid erections. This may cause them to feel "inferior," and any woman who believes that the unexcited penis is a direct index of the excited state and ability may think the same—though what any particular person makes of that is far more complex. But, for some time, we expect the anxieties and the myths will remain the social realities of the beach scene and of any other public nudity or sex. The more that is true, the more people will feel threatened by such things; thus, the more they will try to stigmatize and repress them.

There is also a large group of people for whom the seeing of private parts is inevitably a form of sexual intimacy. This is especially true of some women, who seem to feel that having their sex organs seen by strangers on the beach is a form of intimate knowledge, somehow akin to violation, almost to being "taken sexually." Some men feel this way about their women, and some women feel that way about their men. For others to *see* their genitals, which are for intimate relations, elicits intense jealousy. We find it a little hard to understand how such an attitude prevails in an age when most people are routinely subjected from childhood to tortuously revealing medical examinations, some of them, such as in obstetrics, by whole teams of people. Yet we know sincere people who insist that this is their feeling about beach exposure.

There are also a large number of people who fear that the nude beach will arouse in a mate or lover sexual feelings for other people because their genitals are seen, sometimes in an excited state. Since, as we shall shortly see, the desire to see others' bodies is basic to the motive of almost everyone on the beach, we suspect this is partially true and would obviously arouse great jealousy in many people. Some people new to the nude scene are more intent on watching their mates for any sign of interest—especially arousal—caused by others' bodies. This is no doubt a major reason why women are especially careful to show a *lack* of interest in the nude bodies—and to use furtive means of looking. But it is true to vastly varying degrees, from little to a vast amount. Many people are inspired more by curiosity, and experience sexual feelings mainly in the beginning. Even then, it seems highly unlikely that the sight of another's sex organs or whole body will arouse any significant desire to actually have intercourse with that person. The "sexing-up" that occurs seems most commonly to lead to desire for the lover or mate, not for the stranger. But we shall also see that there is a great deal of casual sex on the beach, so this expectation of arousal toward others can by no means be discounted completely. Rather, it is simply to be questioned whether it is actually so important an aspect of the beach experience, or whether it is more a result of anxiety and the paranoid misinterpretations aroused by that.

Finally, another fear is closely related to this feeling of jealousy at a loved one's seeking sex with others. Many people believe that eliminating the inhibition against being nude with strangers will eliminate all other sexual inhibitions. They fear that joining the nude beach would lead their loved one to "go all the way," that the nude experience will "turn them out" into a whole new lifestyle of casual sex. One young man put this particular theory very well on his first visit to the nude beach.

> "There's just something about having a little mystery with sex—I mean it's really exciting when you're nude and making love. But what happens when you run around nude all the time and it becomes no big thing anymore? Then you'd have to look for something else that's even more exciting. It's kind of like with drugs, you start out getting your kicks with grass, but after a while that doesn't do it any more so you smoke more of it until you finally move on to the big stuff. If you get into the nude scene and it loses its magic—what next? Wife swapping? Group sex? Shit, you could end up where nothing else but bestiality turns you on!"

It's hard to evaluate this theory of all-or-nothing, of the progressive loss of inhibitions and the progressive move into casual sex. But it's not hard to see that beach public nudity in no way completely eliminates inhibitions over nudity and sex. That is ridiculous, since the nude beachers have their own "inhibitions," however much they might hate the idea. Inhibitions on male erections, female opening of legs, or on sex acts are strong. The nude beach experience leads generally to a moralistic hatred of heavy voyeurism, so much so that anyone who has been there long would find it hard to do heavy voyeurism. We ourselves got so scared of being taken for voyeurs that we felt like fiends whenever we took a camera to the beach, and the mere glance of a nude beacher was enough to make some of us de-suit with anxious guilt feelings that made us feel like screaming out, "Look, I'm honest! I'm decent! I have an all-over tan! I'm not a creepy voyeur!" At the least, we became very inhibited about being clothed on the nude beach. The relative lack of inhibition remains largely restricted to the nude beach, however, and does not lead to de-suiting on Newport Beach in front of ten thousand suited people. Nor did we ever feel seized by an impulse to de-suit in the supermarket just because it would be more "natural."

The nude beach experience does not lead to any total sexual uninhibiting. For example, most nude beachers definitely do not get into the ultimate in casual sex, groupie swinging, even when they have led a previous life of relative promiscuity or when they are given the perfect opportunity by proposition. The best indication of this is the comment of a young regular, Jon, who had been on the beach for seven years hunting women. One of the swingers told us they had invited him to a party where he could get plenty of women of all ages, but that he refused. When we asked him about it, he shook his head and said, "No way, man, I'm not up for that." On the other hand, one could speculate that he is now further along toward "that" than he was when he started out on the beach—and that maybe he will be up for it after another seven years on the beach. We could even say that we noted a certain hesitancy in his owning up to his refusal, almost an embarrassment about not being ready for the ultimate casualness.

But we could also say that any such progression could have taken place just as fast, or faster, off the beach. After all, most of the groupie swingers have never been to a nude beach, and most of the people who have been on the beaches aren't about to be ready for groupiness. Some of the naturalists are outraged by the groupies. One young man told us about a girl he met on the beach who took pride in telling him she was "what you could call promiscuous," but when she later found he was in with the swingers, she would not talk to him.

All in all, we suspect the fear that the nude beach will turn one out into all kinds of sex is largely unfounded. By the same token, the hopes of the therapists, both the professional and self-help types, that the scene will uninhibit the overly inhibited is overly optimistic. As a form of behavior modification through reinforcement, it might certainly help them to get over inhibitions about public nudity in the same way forcing yourself to pick up snakes will help you get over a fear of picking up snakes. But the hope that it will solve your sexual problems and open up a brave new world of sensual delights, just like the fear that it will create new problems and open a Pandora's box of evil sex acts, greatly underestimates the complex individual and situational relations between nudity and sex. Certainly there is casual sex at times on the beach, but this is primarily because of the self-recruitment that has gone on thus far. Especially in the early days, most of the people willing to go and thus risk the social stigma of being a "nudist" were already into some form of "disreputable" sex, and they were simply using the nude beach scene as a gathering place to pursue whatever their interests were. The whole argument suffers from the same weakness as the argument that marijuana smoking causes heroin use because there are a good number of people who have done both at some time. The truth is simply that the people willing to smoke marijuana are more likely to be willing to use heroin or any other illegal drug. They are also more likely to be into disreputable sex, sleep odd hours, like dogs, and a lot of other things. But little old ladies also like dogs, and don't necessarily become swingers. Correlation does not prove causality and uninhibiting one form of behavior (nudity) need not lead to uninhibiting another form (sex), especially when the situation is different. Most human feelings, beliefs, and acts are very situational.

Just as profound, secret feelings and sincere moral feelings lead so many people to oppose participation by themselves or by loved ones in the nude beach scene, so they lead many people to oppose the very existence of nude beaches. Some of these enemies of the beaches are absolute moralists, but most of them are probably people who fear that their own loved ones will secretly visit or even inadvertently stumble into the beaches and be outraged by confrontation with the nude bodies. Considering the number of CIA types on the beach, the first fear may be well founded. The fear of inadvertent outrage—of public outrage by accident—is not and seems to be more of a red herring than a reality.

THE QUESTION OF THE OUTRAGED TOURIST

One of the greatest barriers to participation in the nude beach scene on the part of those who might be up for it otherwise is their physical isolation, the initial public ignorance of their existence, and the difficulty of finding such out-of-the-way beaches. The beaches are normally physically isolated from major centers of population, so, until they went nude, very few people visited them. Once they did become nude beaches people often spoke of them only in joking asides, almost with embarrassment that there was a nude beach in the neighborhood. Moreover, for the first several years of their existence, the mass media paid little attention to them, and the nude beachers tried to keep it that way. Most of them didn't want any more people, and the wiser ones knew that public knowledge would arouse political controversy—as indeed it has. This "blessed silence" has now been shattered, and the growing controversy has made most people aware that such beaches exist. Each new burst of publicity has caused an upsurge in the crowds of nudes and voyeurs—and in the controversy. But, since they are beaches which few people have visited thus far, they are still not very accessible. If someone can find the beach marked on a map, he still may not know exactly how to get there.

We have literally seen people risk their lives scaling steep cliffs to get to Eden Beach because they did not realize there was a rough path a hundred yards away from where they started their descent. Many times we've shouted up to these "crazies" to warn them of their peril, only to be ignored. (I have seen a number of people fall from the cliffs. Two broke their backs, and one of them hit the ground only ten feet behind me.) We've also talked to some people who were surprised to learn they had stumbled into Eden Beach by crossing the rocks and tidepools at either the north or south end. This relative public ignorance of the location of and approaches to the nude beaches has raised the issue of *the unsuspecting and outraged tourist.*

One of the most frequent objections to the nude beaches is that some people will be offended by them. The counter-claim of the naturalists is that, if they don't want to see nude bodies, they don't have to come to the nude beach. The counter-counter-claim of the outraged (whom we shall soon see are generally property owners in disguise) is that this denies some of the people use of the public beaches, or, at least, of a small number of them. The third-order counter-claim of the naturalists is that arresting people for nudity on the hundreds of other public beaches denies *them* use of the public beaches, since they are offended by the cover-up of bathing suits and that, besides, hardly anyone comes to the nude beaches except those who want to see or participate in the nudity. The moral brick-bats and arguments defy any factual or reasoned resolution. Besides, as we shall later see, they are largely inspired by anxious feelings of threat and paranoid beliefs, or manufactured as part of the political campaign of the property owners near the beaches to get rid of "lewd riff-raff" parking in front of their houses and "stealing" their beaches. But there are some clear facts about the question of whether unsuspecting tourists wander into the beaches and are offended.

The private nude beaches in Northern California have none of these problems, since they are marked, generally with a sign, as nude beaches, and access is possible only upon payment of a small fee (generally $1.00 or $2.00). It is only the public nude beaches that might have such a problem. Some of these have informal signs indicating where the nudity is, so the problem of the unsuspecting stumbling in is not too likely to arise. Obviously, the potential problem could be largely eliminated at all beaches by signs announcing where nudity begins and ends, but officials have rarely been willing to give the nude beaches such official status. Only Eden Beach has had official signs—and nude beachers destroyed these because at that time officials were using them to prohibit nudity from certain parts of the beach. The real question is whether the unmarked beaches affront the unsuspecting.

For a long time, we assumed there must be quite a number of tourists who stumbled into the nude revolution and recoiled in shock and moral outrage. But after spending numerous hours on the borders of the nude beaches (clothed) watching and talking with the clothed people who cross that border onto the beach, we no longer believe that.

As people come across the rocks, or down the cliff, they spot the nude bodies shining in the sunlight a few hundred yards ahead. If they aren't "up for it," they have plenty of time to leave before they can get any clear impression of the genitalia. And that's what they do. In fact, there is a standard pattern of behavior. These few unsuspecting tourists spot the nude bodies, slow down, stand around or begin to wander around in a circle, and then either move forward or retreat in what is obviously a conscious choice.

The same pattern is reported by a beach patrol at Eden Beach. They say that some families come across the rocks with the intention of going to the nude beach, but, when they see what this actually means, they change their minds and go back. But these people do not seem shocked and almost never lodge a complaint, even when the rangers are standing by and clearly visible.

The major reason for the general lack of shock and outrage is that the nudity, even without warning signs, almost always becomes apparent before people are close enought to distinguish the genitalia. The important point about outrage over nudity is that most Americans today are not inspired with the absolutist morality of missionaries. What upsets them is not the *knowledge* that somewhere there are people running around nude. After all, they know that this peculiar form of behavior goes on among some savages, among some Frenchmen, in nudist camps, on stages and movie sets around the world, and in a lot of fenced backyards and most bedrooms in their own neighborhoods. They are not disturbed by nudity that is not immediate. Moreover, almost no one is ever disturbed by the sight of disrobed figures as long as the genitals are not revealed. It is the genitals that arouse all kinds of emotions—excitement, lust, shame, fear, a sense of organ inferiority, and many more, often all mixed together.

There are a few people who do experience shock or outrage over the nudity they see at the beach. Rangers and lifeguards, to whom the complaints are made, report that most of these are older people. They are generally fundamentalists, morally opposed to nudity anywhere, including among savages. Those inspired with such zeal sometimes do not turn back when they spot the nude bodies. They seek the beach out so that they can experience and express their own moral outrage against it. In fact, one of the most frequent visitors to Eden Beach does precisely this. Jerry is a middle-aged fundamentalist who for a few years brought his Bible, his clothes, and his clothed teenaged daughter and son to the beach every few days during the summer to preach to the nude beachers about the "evils of nudity and fornication." The unsuspecting naturalists are sometimes shocked by his invasion of their privacy. One lovely young girl said, "I was lying with my eyes closed when suddenly I felt this hand on my shoulder and looked up to see this clothed weirdo with a book leaning over me. Nearly blew my mind." Though he may denounce them as sinners, he's civil enough and is up-front about his moral absolutism, rather than hiding behind moral rhetoric, so the nude beachers almost always listen to him. Some smirk because they feel uncomfortable. (An effective fisher of men might understand that to go among the people you must go as they do.) But the beach regulars figure "It's his trip" and he's not hurting anyone. They sometimes show a touch of real affection for him, if mingled with suspicions concerning his "real motives." Some of them remember Freud's rule of thumb, "Behind every taboo there is a desire." We concluded this is overgeneralized, but often true.

There are also a few other zealots who visit the beach to express outrage. The park patrol told us of a little old lady who walked the whole length of the gay beach, then came back and called the park director to demand that "they must be gotten rid of, all of them, off the beach, immediately!" A few people have gone to extremes to lodge complaints. In one of the beach communities, some older people used binoculars to spot nude bathers below a high cliff and then lodged complaints with the police. The case was thrown out by a judge on the grounds that the people had had to go to extraordinary lengths to be offended. But, of course, if one feels the moral judgment against nudity is absolute, one must exterminate it whereever it is, and one must root it out to do so.

In general, we found that the great majority of unsuspecting tourists were either tolerant, even libertarian, or really interested. In fact, we think the best general rule would be that just beneath the surface of *almost* every unsuspecting tourist lurks a smirking voyeur, and that most of them are only "unsuspecting" for public purposes.

The libertarian view was well expressed by two older ladies we came across at the rocks one day. We thought we had surely discovered the outraged tourists when they stopped and asked us what beach this was. However, when we told them it was the infamous Eden Beach, they looked surprised, said they'd heard it was nude, and then said, "Well, if that's what they want to· do, I guess it's okay." A casual teenager couldn't have sounded more libertarian.

One day we saw two young college-aged girls cross the mussel rocks into the north end of Eden and walk along the water in the gay section. As they saw the nude sunbathers, they seemed to hesitate and circle around a bit, but went on. We thought this time we had surely found the outraged citizenry and started after them. But, before we could reach them to record their outrage, one of the girls had taken her suit off. We learned that they had heard about it, that one of them used to sunbathe nude in her backyard in Kansas (to the dismay of her mother, who feared a neighbor might learn of it), and that they had been anxious to come see it.

On another day, we came across two couples, in the short space of a half hour, who were both pretty typical. We were walking toward the rocks that separated civilization from the nude beach when we saw the first two people approaching the beach. We were pretty far back and couldn't make out much about them, but they seemed to hesitate and started staring at the nudes. Not wanting to affront anyone, we turned and started slowly back toward the safety of the nude pack. They came on more resolutely and gained on us. Then they went up on the beach and immediately stripped. Realizing they couldn't be the outragees we had long wanted to interview, we turned around and headed for the rocks again. As we passed them, we realized they were a couple of homosexuals who must have come over for the first time, since they were at the opposite end (the South End) from the gay area.

As we approached the rocks, we saw another couple, close enough to make out that one was a woman. They stopped as we drew near. Thinking of the experience with the first couple, we kept to our path. As we got near, the couple turned around to stare fixedly at the cliffs. When we passed them, we realized they were smiling, apparently about the nude scene. Once we were by, they went on slowly down the beach. Later we were returning to our gear when we spotted them standing on the beach, circling around, presumably thinking of what to do next. As we got near, they did a "tunnel vision thing," looking straight up in the air, presumably to avoid seeing something shameful. We thought surely we'd found the outragees, or at least some smirkers, but when next we looked over our shoulders we saw them quickly stripping, laughing and jumping around as they uncovered their POW bracelets. They had apparently only been feeling the usual mixture of shame and excite-ment of nude beach virgins.

Our continued search for the outraged tourist led us to an old couple from Oregon on the straight beach one day. When they told us they would have loved to go in the water but left their suits at home, we told them they could cross the rocks to the nude beach, just to see what they'd say. They joked about it a bit, said, "So that's where it is, ey?" then, as they were starting toward their car, the man said in hushed tones that back home they went skinny-dipping in the river all the time.

We haven't completely despaired of finding the outraged, unsuspecting tourist, but we still haven't found him, either. In his place we have found many people anxious to join up. We have also encountered literally thousands of voyeurs (often smirking), and we will describe and discuss them more fully in Chapter 4.

NUDE BEACH SEDUCTIONS

A significant minority, perhaps 5 percent at most, of people who now go to the nude beach went there suited-up in the days before it became a nude beach. These are joggers, walkers, nature lovers, property owners for whom this beach is nearest, surfers, divers, and a few people who liked swimming in an isolated area. Some of the people who fit these categories quit going when it went nude, but some kept going, a few as regulars. The great majority of people who go to the nude beaches, either clothed or nude, get to the beach by hearing about it, asking how to get there from someone who has been, or, most commonly now, going with someone who has been before. Most of these people know all about the nudity and come in large part for that reason, since it's almost always too much work to get to the beach without a strong motive.

Regardless of how they get to the beach, once they are there they find great, and often unexpected, pressures to take off their clothes. As officials have been discovering to their dismay, nude beaching is contagious. This contagion factor is especially strong for the people who, whether inadvertently or by choice, find themselves on the nude beach. There is an urge to imitate others, at least those obviously enjoying themselves.

If most people have their suits off consider this to be the appropriate thing to do, look happy, and sometimes glare at you, then you find yourself in a defensive position. You know without being told that they resent you and both you and they feel that you are taking advantage of them by looking at their bodies without offering your own for view in exchange. After a lifetime of feeling natural only with your suit on, and thinking people who run around nude in front of strangers are unnatural, you suddenly find those feelings and morals slowly being inverted. Now, in this concrete situation, you are the unnatural one, the outcast, because you have your clothes on. As a clothed TV cameraman filming the beach said, "Man, it feels weird being clothed down here with all these nude people."

In addition, anyone who is on the beach for long comes to realize that the nude beachers assume that someone wearing clothes is a voyeur, which from their standpoint is a most unfriendly and down-right immoral thing to be. This feeling is especially difficult to escape because anyone who watches the clothed people on the beach knows that they generally are indeed voyeurs. A few nude bathers start staring at you as you slink by and you begin to feel shamed at being clothed. These pressures are combined with the positive motivations of sexual excitement in various forms of *nude beach seductions*, or ways in which people are induced to take off their clothes when they are reluctant. Since some people have a considerable amount of reluctance at first, these seductive techniques are important in getting them to join the beach—to "get honest" and "be natural."

Seducing people out of their bathing suits becomes an exciting pastime for many of the naturalists. Almost all of them enjoy it, but some dedicate themselves to it. They're not at all sure why it's exciting. Certainly it's sexual and provides a voyeuristic pleasure when it's successful, but that's minimal when there are already hundreds or thousands of beautiful nude bodies on the beach. The crucial factor seems to be the seduction. This pleasure is great because the people being seduced are virgins—not sexual virgins, but nude beach virgins—those who have not previously bared their outer-most souls to strangers. The virgins carry the excitement of the unknown, and their clothes titillate sexual feelings by partially hiding that unknown. Most of the seductions are, of course, done by men, of women. Most of the attempts are on the spur of the moment in response to an urge that is simultaneously serious and joking.

For example, one day we were walking along the water talking with one of the regulars when we spotted two sixteen-year-old girls ahead of us. One of them suddenly took her suit off and waved it in the air, revealing her virginal state and jumping and laughing with the excite-ment-embarrassment of being nude—exposed for the first time. As we approached, she ran into the water, still laughing and waving her suit. Her girl friend joined in the laughter, but sat fully clothed near the water's edge. As we passed by, our friend laughingly shouted at the straight one, "Hey, are you too embarrassed to get your suit off?" She laughed and said, "Well, I'm not embarrassed, but I'm not going to get my pants off!" (Denying obvious embarrassment is standard. It's another secret emotion. Shame over nudity implies both fears of body inferiority and repressive moralism, which is "illiberal," so today among casual young people it's embarrassing to be embarrassed.)

Sometimes girls will do the same sort of thing to boys, especially if the boy has sat down to talk with a nude girl but has not presented himself in an up-front manner. After talking for a while, the girl might ask, "Why have you got that suit on? What's it hiding?" Sometimes it's harder for a girl to seduce a boy in this situation than the other way around because he may be afraid of getting an erection if he takes his pants off with the girl watching him. Many boys refuse, but most surrender, and hope for the best.

These sociable exchanges, prompted more by mirth than any realistic hope of success in seducing the virgin, are not the whole story. Some attempts are unrelenting and may engage the interests of a whole group, as we can see in the following account of an attempt to seduce two young girls:

"I had picked up on two young chicks new to the beach, with their suits and all. I brought them over to the group I was with and they joined in. As soon as we got there everyone started asking why they still had their suits on and wouldn't it be nicer to take them off? But that was only the beginning. Throughout the day the group would get to talking about the 'bastards on the cliffs looking down on the nude bathers,' 'how we could screw them up by shining mirrors into their cameras,' 'how the battle to close the beach was led by those who were too up-tight to get nude' and 'what creeps the guys were that walked up and down the beach with their clothes on.' I don't think all this was aimed directly at the girls, but when people are coming down on others with suits on and there you sit hiding behind your suit, you can't help but think they're also talking about you. It really got to the girls because whenever this stuff popped up they would just look at each other and shrug their shoulders—like, what do you say when you've got a whole group trying to get you out of your clothes? I kept hoping they'd cave in under all that pressure—I even threw in a few insults myself—only it didn't work. Too damned bad. They had beautiful bodies and you know here you just have this tremendous curiosity—and it's only part sex—to see 'em all over when they're really beautiful. You know, like you want to see how their breasts are formed and whether their nipples get erections and all. But not that day."

An even more serious form of seduction, because of its more specific sexual aim, is the seduction of the unsuspecting. This is generally done by boys and meets with widely varying results. Boys will bring to the beach girls who either don't know it's a nude beach until they see it ahead or, more commonly, know it is nude but do not suspect, or won't admit suspecting, that their companions will try to get their suits off. Sometimes girls will insist on returning to the straight beach as soon as they see the nude bodies. Sometimes they go alone. More commonly, they stay. Once the boys get them there, they generally tell them something like, "Well, everyone else is doing it, so we might as well." Sometimes the girls are anxious to join in, and in some instances even do the seducing. Often a girl will hold back, smiling stonily into the boy's eyes, as if nothing is going on, while he takes his suit off. Sometimes she will later join up, sometimes steadfastly refuse but enjoy looking at everyone, and once in a while she will leave the boy holding his suit in his hands. But the social pressures to join in, not to be a "party poop," not to be a prude, and not to create an embarrassing scene that might endanger the whole future of a relationship are generally too great for anyone who is reluctant. They generally cross the divide, and most of the time they seem to enjoy it, unless they get sunburned buttocks. Like most others, they soon share the feeling of prestige that goes with the all-over tan, the status symbol of membership on the nude beach.

The most serious form of seduction is the *nude beach rape*. It's not a real rape, just a let's-pretend rape that is raucously enjoyed by all, if a little less by the rapee than by the rapists. If someone steadfastly refuses to get honest, but doesn't really seem up-tight about it all, his or her friends will on occasion escalate their joking demands to the point of pretending to rip off his or her clothes. The victim will often scream in mock agony and put up a ferocious mock battle to preserve his or her mock modesty.

One of the regulars reported such a case to us:

"There were four of us sitting around on this blanket playing cards. Two girls and myself were nude but the other guy still had his suit on. The two girls started asking why he remained clothed. He explained that he was with a friend that didn't do nude bathing and he didn't want to blow his friend's mind by joining the scene. He maintained that he was certainly not up-tight about being nude and offered proof positive—he had gotten nude at the two girls' home. But they said that 'No one sits around in our group clothed!' and proceeded to de-pants the guy. Everyone was laugh-

ing and having such a good time that I said, 'Christ, I think I'll
have to put my pants back on.' "

No doubt the rapists could make a mistake about how up-tight the
rapee is, but we never heard of a case of pants-rape that was forced
further after the rapee raised serious objections. The nude beach rape is
just a helping hand, inspired by lustful curiosity, for those who don't
quite have enough moral fibre to get honest.

There are definitely, however, many people who cannot be seduced.
After all, most people cannot even be induced, inveigled, or seduced
into *going* to the nude beach. The people who come to the beach with
the expectation that they will join and then cop out probably do so for
the same reasons most people refuse to seriously consider joining. The
only major difference seems to be that those who come intending to do
so and then find they can't discover that their feelings about it are more
intense, more overwhelming, maybe even more panicky, than they ever
imagined they would be. Actually, this is not too surprising, since most
people cannot successfully predict how they will feel when they face
such an important and new experience. (If they could, there would be
immensely fewer "bad experiences" in losing one's sexual virginity or
starting any new sexual relationship—or any new job.)

All periods of transition in individuals' lives—and in the lives of
whole societies—are periods of great ambivalence, most especially if
one's life is changing rapidly while the basic rules and the feelings
associated with it have not yet changed much. We have seen people
caught in the anguish of total ambivalence over joining the nude scene.
A classic case was Kay, a young teacher from Kansas. She was visiting a
friend of hers, Diana, a college student who lived near the nude beach and
had been coming for some time. We had known Diana for some
time. She was quite casual about the nude scene (and about sex more
generally—she later became a masseuse and was of great help in Paul
Rasmussen's study, *Massage Parlors*). She suggested to her Kansas friend
that she might enjoy the nude beach. The friend thought it sounded
great and decided to go nude publicly for the first time in her adult life
(she was about 24). The two of them talked a third girl into coming
with them. We ran into them on the border of civilization and accompanied them the mile to the main part of the nude beach (now the legally
nude area).

Kay and the other friend showed the usual signs of the nude-beach
virgins—a little jumpy, furtive looks at the nudes lying along the beach
as we passed, and so on. When we got to the main nude area they chose
a spot and threw down their things. Diana immediately took off her

clothes, as usual with almost no sense of self-consciousness—casually. Kay did nothing and the other friend sat down clothed and stayed that way the whole day, as far as we could see. We offered to show Kay the beach and tell her about it, so she and Diana wandered along the full length of the beach (about two miles) with us. By the time we got to the northern borderlands, we were taking turns slyly poking fun at her embarrassing deviance—clothes. She generally missed the jokes or, more likely, refused to show signs of awareness that she was being lightly shamed. As this failed, we got more direct, finally asking her why she kept her clothes on when there were thousands of nude people swirling around her. She squirmed, "I'm going to! I'm going to! I just haven't gotten up to it yet!" We kept hinting ever more strongly about her immorality as we walked back to her things. Knowing how much easier it is for someone to "get honest" when there are no members of the opposite sex immediately at hand, we left, gently urging her to "keep trying."

Later that day we did see her with Diana in the ocean. As the waves lifted her, we could see she had her shirt off but was holding it in her hand. We watched from a distance to see if she would have the courage to leave the protection of the water that way, but she put her shirt on and came ashore. Toward the end of the day, we were passing by and saw she was still fully clothed, standing in the hot sun. We sauntered up and exclaimed, "Great God! You still haven't done it!" She threw her hands up in the air and laughingly cried, "I can't!" She had no doubt spent the whole day anguishing over her ambivalent emotions, first pulled one way and then the other, finally surrendering to the ancient rule.

Almost everyone who joins the nude beach goes through some of that emotional ambivalence. Probably most who do fail in their quest for new ways of life. Those who do not fail enter a creatively exciting time in their lives, but one that has further problems that have to be solved, if they are to stay in the nude scene for very long.

MANAGING THE FIRST-TIME PROBLEMS

Because it's embarrassing to be embarrassed and the excitement of exposing oneself has always been a bit forbidden, most nude beachers won't admit right away that the first time is an emotional experience. But, as with other forms of virginity, losing your nude public virginity is filled with meanings and emotions, often conflicting ones, for the nude beachers. In fact, just as with sex generally, these meanings and feelings remain important, though less so, in subsequent experiences of de-suiting. Each de-suiting is normally done in the presence of new people, strangers, whose feelings are to some extent unpredictable, so each time has to be managed anew.

In contrast to what we've just said, some people report not feeling anything much the first time they cross the divide. They do commonly take it seriously and see it as an important commitment, but report that they just didn't *feel* much about it. One young man noted that at first he didn't even feel it was very "sexy" to go nude, but after he had been nude for a number of days he began to feel quite "sexed-up" by it. This is an indication that people commonly *clamp down* on their emotions the first time as a way of preventing too much excitement—especially, for men, as a way of preventing an erection. The internal state of no or little feeling is probably the internal state accompanying the "frozen smile" that one sees on beginners. They are carefully overcontrolling themselves to avoid any mishaps that would reveal their excitement, embarrassment, panic, or whatever.

Natural or not, most people don't seem to feel very natural when they first de-suit and they certainly don't act in a manner the regulars would see as natural. They improvise with all sorts of tactics for *easing into the scene,* revealing only a little bit at a time, learning to get over each new bit of embarrassment and/or overexcitement before going on to the next challenge. Women, for example, most commonly ease into the situation by first taking off only their tops, since exposing the breasts is far less laden with emotions than revealing the pubis. We saw earlier how one casual young woman, Janine, managed her emotional tumult her first day on the nude beach.

Another young woman, as reported to us by her husband, revealed the whole gamut of tactics for easing into the scene:

"When my wife finally agreed to come down with me, she made sure that we sat way away from the nude crowd. We went so far up the beach we were almost in the gay area. We plopped our blanket right up against the cliffs—thank God there were no land slides! She was really up-tight about someone seeing her from work and thinking that she was some sort of pervert. She laid ass-up all day, facing towards the cliffs, and avoided the glances of anyone walking by. She propped herself up on her arms, carefully guarding her breasts, and worked on a crossword puzzle. She really does like to work on crossword puzzles, but then I've never seen her finish one like she did that day. I did try to get her to go for a walk along the beach but she wasn't about to . . . that would be much too revealing. She did make a couple of dashes to the water, but they were for urgent calls of nature. She was so good at hiding her body and keeping away from others, that except for her burnt ass, you'd'a thought she'd kept her suit on the whole time."

It's almost hard to believe how sophisticated many people are from the very beginning, with no previous experience in dealing with this situation, in devising techniques for hiding their genitals when they first go nude and for managing any possible embarrassment over the whole situation. Women are especially remarkable, but sometimes the men beat them at it. Women's clothes are sometimes so tight that even on the straight beach they have to sit down to get their pants off, but on the nude beach even some of those with nothing on but loose skirts or bandaid bikinis suddenly discover that the only effective way to de-suit is by sitting down, trying to get both legs in the air at once, and, failing that, wiggling it off a little at a time. Having managed that difficult feat, most of them discover that the only comfortable way to sit is with their legs tightly closed together and pulled up under their chin, and with their arms wrapped firmly around those legs with the chin resting on the knees. And, if that isn't good enough, then the only comfortable thing to do is lie on their stomach. (Sometimes you can see a row of white buttocks pointing up in the morning and the same row pointing up in the afternoon, but red. This is a major reason why there are so many sunburned buttocks on the beach and so few sunburned genitalia or breasts.)

Another popular way to deal with the emotional problems of the first de-suiting is to deceive yourself and others into thinking about the whole thing in some other terms than nudity or sex. (It should be remembered that most of the first timers have no good idea of the hip vision, the naturalist ethos of the nude beach, or of the traditional nudist ethos. They must make do as best they can with their own bag of broken values and disconnected ideas.) Some people seize on all kinds of ideas. One of our favorites was the story of a young woman who "had to come to the nude beach" because she had lost the top to her bathing suit. (But couldn't you have worn a shirt? And wouldn't it have been easier to find a top, or borrow one, than walk down and up that steep path? Besides, once you got to the nude beach, couldn't you have just kept your t-shirt on?)

One young man insisted that he de-suited because his trunks were too "trashy" to put up with any longer. (But we know a huge number of people who have gotten new suits because their old ones became trashy, rather than going nude.)

Most people look at these explanations as "rationalizations" and find them as curious as the motive of someone who leaves a note saying they've committed suicide because they couldn't get the top off the ketchup bottle. Some emphasize the desirability, even sexiness, of the all-over tan to be had at the nude beach. (But, if that is so and the whole thing to it, then why not just go to the really isolated part of the beach where hardly anyone would see you? Why park among all the other nude people?)

A nude beach couple in Santa Barbara insisted in the beginning that they started nude sunbathing because the woman had an operation and the sun would help heal the scar. This seemed strange to us, since her scar would have been sunned just as easily in any two-piece bathing suit. And, sure enough, as the day wore on, and the beer flowed, they began to talk about making the trip all the way from Los Angeles because it really "sexed them up." It was, in fact, common for people to start out giving us funny rationalizations for their nudity and then progressively open up about their sexual reasons as they got to trust us more. Some people are sincerely self-deceived; others are merely warily lying to strangers or potentially shaming friends.

But most people use the *skinny-dipping rationale,* or some variant thereof: I'm-taking-my-suit-off-just-to-go-swimming-so-now-that-it's-off-just-watch-me-dash-into-the-water and play-cooly-with-no-concern-for-the-nude-bodies. One young man made the following confession:

> "I'd just met this chick on the beach and we walked about a mile down the beach where there weren't many people. It was cloudy and cold enough to freeze your balls off, but I wanted to get her suit off, so I said let's go in for a swim. . . . She said fine and I told her I always went in without my suit because I hated to get it wet. . . . I took it off fast in case she didn't want me to. . . . But she was really up for it . . . she took off hers, saying 'Yeah, I always do too.' Only she was really so white all over I couldn't believe her. I think it was really her first time, because when we got in the water she wouldn't let me touch her much, or she didn't seem nearly as friendly, and she made a big show about swimming all over. At least I got her suit off, but that was about all."

Men, especially the very young, have a special problem during the early stages of their involvement on the beach. In the straight world, we have some sexual feelings and intentions which would be quite embarrassing if known because they're out of place at the time. Our clothes allow us to hide these with a bland smile and reserve them for a more appropriate or effective moment. But on the nude beach, a man's sexual arousal is pretty obvious, unless he can find some way to prevent its making a public announcement. Except for the heavy exhibitionists, erections pose a distinct possibility of embarrassment. They also cause a bit of anxiety among some about the danger of arrest, since most people think this is possibly a form of behavior the police would see as "lewd." (We'll see in the next chapter that almost no naturalists think of an erection as "lewd" unless it causes a feeling of threat.)

The possibility of embarrassment, and the fact of it, as well as any feared legal problem, are managed in several distinct ways. The most common way is to keep your suit on, especially if the erection has already occurred from the excitement of seeing the nude women. No doubt most erections are simply hidden this way. Sometimes the offender makes the mistake of standing up or trying to walk away, and it becomes obvious that those with suits would have the same problems as those who de-suit, if they could be seen as easily. Boys will also sometimes tell a girl that this is the reason they haven't taken off their suits. Though it is far more common to see a couple or group in which the male is nude and the female suited or, perhaps even more common, panted but de-topped, there are cases in which the girl de-suits and the male "cops out." There are also cases in which the male, not knowing the ways of the nude beach, will approach a nude girl without showing decent reciprocity. One girl who had been approached many times, and who was generally willing to talk to see what they were like, said she commonly asked the boy why he stayed suited, after giving him time to get decent or, at least, to calm down. Generally, the boys used evasion, but some would admit they were "afraid something might happen." She found that when she gave some hints that she understood such things and might even appreciate them, they would commonly undress without the feared embarrassment. But some would never get honest. Given the prevalent fears of not making a good showing, these might have feared other embarrassments. The fear of not measuring up is probably a source of far greater potential embarrassment for most people in their early days on the beach than that of overreaching the mark.

Probably the next most preferred manner of dealing with the problem is to sit on it for a while, or, more specifically, to lie on it. If you lie on your stomach, no one can see if you're erect or not. You just wait it out. We've seen couples get up to take a walk, realize that something had happened, look a bit sheepish, then decide it wasn't time. One method of dealing with the problem is especially fitted to the cold Pacific Ocean. We've heard friends give a man with a problem the advice to "go in the water and cool it off." Cooling it off works very fast. (Human sex is apparently intended only for warm climates.) However, there may be a backfire problem involved in this method. When the body begins to warm up after leaving the water, the male organ seems to rebound. This method may work only in the short run and force an extended period of sunbathing one's back.

If newcomers aren't aware of how they can cool it off, or don't think of simply hiding it in the water or in the sand, they generally just play it cool by pretending not to notice that anything is going on. Eventually the problem goes away, especially because vigorous exercise, and even walking, impedes virility. A case in point was a threesome of college students (with UC Irvine decals on their shirts), two males and one voluptuous female. They started de-suiting right away, with little easing into it, thus indicating they were either into a heated sex thing or awfully anxious to get into the water. Their POW bracelets made their beach status glaringly clear. This status was confirmed when one of the males promptly proceeded to get an extension that threatened momentarily to turn into a full-scale erection. (It is very important on the beach to distinguish between an extended penis and an erect one. We shall see the variations in the distinction in our later discussion on exhibitionism.) The girl, no doubt recognizing the situation, dashed for the water. The boys, probably realizing the impropriety of chasing after the female in this situation, were forced to put off satisfying their need for the cold water and immediately began a vigorous game of frisbee.

If a couple knows each other better and has more of a sexual relationship, or is simply more brazen, they sometimes just try to joke it off. They might say, "Uh-oh, look what happened," or "What's that?," or "I bet I can guess what you're thinking," or "Now, that's more like it," or "Are you trying to threaten me?" or "Now, let's not get lewd about this." Of course, those who know each other are commonly not at all embarrassed about the situation and may encourage its development, at least if they think they can find someplace to do something about it. And, on a rare occasion, when they feel strongly that it's no joking matter, they may not even worry about being seen by other people.

EVADING SHAME AND MANAGING SHAME

Shame is the universally shared (and genetically inherited) emotion used to enforce the basic social rules. It is a powerful emotion which, when thoroughly aroused, can cause us to "flood out," be paralyzed, and even "wish I were dead." Embarrassment is the same feeling but is aroused not by being caught in violation of a basic rule, but by being ridiculed—by being or appearing to be ridiculous. The rule against public nudity is so overwhelmingly powerful, so almost totally unviolated down through the history of the Western world, because it is enforced by both shame and embarrassment—a double-dose of shame feeling which seems to increase geometrically.

The individual who is seen nude in public is both shamed for violating such a basic social rule and embarrassed out of the fear of not measuring up. Anyone who has ever inadvertently violated the rule—who has literally been caught with his pants down—knows how overwhelming the feeling of shame is, especially if someone actually shames or ridicules you. I suspect my own fears of shame were much greater in the beginning of my experience in the nude scene—and at just thinking about it before doing it—because this happened to me once in the second grade. We had just moved to Orlando, Florida, and, being shy to begin with, I was suffering the torments of the shy new kid in a totally different kind of social situation. On one of the first days of the school year, I got on the school bus, found it crowded, and stood in the aisle. After a while another boy, sitting across from where I was standing, looked at me, started giggling and pointed at me, saying, "Your fly is open." As soon as I saw that I was indeed exposed to the world, I was flooded with the most intense feeling of shame *and* dread at unknowable consequences. I could not think of anything that could possibly retrieve the situation—all was lost. The only thought I seemed to have was that "If I do anything I will confirm their thought that I think I am shamed," which in some primordial way meant that I would be inferior. So I did absolutely nothing and stood there stonily, in total mortification, until the bus got to school. I obviously was not very good at using cognitive defenses, because I have always remembered that—with feeling. We shall shortly see that, like those of most human beings, as an adult my body has subconsciously learned how to deceive my conscious self about very painful feelings, but I still do not seem to be very good at repressing their memory.

If people had to endure the full force of shame in the beginning of their nude beaching, there would be no significant nude beaching. Only fanatics who wanted to shame themselves (as some ancient saints did) or who wanted to outrage society (as some hippies of all ages have done) would "get honest." But, of course, people do not have to endure it. They evade most of the feelings of shame by following the Basic Strategy of Shame Evasion: They begin violating the rule as secretly as possible in an isolated place out of sight of rule enforcers or ridiculers; they deceive themselves in extremely complex ways to avoid shaming themselves; they violate the rule, and recognize their violation of it, only in the least-possible stages so that the feelings of shame are as small as possible at any one time; they vent the feelings of shame they do have, so they remain at a low level; and they proceed from one stage to the next only as they have gotten used to the rule violation and do not feel great shame. If any of these conditions is not met, then the person returns to the straight and narrow world of clothed society— decency.

The ways in which people achieve secrecy—social invisibility—have been seen and are obvious. The main way in which they deceive themselves is by hiding behind the counter morals of the naturalistic ethos—we're only doing evil to achieve a greater good. "Being natural," "sincere," "honest," and "up-front" are themselves basic rules of our society. Insofar as one truly feels that going nude is those things, he has one set of feelings (righteousness) to counterbalance another set. And insofar as he can deceive himself into thinking that he is not on a sex trip, but is only being honest, he avoids triggering the shame of public sex—especially of being a voyeur or, perish the thought, body displayer. Of course, he can rarely completely believe the naturalistic counter- moral front, but it does help. It fronts out some of his own feelings of shame, or, more specifically, counter-balances his feelings of shame, and fronts out some of the possible shaming and ridiculing of him by others. After all, even straights are in favor of honesty, sincerity, etc.

When individuals cannot evade the shame feelings entirely, then they manage them. Probably the most common and most effective means of doing this is by venting the shame feelings. (Just as one can repress and then sublimate the id, so one can repress and sublimate the super-ego.) The basic way in which this is done is by *displays and angry expressions of aggressive counter-moralism* (shame-fury). People who are extremely good shame managers respond to the slightest feeling of shame, or just the situation which they subconsciously recognize will arouse that dreaded feeling, with an almost instantaneous burst of aggressive coun- ter-moralism or counter-shaming. I was walking along the beach one day when I spotted Jerry, the local moral crusader, ahead of me lambasting some innocent with his moralistic preachments against the "evils of nudity and fornication!" As I came up to him and his victim, I smiled and said "Be ye as the lilies of the field, brother," and walked on. Like most people on the beach, Jerry seemed to me interesting and okay. Then a young woman with her top off and bottom on came up to me and said heatedly, "Did that old nut attack you for being nude?" I told her he always did, but he was okay and sincere. She said, "He might be sincere, but he's still nuts." She was really angry at him. I inferred from all this that she was new at the beach (bottom on), still felt uptight about it, and for this reason angrily and moralistically attacked Jerry. I suspected she was suffering from self-deception, but looked at this only as a suspicion to be checked out if she continued to come, which she did not.

Since the nude beach was a scene in which many conflicting groups and sets of rules interacted continually with each other, it was an unbelievably rich source of personal experience and observations on shaming displays, dominance-submission displays, evasions, deceptions, venting of shame through aggressive moralism, and other means of managing shame and guilt. I was able over many years (nine thus far, but only five of which have been nude years) to observe individuals repeatedly dealing with shame and so came to recognize the patterns. (I should point out that my own feelings of shame, especially of aggressive moralism and certain forms of self-deception, long "hid" much of this from me. But I have become conscious of them and am now even watching them. I must admit it was more fun when I was deceived and could more "sincerely" vent my aggressive moralism on those "voyeur creeps" who made me feel shame subconsciously or even momentarily consciously before I could vent it and pull the warm layers of self-deception over myself.)

One of the superb tacticians of moral aggressiveness was Old Pete, a regular who was there almost every day, year in and year out, winter or summer. I had come to know how "testy" he was and how he would bristle when his attention was directed to the clothed "voyeur types."

The very word "voyeur" reeks of aggressive counter-moralism on the beach among the nudes, just as the clothed people often protected themselves against the sexual threat of the nudes by laughing at the "creeps." (The clothed people here were doing stigmatic work, not venting shame, since they felt no shame about being clothed. Nudes would sometimes do shaming displays—laughing back at them, for example—but I don't think that had nearly as much effect. Nudes are easily exposed to shaming because wearing clothes, "covering our shame," is so basic to the whole history of civilization—especially the one spawned by Adam and Eve. It took me several years to begin to *feel* the truth of this understanding and, thus, experience less shame—or less deceit and venting—when these voyeur parties came along and started doing their protective work. I still do *pitying displays* on them in my mind, which is just a lesser form of venting by counter-moralism.)

I first became quite conscious of Old Pete's counter-shaming when two of my sociological colleagues came along one day "walking the dog." (Nudes always look at such accounts as voyeur rationalizations. I look at them as more effective self-deceptions.) I was talking with my colleagues, feeling slightly uneasy in the presence of their coats and ties under the hot sun (note the subtle degrading), being careful not to let my voice quaver and, thereby, reveal my true feeling of uneasiness (let's get honest for open truth purposes—shame). Old Pete came over and introduced himself, looking up and down their coats and ties and pants and shoes, a bit testily. We had a nice little talk about the beach, with Old Pete deftly covering our shame with the warm protective mantle of the naturalist ethos.

Then one of my "creepy" colleagues started "doing ironies" on the nude scene and the deceitful frontwork. He was very subtle about it, but his primordial facial expression of semi-smirking irony made it all too apparent what the subtlety did not say, but meant (besides, Old Pete is a retired wordsmith of great intelligence). Old Pete almost immediately started preening himself, literally growing inches taller, more stately, less paunchy. (It is unfortunate that human hair does not bristle the way chimpanzee hair does when individuals are threatened.) And, of course, in an old pro like Old Pete there would never be a telltale blush. He slowly worked himself into a moral fervor about voyeurs who come down to prey upon all the innocent young girls and don't have the honesty and decency to take their clothes off like us. I tried to deflect his moral vigor (but was hoping he'd really let them have it the way they deserved). After they left, smirking, Old Pete continued to vent with aggressive-shaming directed against such creeps for some time. I have since seen him do this, generally much more subtly, against various other people; and I've seen him do the closely related stigmatic work against people who threatened him sexually (mainly sex-organ-display artists and crotch-watchers who shamed the young women and drove them off. Old Pete was mainly a casual voyeur and sociability type).

Probably the second most important way in which we vent shame feelings is by doing counter-pride displays, deceitfully taking pride and displaying pride in the very thing which has aroused shame feelings. Counter-pride displays are so commonly mixed with simple counter-aggressive behavior to achieve revenge for the aggressive intent in the shaming display that they can be very hard to observe. We all know the feelings involved, though. Consider, for example, the effects on some-one denounced (shame-display) as a "warmongering American." If one feels quite confident in his innocence, he may not even respond because he does not want any trouble. On the other hand, he is apt to feel aggressive just because someone is aggressing against him. But it is only when he is "defensive" about this Americanism—that is, when he in fact feels some subconscious shame about suspected warmongering behavior—that he responds with that sharp "overreaction" of preening himself, puffing himself up (stiffened back, stern look, haughty contempt for the inferior, chest out—all very military forceful), and doing pride displays that we call counter-pride (or pseudo-pride).

A common pattern of this was obvious after years on the nude beach. Voyeur couples would often walk along staring at the nudes, most of whom were young men, whereas the couples were commonly middle-aged. They would often giggle at the nudes or slyly do shame-displays with smirking smiles and other body language perfectly understood after years of intimate contact together. As I said earlier, this seems to be stigmatic work to protect oneself from the very sexual threat of the nude body. It seemed obvious that men were most apt to do the stigmatic work, because, presumably, most of the nudes were young men (and I suspect women feel less jealousy threat than men over nudity); but women alone in small groups would do similar things. In any event, I heard various of the body-display artists even mutter things like "I'll show that bastard," then set off to do close-up body-display spectaculars for the women. I cannot say if such response leads to more protective deceits by the voyeurs, but I would imagine so. Sometimes the nudes even started talking with the straights and seemed to be trying to get the interest of the women, presumably to arouse jealousy in the men, since it seems rather unlikely anything more could happen. This kind of counter-pride display, commonly coupled with more subtle (self-talking?) aggressive counter-moralism, would be especially successful in venting any shame feelings if it worked; it would also constitute revenge, an exquisite delight for the human animal.

We can now see why the naturalistic ethos, like moral fronts in other scenes, is so important to the people in their early days into wickedness. It is both a front to front-out shaming and a counter-moral force. The fascinating thing about the naturalistic ethos is that it is used less and less as people come to live it more and more. That is, in the beginning, when people are most on a sex trip, they talk the most about the naturalist ethos. But, as their sex trip mellows and they come to feel more natural about being nude in public (at least on the beach), then they have less need for a front or counter moral force, so they talk less about it. The most naturalistic people of all, like Big Don—who was so naturalistic that he seemed to be a practicing pantheist and spent much of his life observing and feeling with nature—would only talk about their feeling natural about the nude beach if someone else brought it up. The more people did morality-displays, the less convincing they were.

BECOMING A REGULAR

The problems of shame or embarrassment are not restricted to the beginners. Certainly most people experience a decrease in sexual arousal over nudity, both their own and others', over time. But the time involved can be very long indeed for those unused to nudity or casual sex scenes, and getting used to the nudity only restricts those situations in which arousal occurs to those which are specifically sexy. The beginner is apt to feel sexually excited all the time, whereas the regular is only aroused to a major degree by being horny, by exceptional beauty or masculinity, or by sexy occasions. One beginner said that at the end of the day his penis felt all tired out from all the alerts. The regular is far more apt to feel relaxed most of the time, and, thus, all the more ready to get up for what looks like the real thing. Many examples could be given, however, of the sexy situations on the beach that do get to him. Perhaps the best example is that of Tod, whom we met earlier. By this time, Tod was into the swinging trip (discussed later), but he still ran into some serious public relations problems one day when he decided to turn masseur:

"No, I'd never had any problem with getting a stiff on the beach until one day when I gave this chick a massage. It really is a sexy thing and I really was laying it on—full body strokes running up the inside of her legs, just touching the hair on her snatch. Man, she was really squirming around, obviously getting really turned on by it. She was dynamite! Pete, a friend who was eating it all up, got stiff even before I got to her front side and had to dash for the ocean to cool off. When she turned over, it began to happen—her moans and erect nipples were just too much for me, I really got a stiff. People were walking by and staring at the whole thing. What do you do? I finally had to stop. I just couldn't handle being stiff in front of all those people and besides that's just the kind of thing the fuzz are looking for. . . . Shit, everyone knows what you're thinking about on a nude beach. Only most of the time it isn't so obvious!"

The nude body does not become totally de-sexed for anyone except the un-sexed (after all, neither does the clothed body), and everyone knows that the straight beach is far more a sex scene than the grocery store, even when you've been going to it for years. The obvious truth that a complete de-suiting will lead to even more sexual excitement is, in fact, true. Contrary to traditional nudist public relations talk about "coming to accept the body as simply natural" and "separating nudity from sex," nudists themselves these days commonly admit they have always found the nude body more sexy than the clothed body and that it would be ridiculous to face the possible social stigmatization as a nudist if this were not so. This is even more the case on the nude beach, where sex is so much more apparent than in almost all nudist camps and where you are so much more likely to be spotted by friends or, worse, enemies. Rather than being de-sexed, over time the nude body simply becomes more an object of "constant warm appreciation" than a constant stimulus to strong sexual arousal. If this appreciation should diminish greatly for anyone, then he would probably not continue coming to the beach, for the difficulties and risks would not be worthwhile. Just about everyone who stays on the beach long, then, mellows over the nudity, but remains more appreciative by a good bit than those on the straight beaches. You become "cool" about the nudity and sex, not cold. You are neither too excited nor too up-tight, just mellow, cool, casual.

Newcomers are commonly loners. They are either too excited or embarrassed by their own particular sex trip to take much interest in the other people as people. Other people are nude bodies, not fellow sufferers and enjoyers of the human drama. You do your thing to them, and they do theirs to you. But with the mellowing of time also comes a growing sense of camaraderie with some of the people you've seen on the beach day after day, the regulars. Everyone into the nude scene quickly recognizes that he shares a good bit with other people into it—the shared opposition to the enemies of the straight world; the shared dislike and distrust of the "pigs" (especially when they come down to harass people); the enjoyments of the scene; the shared and growing hatred of the straight voyeurs. But he also recognizes that there are some nude types whom he dislikes and distrusts.

From any one person's standpoint, some of the other nude beachers are predators. Some of the couples and singles come to dislike, or even resent, some of the heavy swingers who proposition all kinds of people for their parties. For example, one young man told us of a budding friendship ruined by his association with a group of swingers:

> "I was sitting with some of the swinging crew when I noticed a
> lovely, tanned, *lonely*-looking chick down the beach. I figured,

what the hell, why not go over and talk to her? Things went really well. I got her phone number and we were talking about sex—shit, she even was saying she was what some might call 'promiscuous!' I was kind of sitting there drooling at the thought of landing this one in bed when the swingers I had been sitting with swooped in, hitting her up for one of their parties. I was kind of pissed off at their cutting in like that, but then she didn't seem to mind and she even said she might like to go to one of the parties. But, when I called her the next day she said she had thought it all over and decided she simply didn't want to get into any of *that*. . . . I tried my best to convince her I wasn't really one of *them,* but the damage had been done. . . . She wouldn't buy my lies. Those bastards had scared her off with their swinging . . . and just because I knew them I lost out on a nice piece of ass."

Some of the couples also dislike the heavy exhibitionists or heavy nude voyeurs. Some of the gays dislike the straights in general. (To the nude beachers, commonly, the straight people are the clothed people. But to the gays, the straights are also the nude beachers who are heterosexual. And, though we have not heard it said specifically, we suspect that to the "screaming gays," or those who flaunt their homosexuality openly, the straights are the covert gays, or those who do not flaunt their gayness to the straight world. There are moral factions within moral factions.)

The covert gays often hate the "screamers" and those who practice open sex on the beach, for fear of repression. And some of the straights dislike the gays, screaming or otherwise, who insist that everyone is at least a closet bisexual (or one who really is bisexual "deep down," but has not yet been turned out by a "really sexy gay guy"). Therefore, it makes sense for them to "cruise the straight (hetero) nude beach" and "put the heavies" on the straight guys.

Given these conflicts among the nude beachers, any sense of shared interests and community remains vague and conflictful. They may have a vague sense of camaraderie or of being commonly embattled, but they do not have a real sense of community, of shared identity, that encompasses the whole beach over long periods. Instead, there are subcommunities (or sub-subcultures) and, more commonly, loose groupings ("tribes") of friends and acquaintances. Just how much camaraderie there is, and how much identification with a subcommunity, varies greatly from one beach to another. Most of them have more sense of community than Eden Beach because Eden is such a big urban scene spread out over several miles and heavily infiltrated by straight voyeurs. But one, at least, had even less. Dunes Beach probably had the lowest sense of community because of the sand dunes which allowed everyone to live separately and because there was commonly so little coming together out on the beach. But even at Eden, the subcommunities and friendship groupings developed, especially among those who saw each other there for months or even years. The mere fact of having been there and having been seen not to be up to something detrimental to each other's interests, leads to a sense of "being in it together," and to the trust so essential to any friendly feelings or sense of community. These groups were partly submerged on the hot weekends when the regulars drifted among the throngs of relative strangers, but they re-emerged on days when the masses toiled in distant bureaucracies, especially on the cooler winter days when the throngs had shrunk to the tens. The fleeting sense of community was heightened by their shared isolation.

For some regulars, the beach becomes the major focus of their lives. This was certainly the case with some of the old-timers at Eden. Old Pete and Fred were two retired guys who met on the beach after making their rounds separately for months. They eventually became close friends even off the beach. The same was true of some of the young regulars, though crossing the divide from the beach to the straight world was often as much of a jump for beach relationships as crossing the divide to join the beach had been in the first place. As Janine put it, "Most people recognize that this isn't the best place to meet someone." At least, it isn't for anything beyond the casual relationship of the beach itself.

The beach is cut off from the straight world, a world largely unto itself. It is a place for escaping and for taking your own trip, for playing out your own particular dream. As uninitiated straights assume, the dreams and the realities of the nude beach are largely sexual, but they are generally very different, cooler, more casual, and far more complex than straights imagine.

3

Heavy Sex

It's obvious to most people who have never been to the nude beaches that they are "heavy sex scenes." Nudity and sex, sex and nudity. The two are irrevocably entwined deep in almost everyone's mind. *Why would anyone want to run around naked in front of a bunch of other people? Sex.* To those who look at the beach only through their mind's eye and do not share a casual vision of the beach or a traditional nudist ethos, the beach is an orgy scene. Why else would anyone go there? What else could it be? Sex. Sex everywhere. One young woman playing with her daughter at the playground admitted to two other young mothers that she and her husband had gone down to see what was going on. The other women looked shocked—the normal response to this self-exposure—and one said, "How could you stand to go down there with all those perverts?" They had never been to see, but they *knew*. The obvious was obvious. After all, how could it be otherwise?

Yet, strangely enough, outsiders who come to the beach to "see what's going on" commonly do an about-face and wind up taking an opposite view of it. Time after time, people have told us how they heard it was a wild sex scene and believed that until they went to see it. Rather than being shocked at seeing a sex orgy, they are slightly shocked at seeing "a perfectly ordinary beach scene." As one straight young man who had been jogging at the beach for several years said, "I've run at the beach a great deal over the years and I've never seen any sex there. You even see a lot of families and even older people sunning or swimming nude. It's not really a sex thing." One young woman, a doctor's wife, commented at a dinner party that she found it *depressingly* normal: "They simply aren't all they're cracked up to be. You hear about all the beautiful young nudes running around, so we went down to see. And here were all these old guys just prancing around—not very exciting."

This same view was expressed by a young couple who showed great surprise that the beach was so different from what they had expected. As the husband said,

> "I really imagined all kinds of people piled on top of each other fucking and sucking and all that—I mean a real *orgy*. But all I've seen are families playing in the surf, guys walking up and down the beach, and girls laying on their towels getting a tan . . . no sex at all . . . not even a little necking or caressing. What a disappointment! This place is so tame you could even bring your family here, no sweat. It really is a pleasant family thing."

This view of the nude beach as a family social, or a young people's health clinic is aided and abetted by some of the news stories about the beach. As we shall see in Chapter 6, we've seen some fantastic instances of newsmen coming down to the beach, almost ignoring the thousands of hip young people, and even one instance of heavy sex going on literally under their noses, while shooting hundreds of feet of color film of a few two-year-old nudes building sand castles. These two-year olds and their families constituted about one-hundredth or less of the people on the beach, but the TV camera made them look like the whole nude scene. The family social image of the beach probably springs largely from the simple contrast of the actual scene with the orgiastic images people had picked up from the atrocity stories circulated largely by property owners. The reality of the beach comes as a great shock. People are not doing genital, oral, or anal sex all over the beach; instead, there are hundreds or thousands of people standing, lying, walking, swimming, running, kissing, picnicking, playing frisbee, and doing all the other things Americans at leisure do clothed.

At first glance, the only difference seems to be that these Americans are nude, and that's largely because most of the social forms of clothed life are more or less carried over into nude life. It is also because people who are in fact doing something deviant from the rules of clothed life (beyond the obvious one of going nude) are especially anxious to look like they are doing respectable or normal things. They *normalize* the appearance of their activities, and, in fact, commonly exaggerate the normalcy of their behavior so they can use it as a front for their deviance. (The people who feel threatened by the nudity *abnormalize* the whole thing both because of paranoid delusions and for the rhetorical purpose of making it look as bad as possible.) The exaggeration of normalcy is to make sure people see the signs of normalcy; but once you know that, you can use exaggerated normalcy as a sign or index of deviance. (As it has been put, "Methinks the fellow doth protest too much" that he is innocent.)

Typically, a voyeur who is feeling shame at spying on people, or feeling fear that someone might attack him (not unheard of), looks fixedly *away* from the nudes so that when he does stare at them his attention will not seem to be undue. "See how I am concentrating on the ships at sea. That's what really interests me, as you can tell by all the time I watch them with my binoculars. So when I casually turn the glasses down the beach toward those nude girls, you can tell it's only a mere accident." No one on the nude beach will believe that binoculars are for anything but the obvious. (And, in fact, the only time I remember ever seeing anyone using binoculars and believed that he was sincere about bird-watching was when I saw Big Don. I had known Big Don on the beach for about four years by then and I knew him to be one of the ultimate old-timer regulars and a member of a local communal group. He was very casual, worked in a natural food store, and held that the nude body was an object of beauty. He was then 35 years old but looked 25, built his body carefully, but also avoided any overbuilding. He was one of the beautiful nudes and very successful with women. His latest girlfriend was with him the day I "caught" him with the big glasses, sleeping a bit while he watched the birds. Don was one of the many unlabelled pantheists among the naturalists. He had a loving interest in the birds and the little fish swimming in the rippling currents, just as he did in the beauties of the human body. But his loving interest seemed to be a sincere, gentle interest, far more gentle than I have yet managed to become. He is at the opposite extreme from the voyeur—a sincere naturalist—something very hard to become when you have not been born into the nude life.)

There's a big sign at one of the northern nude beaches proclaiming emphatically and proudly—*Nude, Not Lewd*. The owners of such private beaches know from past political hassles with local officials that it is vital for the public to see the nude beach as "respectable"—that is, non-sexy—if they are to avoid trouble and, possibly, simply to keep open. They know this is a tremendously difficult task because of the strong tendency for political enemies to assume the beach is an orgy scene without ever looking at it or, even worse, to report atrocity stories after one look.

One of the owners of such a beach told us about a local politico who came down to the beach because of the atrocity stories and spread his own:

"The county tried to stop this for a while; it wasn't with laws, just a bunch of talk. One county supervisor claimed he made a trip to the beach and that thirty women had approached him. But at that time we were 97% homosexual so we knew that we didn't even have that many women down on the beach. It was supposed to have occurred on one of those foggy, horrible days—we just knew that it didn't happen. . . . He was trying to close down the beach and had to say something."

These owners know—and so does just about anyone involved very much in the nude beach scene—that any lewd behavior would be a clear violation of state laws against indecent exposure. For this reason, they carefully cultivate the view of the beach as a "Victorian beach." Like some of the more savvy and cynical property owners, they lie. The same tactic of carefully presenting a false front about nudity as "asexual," or even Puritanical, was used very successfully by the old-line nudists to protect their camps. A few of the central people on the beaches are these same old-line nudists, and they are very consciously cultivating this asexual image of the beach. Some of the very people into heavy swinging on the beach issued grandiose proclamations in the news media about how slanderous it was for outsiders to see the beach as a sex scene. These fronts often take in nude beach virgins, but, as is true of virgins generally, they are not taken in for long. If they join up without knowing, they quickly learn the truth and, if they embrace the scene, they become supporters of the public front. Like all embattled groups, the nude beach naturalists feel the necessity for a common front.

There are, then, two polarized public views of sex on the nude beach: It's either an orgy scene or a family social. Hardly anyone, for public presentation purposes, takes an in-between position on sex at the beach. Whatever the reasons, both of these polarized views are just as wrong as extreme views are generally. The realities of sex on the nude beach are very difficult to get at, though not nearly so difficult as getting at the truth about sex in our everyday lives because one who watches and understands the emotional body-code can "see" a vast amount of "secret" life on the nude beach. It can be our periscope into the secrets of human nature. Those realities are very complex and, contrary to popular opinion, are not commonly "out in plain sight." Having spent many years unraveling these mysteries, we ourselves were left with our own sense of shock—shock that everyone could be so presumptuous as to assert, after taking one look or none at all, that they knew the truth about anything so emotion-laden and complex. While we were shocked at both sides, we were most shocked at those who accepted and perpetrated the atrocity stories, because they branded thousands of people as perverts or panderers to perverts on the basis of a relatively few stories, most untrue, and all ripped out of context.

SEXUAL ATROCITY STORIES

Those who hate the nude beachers because they have "stolen our beach" or threatened them sexually by "flashing their nude bodies in the sunlight" look at (or merely present) the beaches as truly menacing orgy scenes. Out of the deepest fears and hatreds spring the atrocity stories that mark all great human conflicts, as well as all small but intense ones like that over the nude beach. (The atrocity stories told in divorce courts are almost as blood-curdling as those told on battlefields.)

The nude beach atrocity stories are all sexual. This is especially revealing because, as the police contend, there are also a lot of drugs on the beaches (both nude and straight). It's heavy sex, not heavy drugs or anything else, that scares these people. Many of them have come to accept, or even take part in, the experimentation with one's mind and body involved in some drug use, but the experimentation with casual sex "blows their minds"—and often enrages them.

Most of the atrocity stories come from older ladies, though older men will sometimes join in, and younger men and women will not infrequently joke about them. Nothing reveals better the deep roots of these stories than the venom (and occasional screams) with which otherwise demure ladies recount them.

The first atrocity story we heard was calm enough, perhaps because of the setting. We were at a cocktail party when we heard a woman behind us telling another woman that her teenage daughters found it impossible to go to "their beach" anymore because they were afraid of the "nudists" who had taken over the whole beach. (Always remember that anyone who calls nude beachers "nudists" is either a nudist or an outsider, because they almost never call themselves that.) We joined them and asked innocently, "What sort of things are they doing down there?" She said she and her husband hadn't been down for months because the last time they were there it was so gross. They'd just gone to the foot of the private drive leading to the beach and stood there watching the "nudists." "It's really ridiculous the way some of the men just run up and down with nothing on at all. But the ones who wear a shirt and no pants are really something." Her greatest sense of outrage, however, was reserved for three clothed men who came down to the

foot of the road drinking cans of beer. She said they went over to a
young mother with her child, both nude. The men started saying
"offensive and suggestive things" about her body. She didn't look at
them, but her unhappy expression led the men to say that "any woman
who would come down here nude is ready for anything. The nudism
just attracts the worst possible kinds of people." She then repeated the
"liberal line" we were soon to hear from many people who felt
threatened: "I don't think there's anything wrong with nudity. I mean
it's your own decision. But when people do the kinds of things these
nudists do, the public has rights too and should be protected from
them." She then told of the political moves being taken by the
property owners to end the "nudist takeover."

We were to hear many more of these atrocity stories up and down
the coast, most of them far more blood-chilling. The most venomous
came from the wife of a famous scientist. She verbally attacked one of
the nude beachers who had become involved in the political attempts to
"save the beach (for nudity)," insisting that there were many perverts
on the beach. As the nude beacher, a young woman, told it,

> "She was just really upset and she is a funny little old lady, like with
> tennis shoes, and you could just see she was that type and, you
> know, the story she told she didn't even want to repeat on the
> phone—people that park on her property and park on her lawn
> and come in and knock at her door and want to use her telephone
> and ask to use her bathroom and people that shit in her
> bushes. . . . She used to go down to the beach, she said, and every
> time she would go down there, the things she would see—indecent
> and immoral things that are going on right down there on the
> beach. She said she even has seen three men just standing there
> masturbating on the beach and laughing at her. She said she's seen
> people copulating. But the biggest thing that she was upset about
> was that her daughter went down there this summer walking her
> dog and got thrown in the paddy wagon and taken down to jail
> and was booked for seven hours for just walking her dog. And
> people were so rude to her. They would call her shit-face and
> stuff like this . . . and here her daughter got busted right there
> with all the other 'perverts' that they didn't do anything about. I
> mean, she kept screaming, 'What kind of justice is that?! All those
> perverts and they arrest my daughter?!' "

Some of the same themes revealed in these stories were repeated up
and down the coast, though sometimes with less venom and with a bit

of humor. Typical of these were the stories we heard in a country bar near the Northern beaches. We had just been to the private nude beaches and had stopped off for a beer before spending what turned out to be a very cold night on the beach. The bartender was an old-timer, so we figured if anyone knew anything about the nude beaches, he would. He claimed he never had gone down but had heard a lot of stories from the guys that came in. His favorite one came from Bud, a local but well-known "tall-tale teller."

> "Bud had talked it around town that when he went down to the beach he was propositioned by three young girls, that they were all a horny bunch just waiting for him to lay them. . . . You can't always believe Bud but then Bud's wife heard the story and really gave him hell, damned near threw him out of the house. She wanted to know what the hell he was doing down on a nude beach to get propositioned!"

EVALUATING SEXUAL ATROCITY STORIES

Atrocity stories are almost certainly born in part of the great difficulty anyone has in interpreting the meanings and understanding what they see on the nude beach. The straight beach scene is one in which the patterns of behavior and their meanings are reasonably clear to everyone from years of experience. In contrast, the nude beach scene is new to the vast majority of people taking part, especially because there's a pretty high rate of turnover. Moreover, the people there are up to many different things, some of which we don't normally encounter on straight beaches. (For example, all the nude beaches have heavy homosexual scenes. There are some gay cruising scenes on otherwise straight beaches, but these are often cut off from the big public beaches, and the cruising may be less heavy.) Both of these facts make people more uneasy about what people are up to on a nude beach than they would be about what people are up to on a straight beach.

There is also vastly more lying on the nude beach. It's a scene in which many people have reason to hide their participation from their home life and where, as we shall see, everyone knows that most people are "up to something" they wouldn't want to come out and talk about with strangers, especially since they often suspect there are "plain-nude cops" on the beach. As a result of all this, the nude beach is a *scene of suspicion* and of continual misinterpretation, even on the part of those who are into the nude scene.

We ourselves were continually aware of this and, therefore, of the need to check out our own interpretations of what we thought was going on and of what people told us they were doing. An example of the problems even we encountered makes this starkly clear.

We had already observed the slow development of the nude scene for several years and had been deeply involved with the people for some months when we went down late one afternoon to take some pictures of the beach at sunset. We had chosen this late hour both because the beach is very beautiful at that time and because we were normally very anxious not to be seen with cameras, which would immediately tag us as heavy camera voyeurs with most people. (The few times we had to take our cameras down on the beaches, we hid them in plain brown bags.)

Having finished taking our pictures of the cliffs and ocean, we walked back down the beach toward a steep and treacherous path leading to the car 300 feet above. Just before we started up the path, we passed a young nude couple lying on the beach. He was lovingly caressing her. A little bit down the beach we saw Ben jogging our way. We said hi to him, and started up the cliff, exchanging some comments about his being one of the heavy exhibitionists and pick-up guys on the beach. (This was a rare combination, because the exhibitionism prevents success in heterosexual hunting, though not in gay hunting. Ben later gave up exhibitionist displays and even began wearing a swimsuit.) We'd seen him try to cut girls out from their dates, and, since this and exhibitionism (organ-displays) are two of the really heavy acts on the beach, we'd been watching him for months and comparing notes. When we got about halfway up the cliff we came to a young couple ahead of us on the path catching their breath for the final ascent, so we stopped and looked down to the beach. Ben had stopped at the nude couple and was kneeling, talking to them. The nude couple immediately got up and dressed and headed for the path. Ben took the girl's hand as they sped along, then he put his arm around her and hugged her and caressed her. She didn't seem to respond and kept walking fast. The boy didn't seem to look, but stayed at her side, moving fast. As we watched this scene unfold below on the now deserted beach, we immediately interpreted it as a pretty heavy scene. We muttered things like, "Jesus Christ, will you look at that." As it got heavier, our concern mounted.

As the three neared the beginning of the path, they disappeared under the rim of the cliff. At that point, we were really worried that Ben might try to use force to keep the girl on the beach. We agreed that we couldn't see why the boy didn't put an end to it, but then decided that he might be scared, since Ben was far more powerfully built and

much bigger. We were debating whether we should go back down to see
what was happening when the couple came over the lip of the path
toward us. Ben ran out from under the cliff at a rapid pace, then turned
and waved up. As the couple got to us, we said, "Hey, is that guy a
friend of yours?" The girl looked up, kind of surprised and said a bit
tentatively, "Oh, yeah." We figured they could have been embarrassed
and hid it from us, but why? And they did seem unconcerned about
anything other than the panting ascent, since the girl laughingly joked,
"I'll never make it." We felt forced to conclude that Ben did know her,
that he did try to cut her out from the boy, that for some reason the
boy didn't feel he should complain, but that Ben wasn't up to anything
as heavy as we thought when we assumed he was a stranger to the
couple.

We started up again, then came to the couple who had been ahead of
us earlier. The boy started to talk with us about our cameras, and we
had a very nice talk about shooting the natural beauty of the beach,
something we emphasized we'd been doing for years. As we started up
again, with the warm feeling of a friendly encounter inspiring us, the
camera bug said, "Yeah, I'll bet you really love it when the beach is
crowded." We left them smirking at a couple of labelled camera
voyeurs. All we could do was laugh at our latest evidence of the
difficulties of figuring out the meanings of what is seen on the nude
beach—and of avoiding unwanted meanings.

If we had that much trouble figuring out the meanings of what we
saw after years of casual observation and months of intense involvement with the people on the beach, how easy it is to see why casual
observers of the scene, who never even talk with anyone on the beach,
would sometimes look at the whole scene as an atrocity story. It is even
easier to see why nearby property owners inspired by hatred of the
"beach thieves" or "perverts" would see the whole scene as a "mind-
blowing orgy."

We find it especially hard to evaluate atrocity stories because we
commonly have not seen the events supposedly reported by the stories.
But we can evaluate them in terms of their similarity and dissimilarity
to the immense number of other events we *have* seen on the beach. This
will reveal how unrepresentative such stories are of the realities of the
nude beach. After all, one obviously does not want to judge the whole
nude beach in terms of a few events, any more than we would want to
judge all of American society in terms of the eight to ten thousand
murders that occur every year. We can also evaluate the stories in terms
of how distinctive they are of the nude beaches today. That is, is any
heavy sex on nude beaches today really different from what went on at

such isolated beaches in earlier days and on straight beaches today?

These evaluations reveal complex realities. Like all atrocity stories, the stories have some basis in real events. They are not totally unrelated to things we have seen on the beaches or heard from reliable naturalists themselves, though they are undoubtedly exaggerated. But, unlike what the property owners and other enemies of the beach might think, these stories do not distinguish the nude beaches from other beaches to as great a degree as they maintain. They do not know—or have not bothered to investigate—the full realities of clothed beaches.

THE QUESTION OF VIOLENCE ON THE BEACHES

Given these cautions about the difficulties involved in evaluating the atrocity stories of the beaches, let us begin our comparison of the beaches with the heaviest acts of all. Almost everyone on and off the beach would agree that these are the violent acts, and that the only forms of "super-heavy" sexual acts would be rape and sadism. We suspect that most people who see the nude beaches as orgy scenes might offhandedly expect such acts—especially rape. After all, they might reason, surely some people would be so inflamed by the sight of nude bodies that they would go to any extremes to quence their animal passions.

Yet, for some inexplicable reason, as far as we know, there have been no atrocity stories about rape or violent attacks on the nude beaches. There was one death due to knife attack at Eden, but so far as police could determine it did not involve the nude beachers and it did not appear in any atrocity stories we heard. It is hard to see why there have not been actual cases of rape on the highly isolated beaches. Some parts of the big ones are miles from civilization and in the off-season are unpatrolled by the police. In addition, there are canyons where those with a violent bent might lie in wait for any woman willing to tempt fate by walking alone in such isolated places.

Nor do we know of any instances of reported physical attack, other than an unsubstantiated report of one camera voyeur being stoned at a nude beach near Los Angeles. Many times we've seen thousands of young nudes milling around, miles from any police patrol (unless there were indeed plain-nude cops doing undercover work nearby, and we doubt that), but we have never seen any fights. The only shocking instance of physical brutality we observed was on a straight beach (a state park) in San Clemente. We were talking with some surfers and young couples in search of a wildcat beach we'd heard about but couldn't find. Suddenly we heard a woman screaming and looked over to see a big, burly, middle-aged man hitting her, then kicking her as she lay on the ground. He and another couple then walked off, leaving her moaning in the sand. (The other man remarked that she deserved an academy award.) The people we were talking to said they were married and it didn't mean much. We decided we'd better get back to the relative safety of the nude beach.

I have learned of at least two acts of near violence connected with the beach. Wendy, of whom we shall learn a good bit later, was one of the beautiful regulars for about four years. She was also one of the most reliable of our informants, since everything she ever told us that could be checked out did check out. She told me that Ben once came up to her, and, with no overtures, put his arms around her and kissed her. Jon, her boyfriend (whom we shall also hear a great deal about), was standing nearby and glared rather ferociously. Ben then withdrew. I can well believe the story because I have seen Ben run up to strange women on the clothed beach and take their hands. Wendy had a bit more scary encounter with an unknown assailant late one afternoon about dusk, as she was climbing up the canyon to return home. Schmidt Canyon is very isolated, with only a steep clay path through the underbrush. As she was slowly wending her way upward, a young man reached out from under a bush and grabbed her ankle. She did not recognize him and managed to break loose and run.

Why is there no violence, or so little we haven't yet found it? Since the moral conflicts can be very great on the nude beach, and there are no officials to mediate conflicts, why do there seem to be none? Perhaps it's because of the animosity toward violence and the general peacefulness of the casual young and the well-educated who predominate on the beach. The lack of violence on the nude beaches is especially striking in comparison to what has happened on some supposedly straight beaches. Certainly there have always been some rapes on straight beaches at night, and there have been bludgeon murders of overnight campers on Santa Barbara beaches in recent years. We would expect the reason for the lack of violence thus far is simply a matter of probabilities. Violent acts of that sort are rare events anywhere, and they occur independently of anything like nudity or non-nudity.

HEAVY SEX ACTS ON THE BEACHES

Beyond acts of violence, there would be great disagreements over what constitutes "heavy sex." Some straights, of course, would insist that all the nudity itself is heavy, or evil, regardless of what else it might or might not be associated with. There is, of course, no arguing with such extreme differences in standards, so we shall leave them aside. There is, however, a great middle ground in which some of the disagreements are partly a matter of different standards and partly a matter of different ideas about what is actually going on. There are some people on the nude beaches who would not consider some of the things we shall consider here to be instances of heavy sex. They would see almost any nonviolent sex as "their own thing," whether done privately or publicly. On the other hand, most people in the nude scene and almost everyone off the beaches would consider them so and it is their charges, especially in the form of atrocity stories, that we are considering here.

Public sex acts—anal, oral, or genital—are probably the three forms of sexual behavior which most people would see as the most offensive. Public masturbation would probably be next in line, with male erections and sexual propositioning causing the least sense of offense and the most disagreement from most people. Let us consider these three major forms of sex on the three different types of beaches—nude, isolated (but largely straight), and straight.

Some people would be offended by the mere existence of such sex acts, whether or not they were done in such a manner that they could be seen or done out in public. If this attitude is taken, then, as we shall see abundantly in the next two chapters, the nude beaches are indeed heavy sex scenes, at least in certain areas. The big beaches have canyons, and "going up the canyon" is a recognized pattern, primarily in the gay sections. Heavy gay sex of all sorts, short of violence, goes on in the canyons.

But even this form of behavior is not new or unique to the isolated beaches. Some of the same canyons and caves were used for the same purposes by homosexuals for decades before the beaches were "liberated." They have also been used by the heterosexuals for every possible form of sex. But considering private forms of sex, rather than forms of sex openly visible to strangers or the general public, also eliminates the major distinctions between the isolated beaches and the straight beaches. The straight beaches are systematically used at night for all kinds of sex. But the same is true of private sex in the daytime. The straight beaches are used for pick-ups and sexing-up partners all the time. The only difference is that, instead of going up the canyon, you go to your nearby hotel room or apartment.

One young man on the nude beach reported a close similarity in his use of the straight and nude beaches for sexual purposes:

"I used to hang out with the surfers on the beach. We'd just sit around and drink beer and rap. . . . One day two hip chicks showed up that I'd seen around some. We shared our beers with them until it became pretty obvious that they were hot to go. I grabbed a surfer friend and some more beer and the four of us headed on over to their place. We sat around and smoked some dope and drank some beer . . . really getting stoned. Then, we all started wandering around, not knowing where we were going— making trips to the john, fixing cups of tea, working on some leather goods. Finally, one chick and I ran into each other, alone; I took both her hands and motioned toward the bedroom . . . she said she was really nervous . . . I said let's go and directed her to the bedroom. We got it on and then joined the others. It works pretty much the same way on the nude beach."

Given this relative lack of differences between the types of beaches and private sex acts, we must restrict our comparisons to those acts which are open to public view and might, therefore, constitute legally lewd behavior. (Besides, it is only publicly visible sex that concerns most people.)

It sounds simple to determine whether there are public sex acts on the beach. Either you see them or you don't. But, like most of the other realities on the beach, it's not simple. The heavier forms of public sex aren't often simply "out in plain view," for there are degrees of hiding. For example, almost everyone walking on the beach walks at the water's edge. On most beaches, the edge of the water, especially at low tide, is below the level where people sit and lie. On the big beaches, the water's edge may be a hundred yards or more from the sunbathing nudes. If people lying on the sand are engaged in sex acts, the people walking by would rarely be aware of it unless they very carefully went out of their way to see such things. Again, couples may have intercourse under a blanket. We have even seen couples lying on their sides having discreet (nonvigorous) intercourse with a friend or two largely screening them from the view of people walking by at the water's edge. Is that public sex or not? It is quite problematic.

Given the complexities of these realities and the unreliabilities of most witnesses, we were always careful to believe things only when they checked out with what we ourselves had seen and what a number of other witnesses had told us. Using this as the basis for our conclusions, we think we can be confident of a number of things about the heavier forms of public sex on the nude beaches. We can be confident that such acts do occur; that they *almost* always involve some degree of concealment, so they are not simply "open to plain view"; that they are far more frequent than on the straight beaches (in the daytime); that they are probably less frequent than on isolated beaches that are nominally straight; that they are reasonably rare; and that few people other than voyeurs (including research voyeurs) ever observe these acts clearly enough to be offended. (The situation is quite different for erections and propositions.)

We have never observed any behavior that could even remotely be interpreted as actual anal intercourse, nor have we heard of any atrocity stories involving anal sex. (Maybe it's too heavy for most people's imaginations.) We were, however, informed of one instance of public anal sex by a gay guy who appeared to give very good information about everything we could check out.

> "It was on a gay beach . . . and there were about a hundred people on it . . . just before sunset. There were these two guys that dashed out into the water nude. They played around for a while and then got into it . . . one guy behind the other. It was in the water and you couldn't see for sure, but the position and the motions proved what they were into . . . going Greek right there! There's a lot of sex that goes on at the beach . . . especially late in the afternoon . . . but you don't see much anal sex out in the open, even on the gay beaches where you'd figure it would be more likely."

This act was reported to have occurred at a gay beach where nudity was practiced commonly, but where the police make arrests whenever they can catch people. Such an open event is rare enough to astound the gays themselves.

We ourselves did not observe any definite instances of oral sex out in the open for the first several years. We first observed one instance on a gay beach in which a gay guy *appeared* to be performing oral sex, but we could not be sure from where we were (at the water's edge walking by) and did not go near to check out the scene. In recent years, however, we have seen instances of oral sex, several by gays and once by a young couple. The instances we saw were away from the main areas so there were few people, but they were not concealed acts. As a matter of fact, the young couple attracted several voyeurs who stood at a distance to watch.

We were told by reliable witnesses of three instances of oral sex that were more open to public view. One guy who had been involved in the

gay scene at one beach for ten years reported two instances. He said
that at one point the beach was invaded by a bunch of "screamers"
(gays who publicly flaunt their homosexuality) who had previously
hung out on a straight beach:

> "One weekend they really cut loose. They didn't bother to go up in
> the trees or up the canyon or anything. Man, they were just doing
> sex all over the place, blowing 'em right out in the open. . . . I
> don't know if the people walking by saw it or not, but anybody
> who came up on the beach sure could see it."

This same informant reported an instance of a bisexual who mainly did
exhibitionism, but who one day propositioned a sixteen-year-old guy
and, when accepted, "popped him up against the cliff right on the
straight beach (i.e., the hetero nude beach) and sucked him in view of
some straight couples."

Another generally reliable witness told us an instance of public oral
sex among heterosexuals:

> "I'd been working on my wife for a long time and finally got her to
> come down and see what goes on. We sat near a group that was
> getting swacked on wine. My wife was really uptight and just sat
> there with her suit on while the party kept getting wilder. One
> couple began to play around—she was jacking him off and he was
> playing with her breasts. What a time for this to happen! I'd been
> telling my wife all along that nothing ever goes on down here and
> then right next to us this couple gets it on . . . but that wasn't all.
> Man, this flaky chick was so drunk she went down on him right
> there. . . . She blew him in front of us all—she didn't even try to
> cover it up! Can you believe it? The one and only time I see
> someone giving head and it has to be the same day I bring my
> wife."

We have received a number of similar accounts in recent years, but it
clearly is still rare.

Publicly open sexual intercourse, as opposed to the partially concealed variety, is rare, but happens on the beaches. Intercourse has
always occurred on these isolated beaches, simply because their isolation made these acts less visible. Anyone running along the water's edge
in the days before they became legally nude would occasionally notice
a couple up against the cliffs making love. This was generally done
under a blanket and may have been noticeable only because a runner

comes up on someone too fast to allow complete concealment. Since the nudity on these beaches has become legal, the vast increase in population has probably decreased intercourse, except in the early morning or late evening hours, when there are once again very few people around. Since the nudity became legal, we have only witnessed two instances of what appeared to be intercourse when there were many people on the beaches. In both instances, while there were no blankets used, the actions were so muted that we could not be certain of what was happening.

As we noted above, commonly an observer can only see that a couple is lying beside each other or a man lying on the woman with their legs entwined. For example, we observed a young couple, probably college students. They were lying near the water's edge and, thus, were clearly visible to the hundreds of people milling about and walking along the beach that day. They were lying on their sides with her leg over his body, embracing each other passionately. Their body motions were suspiciously intimate. They were simply oblivious to the world teeming about them, until a half-hour later they got up with sheepish smiles and quickly disappeared down the beach. In recent years, we have seen a few instances of very open intercourse. They probably "lost control" of themselves, rather than purposefully "perpetrated a lewd and indecent act upon the public." Everyone, except a few heavy voyeurs, and we research voyeurs, seems careful not to notice what is going on. *Studied inattention* to such sexual events is the order of the day on the beach, but is systematically violated by heavy voyeurs and, less systematically and with more misgivings, by nosy researchers.

Probably because the vast majority of nude beachers, like anyone else, are unwilling—perhaps unable—to perform sexual intercourse publicly, there are more instances of quasi-public masturbation. We definitely observed more instances of couples satisfying each other sexually by hand or by other parts of the body than by genitals. This was always done while lying or sitting, and with such discretion that, once again, most passersby would not have noticed. The common pattern was to suspend the heavier operations and shift to caressing a leg until the intruders had passed. Less commonly, a towel or piece of clothing might be discretely draped over one's intimate activity. We did see one young man, Jon, masturbating different girls on several different occasions and making no attempt to hide it from us as we passed by. In fact, we had the impression he wanted this bit of intimacy observed. We knew him well and suspected he was simply flaunting his ability to score. He was the most committed sexual hunter on the beach.

In recent years we've seen several instances—maybe ten—of what appears to be a pattern. We've seen men sit down about ten yards or more from attractive girls, generally in a slightly isolated area, and start masturbating in their view. The girls almost always quickly leave the area. One day I was standing in the shallow water when I noticed three girls about 30 yards further along. Midway between them and me was a young man kneeling and turned toward them at an angle that hid his genitals from both me and the many people on the beach. But his arm was moving, so I moved further into the water to check him out. He was masturbating, and I've seen him do this several times since then.

One day I was talking with Big Don and several other old-timer regulars when Barbie, another old-timer, came up shaking her head and guffawed in disbelief, "Hey, you see that guy laying beside that chick over there? He's just laying there jerking off and she's laying there watching him. I wonder what in the world she's doing—I mean, what's the kick in it for her?" We stood around some time jokingly speculating on the perturbations and convolutions of human eroticism. Even old-timer regulars might not understand sex acts they see and seek understanding from others, all of whom have some experience in observing sex on the beach. (Barbie herself had a good bit of experience, but, while she was distinctly casual, she was continually astounded at the things voyeurs would do.)

In spite of the atrocity stories, public male self-masturbation appears to be quite uncommon on the beach, though, as we shall see in our later considerations of erections, there is a great deal of less extreme shaking and caressing for display purposes. This form of public masturbation is an extreme of male exhibitionism and, as Phillip and Sharon Davis have shown, can be found, though rarely, throughout society. Campus police report a good bit of it at colleges, though how much goes on is completely obscured by the almost universal lack of reporting of it by female observers. On the beach, isolated spots are generally chosen, obviously because such behavior can lead to arrest for indecent exposure. It is quite likely that isolated beaches generally get their share of this exhibitionism. Though we cannot be sure, we were convinced that in the pre-legal days there were two exhibitionists into this on one of the isolated beaches. Once the nudity became legal and the population exploded, these two joined the beach and seemed to get out of their early heavier exhibitionism into the lighter forms that are universal on the beach.

In the early years, we never actually observed any instances of masturbation once the beach nudity became legal. We picked up other reports that seemed reliable, one a self-report.

One day we were walking along the beach when the "pig-van" (police van) came along giving out $35 tickets to all the dog owners. We stopped and watched them. At the same time, we were watching a man about forty doing what appeared to be his exhibitionist thing. He was unshaven (but not bearded), wearing a straw hat, and a shirt down to his hips, but no pants. He was following two lovely girls into the water and stopped them to talk, all the while sporting a near erection. (By going in the water, he not only did his thing, but also avoided the scrutiny of the police, since his back was to them.) After the police went by, he came over to us and, presumably because he noted our displeasure with the free-handed distribution of citations to dog owners, he said:

> "Man, you see those damned cops? They try to kill anybody's fun. Last week they arrested me for masturbating on the beach and I wasn't bothering anyone at all. They said it would be okay if there weren't any people but that there were some girls watching. There were too. While I was doing it, these ten girls came over to watch and really ate it up. They were really excited about it. But the cops put me in jail for five days. Son-of-a-bitches!"

His outrage seemed to be the result of his failing to see anything wrong with the activity and not knowing there was a law against it. He wandered off down the beach in his peculiar outfit and never showed up again.

We also got a reliable report of a similar instance on one of the beaches to the north that almost resulted in an arrest.

> "The sheriff's department does come down every now and then. On a real crowded Sunday I saw this really ugly-looking guy sitting there on the rocks playing with himself and along came the sheriffs behind him. He was just sitting there waiting for anyone who came along. . . . But he didn't see the sheriffs and they didn't see him. He was really lucky. They almost caught him."

All other forms and degrees of exhibitionism are found more frequently on the nude beaches, from waving erections and, rarely, women's spread legs to flashing bodies in the sun. All other forms of sex are also found on the beaches, from straight-out propositioning and swinging to very indirect approaches and simple dating. But all of these other forms are more subject to argument over whether they constitute heavy sex acts that affront most people. We shall reserve detailed consideration of them to the next two chapters.

All of these distinctly heavy forms of sex appeared to be more frequent, especially in proportion to the number of people involved, on the isolated beaches before they became legally nude and on those where nudity is still illegal and, thus, dangerous. The reasons are simply that the heavier forms of public sex are either offensive to most nude beachers when done publicly or else felt by them to be enjoyable only in situations where strangers aren't likely to observe. Though the total number of incidents may increase over time because the total number of people is rapidly multiplying, all nude beachers recognize the danger of such acts to the legal status of the beach.

While it is true that all of these heavy acts occur on the straight beaches, especially on off-hours, and some of them may even be more common on some college campuses, it is clear that they occur more frequently on the nude beaches than straight beaches. But it is equally clear that they are rare even there; that most people do not observe such things unless they go out of their way to make systematic observations in the manner of the heavy voyeurs; and that, consequently, heavy sex acts do not make the nude beaches public outrages.

And we must certainly keep all of this discussion of heavy sex in the total context of the nude beach experience. We have dealt with the questions of heavy sex at some length because these are a major part of the social controversy, especially of the politics, over the nude scenes. We have stressed repeatedly that these are rare events. We must keep it constantly in mind that on hot summer days, and now even on those unusual hot winter weekends, there are 10,000 to 30,000 people on Eden Beach alone. (Moreover, as we shall see later in considering the effect of the different environmental situations on the types of beach experience, Eden is the "heaviest" of the major nude beaches. By contrast, some, especially the ones around Santa Barbara, are very "mellow.")

I have mentioned that we have observed several instances of public intercourse and oral sex, though almost always away from the main crowd. I could have mentioned that during the same period there were as many drownings, half of which have nothing to do with the nude scene (because they involved a scuba diver, surfer, or party goer), and as many deaths and serious injuries from cliff climbing and hang-gliding. To the people on the beach, and to anyone who is not so severely threatened by sex as to dread its observation, those are the painful rare events that are hard to forget.

I especially find it agonizingly difficult at times to forget the young man who fell from the cliff to only about ten feet behind me and broke his back. The look of stark terror on his face cannot be erased, nor the memory of his futile attempts to move himself, nor my trembling as I rushed to find the lifeguards. Those are the terrors and tragedies of man's natural condition. Even people who are at first shocked or excited by observing public sex acts quickly adapt to them, unless there is that sense of dread or the imprinted ambivalence that lies behind eroticism in seeing others' sex instead of doing one's own. Nude beachers do not concern themselves much with such sex acts, both because they are rare and because they have little or no feeling about them. They "don't matter" and are "natural." All of this, however, does not mean that the nude beaches are not sex scenes. They are. What it does mean is that the nude beach sex scene is a casual scene, not a heavy one.

There is one exception to this conclusion. There is one form of sex on the nude beach that, from the standpoint of the nude beachers, is deeply offensive, that is certainly pervasive and massive, and yet it is completely legal in its heaviest forms. Indeed, it is a sex act even indulged in by a few of the police. Heavy voyeurism is probably the most hated sex act that is a common reality on the beaches.

4

Voyeurs, Body Fetishists and Exhibitionists

From the standpoint of the people who have been on the beach long enough to understand what people are up to, there are roughly three types of people on the beach. There are the straights or outsiders who come fully clothed, do not take part in sunning or swimming on the beach, but do the *heavy voyeur trip*. There are the people who come clothed, but do take part in the leisure activities and do not do the heavy voyeur trip. This second type is largely a limbo group made up of those with different motives for being there. On some beaches, they are young surfers with no major interest in the nude scene, though the older surfers often eventually give in to the temptations and pressures to join up. (Many nude beachers who do not know the surfers consider them voyeurs. This is in part a reaction to their feelings of surfer hostility to nudity.) Most of the clothed people on the nude beach are literally in limbo from their own standpoint—ambivalent, undecided how they feel about the whole thing and whether they should join up—and in limbo from the standpoint of the naturalists. The third group, of course, is the one cohesive group formed around the nude scene—the naturalists themselves. Each group has its own motives for coming to the beach and tends to share common feelings and ideas about the whole nude beach scene. The type with the most obvious and simple motive are the straights, the people commonly seen by the nude beachers as heavy voyeurs, though they make many situational distinctions in the degree of "heaviness."

STRAIGHTS ON THE BEACH: THE HEAVY VOYEURS

Straights look at voyeurism from two different standpoints. On the one hand, there is the moral question of the effects of voyeurism on the voyeur himself. This is really the question which concerns straights most. In this sense, nude beach voyeurism is looked at largely the way pornography or totally nude entertainment might be. It is seen by many as exciting sexual interest in the voyeur by people other than their legitimate sex partners, their spouses, boyfriends, or girl friends. As we saw earlier, it can thus arouse intense feelings of jealousy, actual or anticipatory, and from such feelings of jealousy flow the most absolute forms of moralistic judgments in many people.

This fear of sexual arousal also leads parents to fear that their teenage children will be led into deviant sex by the nude scene, especially when they believe the common stories of heavy proposition- ing on the nude beach by the males and females alike. This fear of sexual arousal and its consequences leads many people to issue orders to their loved ones not to go to the beach and, most importantly, not to indulge in voyeurism.

On the other hand, voyeurism generally concerns straights as well because of its effects on those being observed. This is quite clear in the case of traditional voyeurism. The voyeur in the grand tradition is the "peeping-tom"—a name still used by many people, both nudes and straights, to describe the beach voyeurs. Variants, such as "peepers," are also used. The peeping-tom has always been seen as a weirdo who only wants to see others' nude bodies by stealing a look, a "flaky deviant" into "kinky sex." Because of this weirdo view of peeping- tomism, it would be extremely embarrassing, or downright mortifying, to anyone to admit he or she has done it, though it seems likely that a high percentage of people have done it at some time or other. Some sociologists have even found that high-rise construction workers develop group norms about voyeurizing people in adjoining buildings.

This weirdo view of peeping-tomism has been partially transferred to nude beach voyeurism and is probably responsible for the silent and shadowy nature of the heaviest voyeurs, the *cliff-dweller voyeurs* who spy down on the nudes, both with the naked eye and with binoculars. We were never able to successfully engage these "super-heavies" in conversation. When we approached them, they slid away or, even more commonly, they would switch to peering intently through their binocu- lars at some distant object, as if to say, "Wow, can you see the lines of that beautiful ship." If we got heavy in our questioning, just to see what they would say, they never surprised us—their words said what their patterned body actions belied.

Typical of this type was one man we observed one day looking down the beach with his binoculars, obviously to get some good close-ups. We asked him why he was using his binoculars on the beach when he could just as easily go up for a naked-eye close-up. He looked shocked at our suggestion that he might be there on a peeping-tom trip, and countered, "Oh, I was just looking at the village in the distance on the hill there. It sure is hazy this morning and you can barely make out the lines of the buildings. Sure wasn't this hazy earlier. Wonder if it will clear up." The haze didn't seem to obscure the nearer objects, since we later observed that he had returned to his high-powered scrutiny of the "lines" on the beach.

While the peeping-tom stigma still clings to the heaviest beach voyeurs, they try to evade it or vent feelings of shame by a moral counter attack. (This is an instance of what I call counter-shaming: Shaming others who do or might shame you.) The gist of this argument is simple: "It's not us who are the weirdos; look, we've got our clothes on. We're respectable. It's them who are the weirdos; look, they don't even have any clothes." Those who are stripped of clothes are stripped of moral status—or, worse, imputed the status of a worse stigma. The argument is pushed even further by some to the point at which voyeurism is seen to be a favor done *for* the nudes. This argument is also simple: "They're all a bunch of exhibitionists. They want us to look at their nude bodies. The more we look at them, the more they like it. That's why they come here in the first place." At its extreme, this view of the nude beachers supports almost any heavy sexual preying on them by asserting that "anyone who would go naked in public is up for anything sexual."

The heaviest voyeurs come in many forms. The cliff-dwellers have loomed over some of the beaches for years. Long before any of the beaches became legally nude, the cliff-dwellers plied their lonely pre-occupations. On warm, sunny days, when there was likely to be some skinny-dipping or surreptitious love-making at the bottom of the cliffs, they would man their stations hour after hour, sometimes throughout the day. On a long beach like Eden, they would even run along the top of the cliffs, where there were paths, scanning the sands for a cherished "beaver shot" (a glimpse of the female pubis) or a more fulsome look at voluptuous young breasts—or maybe furtive love-making by an unsuspecting couple. Once we took some binoculars down on the beach to do a voyeur thing on the voyeurs. As soon as they spotted us peering up at them, most of them would duck or walk away, revealing their lingering sense of shame at being peeping-toms, or possibly a fear of being identified by people who might hate them. Some would peer back in a battle of the binoculars. None ever waved in a sign of friendship, as non-voyeurs sometimes do.

Those public nude beaches with low cliffs are the ultimate delight to any true cliff-dweller, because they can stand directly above the nudes and peer down on them from a mere 50 feet away. Cliff Beach and another small cove beach near Los Angeles were surely the happy hunting grounds of cliff-dwellers. These used to be beaches near large urban populations so they were accessible to voyeurs. (Political opposition has closed them down for now.) Here the voyeur could stand for hours and peer directly down on lovely young things cavorting on the sand and in the sea. The lunchtime voyeurs became an especially common sight. On any warm day when the nudes were out, the construction workers in their hard hats, the linemen in their boots, and the rotund, middle-aged executives in their status-symbol ties could be seen lining the cliffs. Many of them munched their lunches from brown paper bags, while some gulped a cold beer, and others licked an ice cream sold by an enterprising vendor who had discovered the popularity of the nude beach scene. Some peered through long binoculars, hoping for the ultimate beaver shot. The camera-voyeurs had a field day, snapping away with their telephoto lenses, bringing the lithe young bodies up to full life-size—in color, perhaps for dreamy hours of self-induced enjoyment later.

One beautiful summer day, we seized the opportunity to rush over to Cliff to record for history the titillating, erotic pleasures of our age of transition, the excited wanting to see but daring not to do which is the wellspring of voyeuristic eroticism. We took our own telephoto lenses and, by standing far to the side on the rim of the curved cliffs, we got hundreds of beautiful pictures of the whole cove beach, with the nudes lying in the sun and playing, and the little crowd of noontime cliff-dwellers peering intently down. To those who understand the scene and its total social context, those pictures communicate a great deal about our social situation today. In the background, one can see a few of the houses in which live the people who are working furiously to ban the nudity because it creates "environmental pollution" for them (both a bother and a threat). On the cliffs are the erotically ambivalent. On the beach below and in the beautiful Pacific are the many types of nude beachers—the relaxed (casual) naturalists, the gay hunters, the casual body displayers, and the beach-patrol voyeurs.

The long beaches, with plenty of air-space, provide another and truly special form of technological voyeurism—*airplane voyeurism*. Piper

Cubs skim along near the water's edge, pilots and passengers peering intently out at the people below, sometimes endangering their lives for a momentary and tiny beaver shot. The sheriff's helicopter, with no jurisdiction on a city beach, would often buzz by at low altitude. Far more commonly in San Diego, marine and naval helicopters would come in close to the cliffs for some zippy reconnaissance, even though, according to sailors and marines on the beach, military regulations forbade such close-in flights. Sometimes the Goodyear blimp would cruise slowly by below the cliffs, no doubt showing the tourists the different varieties of kelp on the beach or looking for shells.

Many of the nude beachers hated the airplane voyeurs more than any of the many other varieties, though in time they got habituated to their presence. They hated them partly because of the noise pollution, but for some the hatred ran deeper than that, to the idea that someone would use these vastly expensive, complex machines of modern technology to explode their privacy.

A few in the early days even distrusted the airplane voyeurs in the same way they sometimes distrusted all the camera-voyeurs. They suspected they might be "pig-voyeurs," taking pictures for secret files on weirdos and sex-deviates. (Some knew helicopters had been used to "raid" an L.A. nude beach.)

One day as we were walking along the edge of the water at Eden, we stopped to look at a helicopter hovering at low altitude a short distance off the coast. One of the regulars, a middle-aged engineer-type, came along and we asked, "Hey, what do you think they're up to out there?" He laughed a bit and said, "Who knows? They're probably just enjoying the nudes, but they might be bugging the place. . . . Maybe you'll see yourself in the next Watergate." In a society in which "covering your ass" is both a basic bureaucratic strategy and a matter of public decency, those who are up-front and who have public positions to worry about, have reason to be suspicious of straights, including those hovering over them. Voyeurism might be another cover for the official-dom of Big Government out to get them.

This fear of exposure is especially great when a camera is around. It reaches its zenith when cameras are clearly in the hands of the "pigs." On beaches like Eden, the police used telephoto lenses from the cliffs to get evidence against nudes in the days when the nudity was illegal. They would park on a point that overlooked almost the entire beach, survey the scene with binoculars, and once in a while try to get telephoto shots of the offenders, especially the homosexuals. It was a common belief among the regulars that some cases against the nudes had been won with these shots.

After the nude scene was more or less legalized, there were still definite instances of police taking telephoto shots of the nudes. We saw one uniformed university policeman doing this from his police car with what looked like a four-hundred millimeter lens. We also got at least two good reports from other people. One vice squad cop told us that the police were continuing their telephoto work on a sporadic basis, and a park worker upstate told us that the police, with whom he was very good friends, frequently took telephoto shots from the cliffs above a big wildcat scene. Both of them told us that the photos were used only for personal reasons.

"The pigs are just getting their jollies," as the park worker put it. But they also informed us that the police hoped it would also "keep the assholes hopping" and help "keep the lid" on the whole thing. It did help keep the "assholes" uncertain, but it made them hopping mad rather than unwilling to take part in the scene. But these stratagems and feelings wax and wave as do the politico-legal battles. Right now (1977) they are hot around Santa Barbara, but cool elsewhere.

Regardless of their suspicions of what the pig camera-voyeurs might be up to, the nude beachers were even madder at the straight camera-voyeurs who would come down on the beach to get their jollies. Some of these beach-patrol camera-voyeurs would come over the rocks decked out from head to toe with technological gear that made them look like some sub-hunter on a navy picket line.

When we think of camera-voyeurs, we always remember the heavy-set middle-aged guy who came over in his straw hat and Bermuda shorts. He had a 35-mm. camera slung across each shoulder, a 200-mm. lens dangling down the front, a pair of super-powerful binoculars swinging from his neck, and a big cigar in his mouth. We felt he was one guy who wasn't about to miss a single pubic hair on the beach. Sometimes the nude beachers would express vague fears that the voyeurs might be *plain-bathing-suit cops,* but most of the time they just saw them as real heavy or flaky. (A few regulars, mainly gays, knew the police did such things in the old days to capture nude gays.)

Most camera voyeurs start out timidly. Like anyone else, they suspect people in that scene might not like having people going around taking their pictures and they are very circumspect. Some of them scout the scene carefully in their CIA outfits before bringing their cameras. Then they might sit on the sand somewhere and use a telephoto lens to shoot distant nudes. But as they find that no one gets physically attacked and that, indeed, under some circumstances, many of the nude beachers are quite willing, even anxious, to have their pictures taken, they grow bolder. Some of them sit or lie on the sand

and take quickie hip-shots of the nudes lying nearby or walking along the water's edge. Some do it as great sport, a way of making fun of (smirking at) the "nudists."

One day a straight guy lying behind his girl friend cautiously poked the lens above her rump and took a quickie of me as I was walking at the water's edge. He quickly hid the camera under a towel and lay beside her chuckling. Not enjoying being the butt of his little joke, and disliking the camera-voyeur sport, I wheeled around and walked briskly in his direction. He stopped chuckling and burrowed into the sand behind the girl. I walked right past him, almost stepping on the camera, and stood just behind him staring at him. He apparently immediately fell into a deathlike sleep, since he did not open his eyes or breathe. After a few minutes, never having intended to do more than make him think seriously about "getting his jollies" in this way, I strolled off down the beach chuckling. (I was not then aware that I was still ambivalent and easily shamed about nudity. I was counter-shaming the camera-voyeurs to vent my own feelings of shame.)

As they got more daring, some of the camera-voyeurs would come in for close-ups. They would walk along the water's edge with their telephoto lenses at the ready. As they came abreast of some sunbathing lovely, or some muscular young man, depending on their tastes, they would stop and zero-in for a close-up. They were generally interested in beaver shots, so they were intense *crotch-watchers,* ever on the ready for an exciting shot of carelessly (or purposefully) parted legs. Some of them would walk along taking 8-mm. home movies of the nude scene, perhaps to delight their guests after dinner or to "get their rocks off" on lonely evenings.

One of the heaviest bits of voyeurism we ever saw on the beach was perpetrated by a couple of straight camera-voyeurs. We were walking along the water's edge when we saw three lovely nude beachers, all about sixteen, approaching us. About twenty feet behind them came two straight guys, both in their middle twenties, with their 8-milli-meters rolling, zeroing in on the girls' tanned buttocks. The girls were looking back furtively, disgust written all over their faces. The guys either didn't understand the body-code message or didn't give a damn and kept coming. The girls tried desperately to escape by walking briskly up into the crowd to the cliffs. The straights followed them, zeroing in for their close-up beaver shots as the girls whirled to confront their tormenters. One of the girls, apparently maddened beyond con-trol, shouted out, "All right, buddy, fuck off!" The straights beat a hasty retreat, but kept their cameras rolling. We later observed them sitting down the beach, shooting any female nude who moved.

There are two other kinds of camera-voyeurs sometimes seen on the beach, but these two, while seen as voyeurs in their own right, are not resented by most of the naturalists. In fact, they are sometimes appreciated, especially by the more exhibitionistic or those into casual body-display. There are a few camera-voyeurs on any beach who have joined-up. If they go around shooting at will, they are sometimes resented, though not as often or as much as those who refuse to go up-front. But if they ask people if they can take their picture, the naturalists are quite willing in about half the cases, either with no questions asked or a simple assurance that it's for personal use (i.e., no plain-nude cop at work and no unauthorized public display). We were talking to a young secretary one day when we were approached by an omnipresent nude camera-voyeur, a small guy who prowled the beach endlessly looking for good shots, almost always with a shirt on (no pants) and a plastic grip with his camera in it. He asked if he could take our picture, but it was obvious he really just wanted her. She'd just been telling us this was the first time she'd ventured to get all-nude on the beach, so we were a bit surprised when she said, "Well, as long as it's just for personal use, it's O.K. with me, only I'd rather you shoot me sometime when I don't have to pose. Get me kind of natural-like and when it's no bother." We even saw one case like this in which a couple of straight camera-voyeurs got a warm response from a married nude couple because they asked their permission and were very friendly. The couple they asked happened to be getting into casual sex, at the husband's insistence, so they even let the guys fondle the wife and pose with her for shots.

The final kind of camera voyeurism, and one greatly appreciated by many on the beach, while deeply resented by a few, is *TV-news voyeurism.* As we'll see in Chapter 6, television news programs became a major weapon in the struggle for control of Eden Beach. TV camera crews came down on the beach several different times to do major feature stories about beach nudity. When they came, they asked no one's permission to film anything, except when they also did inter-views. We already knew most of the reporters and camera crews from an earlier study of TV news, so we were able to go along with them and talk about what they were doing. One crew was filming everything in sight, no holds barred. We knew they wouldn't be able to show adult genitalia on the air, but they were clearly going to show enough to reveal the identities of nude people, so we asked if they felt any need to get legal releases for broadcast.

"Naw," jeered the cameraman. "Man, this is all public and we can show anything that goes on here. No one's ever won a suit against a station for showing public events." He didn't seem perturbed at the thought that most public events are not stigmatized by some of the public. He didn't even pause when a young nude he was filming from afar, realizing he was being shot with a giant camera, shot back an articulate finger as a sign of his resentment. The camera crews were largely vindicated by the fact that most of the nude beachers were happy to get on TV. Hardly anyone refused to be interviewed face to face, à la nude. When a cameraman asked two nude teenaged girls lying down if they'd like to be interviewed on TV, they jumped up smiling, quickly let their hair down and began brushing it to put their best face forward on TV. And when the crews shot anyone, the nudes would generally shout out, "Hey, when are we going to be on the air?"

While the straight camera types are among the heaviest voyeurs, they are by no means the most numerous. Certainly that distinction goes to the *hobnail boot voyeurs,* the *shirt-and-tie voyeurs,* and the *swimsuit voyeurs.* The hobnail boot voyeurs are often heavy, "panting types." They come in their work clothes or uniforms, commonly at lunchtime. We've already seen that they constitute the major force of the cliff-dwellers. But the most panting kind come down on the beach and cruise along among the nudes. Rather than walking at the water's edge, where most others do in the summer when the beach is thronged, they walk up on the beach near the cliffs where the nude beachers lie in the sun. They also meander around, carefully looking ahead to observe where there are any nudes and making their way in that direction. Sometimes their paths follow a wavy pattern as they weave back and forth, getting as close to each nude female as possible. (The heavy, panting types are always male and *almost* always heterosexual.) Sometimes they will stop and stare for many minutes. A few specialize in stopping several feet from a woman's feet and giving her the heavy crotch-stare. ("Crotch-watching" is a term commonly used by regulars.) Regardless of their age, they are on a panting trip and seem to expect the women to be turned on by their virile appearance.

One of the binoculared cliff-dwellers we observed at Eden came down on the beach and decided to add an exhibitionist frill to his voyeur trip. He would walk around, never speaking to anyone, and stand up close staring at the nude women, all the time with a nearly complete erection. We eventually got Al to talk a bit and learned that he was a construction worker. He was about forty-five, white, and stocky. He was pretty representative of the hobnail boot types (though in this case minus the boots) and he revealed in stark detail how exciting the beach is for them. It's generally a far-out, mind-blowing sex trip and, presumably, it provides the images on which their dreams feed. (We shall see in Chapter 6 just how far this construction worker went on his dreamy sex trip.)

The nudity is probably mind-blowing to them, in part because of their backgrounds. Unlike the nude beachers, most of whom are young and college-educated or street types who hang around the college world, the heaviest voyeurs, especially the cliff-dwellers, are predominantly middle-aged working-class types. Studies of sex attitudes have shown that middle-aged working people tend to look at nudity as more evil, hence, very exciting or, for the thoroughly repressed, very threatening, hence, dreaded and stigmatized. Even those workmen who use prostitutes on a routine basis are likely to see the nude scene on the beach as wild and mind-blowing. Very importantly, they are also apt to see the young women involved in the nude scene as "up for anything" and, perhaps, as the embodiments of their dreams of "nymphomaniacs," about which they tell so many stories. They are, then, much more apt to expect their voyeurism and/or exhibitionism to be exciting to the "voyees" and "exhibitionees" than is the case. The heavy voyeurs are apt to look at their actions as "giving 'em what they want," while the nude beachers are apt to feel that they are predators, people using them for their own secret desires. It is even likely that some of the heavy voyeurs find the secret evils of voyeurism to be an exciting thing in itself. Rather than being turned on by the nude bodies, they are excited by *spying on* nude bodies, by the secret evil of seeing nude bodies which otherwise would not be revealed.

This is the only way we've been able to make sense out of much of the behavior of the heaviest voyeurs. Why otherwise would they prefer to hang from the cliffs, when they could more easily come down for closer views? It could be embarrassment at facing people directly. But there is even a type that comes down on the beach, plants himself among nude bodies, then uses binoculars to spy on nudes further down the beach. This type would experience any such embarrassment and a more meager image of the nude bodies—but they also get the thrill of spying on nudity (the thrill of secrecy, of spying secretly on the unknown). Spying seems to be the excitement in itself, especially when it is seeing the unknown *and* is titillated by sexual eroticism.

The shirt-and-tie voyeurs are more discreet. Rarely do they walk among the nudes. Instead, they walk by on the shore surveying the scene, commonly with a distracted look. Sometimes they bring young women down with them on a luncheon date to see the local sights. No doubt they are on a sex trip as well, but it is more discreet, less panting, with more curiosity mixed in.

One day we saw three heavy, middle-aged men who seemed to be a special subspecies of this middle-class type. They were *super-tourist voyeurs,* each one wearing a straw hat, street shoes, Bermuda shorts, and a fiery sport shirt. They crossed the rocks and slowly made their way along the beach at the water's edge, occasionally looking timidly out from under the brims of their hats at the nudes when they didn't think they'd be seen peeking.

After about a half-mile of this casual pretense, they came abreast of a fabulous young woman who was just beginning to disrobe about twenty yards from them. She must have seen them out of the corner of her eye and decided to put them on. Without ever looking directly at them, she slowly took off her shirt, folded it, placed it on the ground. Then she unsnapped her bra, and slowly let each super-sized cup slip down, one at a time. We ourselves momentarily lost our deep veneer of casual composure, while the three straights stood there transfixed, not breathing, their heads screwed around at dangerous angles from their trunks. She bent over to lay the bra on the ground, and then she slowly undulated out of her tight pants, raised one of her supple legs shoulder high, and laid her arms and head along it in a beautiful dancer's pose. We thought the three straight guys were going to faint. Somehow, they eventually managed to get control of themselves and stumble back to the humdrum of civilization.

The greatest number of straight voyeurs come in their swimming suits or, once in a while, in their CIA tennis outfits. The swimsuit types come alone or in groups of up to eight or ten people. Those who come alone are commonly discreet. They walk along the shore, seem intent on not staring too much, and show little expression. In fact, their faces seem frozen in a mask of unconcern: "Nude bodies? Oh, yes, I hadn't noticed . . . ver much. Curious, isn't it?"

They sometimes walk up and down the beach several times at a brisk pace, seeming very anxious not to talk to anyone, especially not one of "them." Women who are on the voyeur trip are especially up-tight about it, and none are more up-tight than those with wedding rings. This type will sometimes walk up and down the beach several times. If approached by one of the regulars, they often will skitter off down the beach, too intent on their quest to exchange a friendly greeting.

The swimsuit voyeurs, who come from the straight beaches beyond the rocks, are highly variable in their approaches and have complex strategies for dealing with the situation. Some of them are willing or even anxious to be seen looking at others' genitals, since they hope it will lead to something even more interesting. ("Putting the heavies" on a female is even used by other male primates, especially the chimpanzees, as Jane Goodall found, to communicate a desire for intercourse. Little wonder that *unwilling* human females feel intensely uneasy when a man "stares" at them, especially at their nude crotches on the beach.)

Most swimsuit voyeurs are in conflict: They want to score voyeuristically (erotically and/or curiously) without being put down for being a "flaky" peeping-tom. There are many complex strategies for dealing with this conflict, but the most common is a simple pattern of fixing a nude in your vision straight ahead (since turning to look at them shows how interested you are), looking "impassively" at the nude from a distance, then averting your eyes as you get near enough to be seen looking, looking straight ahead (with tunnel vision) until you come almost directly abreast of the nudes, then flexing the head forward to look at the ground in front of you so you can make a quick, furtive, hopefully unobserved, score just as you pass by. This pattern is very effective. It allows scoring and really "eating 'em up," but avoids detection better than almost any other device at close range. It sometimes deceives the inexperienced nudes, who are often still thinking others, if not themselves, are not there on a sex trip. (The virgin is very apt to be deceived by the normalized public appearances and thus to fear "I'm the only creep in the world.")

For example, one day we were standing at the rocks at the borderland talking with a young nude beacher when he pointed to a group of five teenage girls approaching and said, "You know, it's really surprising how uninterested some of the straight women seem to be in the nude men." We told him to keep watching the girls as they approached. As they got within about fifty feet, where we could see the direction of their eyes, he recognized that all but one of them was looking at him, straight-on. As they got within about twenty-five feet, one of the four voyeurs tilted her head down and the others did that or averted their heads to the opposite side, one after the other. As they came alongside, he noted that two cast quick sidewise glances and scored for a number of seconds, both under the guise of talking to one of the other girls between her and himself. Four out of five were straight voyeurs, but none could be convicted in court.

Of course, it's not court conviction that concerns voyeurs, since the laws are all against the exposed rather than the exposees. (The people who wrote the laws must have known implicitly that almost anyone, but definitely not everyone, who gets the chance to see a nude body will do so, even if they then scream in outrage and agony.) They are concerned with avoiding conviction by the friends or loved ones who accompany them. This concern is especially great for women, since men are apt to be far more jealous of their interest in nude men than women are of their men's interest in nude women.

The straight women voyeurs have developed two major strategies for dealing with this problem—which go beyond the simple tunnel vision strategy we've discussed. The first is to evade the observation of the boyfriend or husband. This can be done in a number of ways. Most commonly, they will choose the best moment to quickly drop behind him, where he cannot see their eyes, and simultaneously rip off a quick score, sometimes with a full-face, appreciative stare, and even on rare occasions a warm smile. This is easily done when they are both walking along by dropping back a step, turning to walk behind the man to get on the other side of him, simultaneously scoring on a nude walking past in the opposite direction.

A variant on this is the oh-look-what-a-lovely-shell-I've-found strategy. By this device, a woman is able not only to fall out of step, get behind him, or face in a direction where he cannot observe her eyes, but also to get down to genital level for better close-ups without encountering the eyes of the nude. If the boyfriend or husband is using the nude scene to sex-up his woman, as sometimes happens, he may aid and abet these evasive strategies to give her maximum opportunity for voyeuristic excitement without embarrassment. He may even sometimes go so far as leaving her alone while he reconnoiters down the beach.

The second strategy is to pooh-pooh (smirk at, ridicule) the nude men, often by merely turning down the sides of the lips, while eating them up with your eyes. These are the *smirking voyeurs,* those experiencing the most ambivalence either because of internal repression or fear of shaming by friends. Smirking at the nudity is common among couples or mixed groups, but almost never exists when the straight is alone. The smirk is not for the nudes, who might be (and often are) angered by it, but for the loved one or friends with you. It is meant to show that you are not really interested in the nudes and that, above all other things in the world, you are not excited by them and their "gross exhibitionism." The smirks sometimes accompany a running commentary about the grossness of the nudes, whispered as an aside to the one next to you.

"My God, Harry, did you see that hilarious fellow back there with the big erection? He must think he's God's gift to women. I bet he doesn't even know how disgusting he looks waving that big thing around in the air like that. Tee-hee-hee."

"Hey, Betty, do you see the one over there taking a pee against the cliffs? Lord, they have no sense of decency at all. God, they're funny. Every creep in town must have crawled out of the woodwork when they heard about this place."

The smirking seems to be done by women to show their men that they are not excited by it, and by the men to show the women they shouldn't be (and better not be) excited by it.

"Hey, Lois, look how dinky that guy is. He sure wouldn't do much for *you*—ha-ha!"

The nude beachers get especially irate about the smirkers. Some have even confessed to seeking revenge by coming up close to the woman and trying to will themselves into a more attractive state (i.e., "get a mental on," "get psyched-up") for her benefit or by engaging the couple in discussion and playing up to the woman. As one man said, "That'll teach that guy a lesson."

The latest wrinkle in voyeurism seems to be the *voyeur party*. With growing frequency, the straights have been visiting the nude beaches in groups of about four to ten. They commonly come in tennis outfits, either because they've been playing a set of doubles and then decided to go for something a bit more steamy or because they feel the need for CIA protection. They also sometimes bring along their drinks—beer, wine, or cocktails. They drink as they walk along commenting on the nude scene, sometimes pointing out an interesting nude phenomenon with a wave and a slosh of the cocktail.

"Dick, did you see that guy? He was really getting there—almost a complete hard."

"Yeah, that's what the girls are hoping for. Hey, you got the wine back there?"

The voyeur party is generally more sexy, or, at least, relaxed. They're having fun and, maybe sexing 'em up so they can get it on back at the hotel, rather than smirking to protect themselves. One nude beacher put it pretty well when he said, "They've seen 'Deep Throat,' so now all that's left is to see the 'Nude Beach.' "

NUDE BEACHERS LOOK AT STRAIGHT VOYEURISM

Voyeurism, or the desire to see others' nude bodies or genitals, poses a dilemma for the nude beach naturalists, those who share in some vague way the hip or casual vision of the nude beach. The casual vision makes no allowance for the conflicting interests of the world, for the ways in which some people make use of others. It is assumed that in some way each individual can "do his own thing," "take his own trip," without coming into conflict with the trips of other individuals. Total freedom and equality for everyone is both the motto and the goal. Repression of an individual, especially through the use of any degree of force, is the greatest evil. As a consequence, no provision is made for using force against those who seek to repress or use someone else's trip. One can use expressions of contempt, or pity, but not force.

But what happens when someone preys upon you, when his trip is using you? The public nude beach, where there are no owners to exclude predators, shows very well what happens: You get used, maybe even walked on. From the standpoint of the nude beachers, voyeurs have become the plague of the nude scene, but the naturalists see no way to prevent the plague.

The abstract casual vision of the beach does not see it as in any way a sex trip, but the casual vision of life in general certainly does not exclude or downgrade sex. Almost anything goes *if you don't use others.* The problem is that voyeurism and exhibitionism do use others—they possess strangers, or score on them with the glance, and they present sexual excitation, especially in the form of an erection, to them, even if the feeling isn't mutual.

While the degree varies greatly, most of the casual people on the beaches feel used by straight voyeurism and nude exhibitionism, and this is in direct conflict with their vision of what the beach should be. One college girl showed this conflict very clearly, as reported by the friend with whom she went to the beach.

"Joanie was really anxious to go to the nude beach. She'd heard about it and thought about it a lot. She was all in favor of the naturalness of the nude scene, you know, being honest and all. But when we got there, right away she felt it wasn't what she expected. She was really upset. She kept saying, 'This is really vulgar. This isn't natural nudity—it's a bunch of exhibitionists and people staring at you. Wow! There's nothing honest in that.' She didn't leave the beach. We stayed all day and did some reading, but she kept being upset by it. She didn't take off her suit at all and she made me feel so uneasy about it I didn't either.... A couple of guys came up, nude, and asked if we'd watch their clothes while they went in swimming and I said, 'Yeah, if you'll give me one of your beers,' because I was really thirsty and

there's nothing to drink down there. They did and they were kind
of nice enough, but Joanie made it clear she didn't want to have
anything to do with them or anyone else. She just kept feeling it
was a vulgar scene. Yet she was kind of interested in it, maybe
excited sexually, I don't know. She was a bit overweight and
maybe that's really why she didn't want to get nude. . . . But we
stayed all day, with her complaining the whole time about it's not
being natural and honest."

Even when they feel all used-up by the actions of others, there is no
provision in the naturalistic, casual ethos for what to do about being
used in this nonviolent way. The implication of the casual ethos in
general about sex is clear enough to almost all casual people. "That's
their trip. Let 'em alone." As with almost all other aspects of life on the
beach, there is considerable variation in the interpretation of this
let-them-do-their-own-thing idea and in the degree to which those who
share it live up to it. There are some dedicated casual types who do
seem to live up to it, even under great stress of being used by voyeurs.

In her classic statement in the Berkeley *Barb,* Gina Shepard recognized the emotional problem caused for the earlier hip types by the
voyeurs, but then quickly concluded, "If it's their thing, just let 'em
leer":

The total experience [of being nude on the beach] was a combination of sensual and mystical responses. Being nude put me on
the same footing as the rest of creation. I understood Lear on the
heath. There was only one ugly thing on the beach. A group of
boys had apparently entered with the intention of peeking at
some nudies. Since I was the only woman there, they congregated
around me. This wouldn't have bothered me at all if they had
been nude, too. But they remained clothed in their surfer suits.
At first, this seemed a prostitution of the purpose of the Beach—
they were being "dirty" about it and it almost made me feel that
way. But after a while I realized that if I gave them pleasure by
looking at me, then that was a fine thing. If their thing is to look
at nude women for a charge, I certainly am not one to stop them
from doing their thing.

This dedication is especially called for at the small, public, cove
beaches with close, low cliffs. Cliff Beach in San Diego was probably
the ultimate test of the casual vision until it was repressed. It was ideal
for masses of cliff-dwellers, who could really get close to anyone on the
beach, and it was very near the major youth culture community of San
Diego, Ocean Beach (and nearby Mission Beach). Aside from the tiers

of cliff-dwellers haunting Cliff there were even two regulars on the beach itself who surpassed almost anything we've seen anywhere. They drifted along, not talking to anyone most of the time, looking real innocent, and coming up to stand right at the feet of any nude girl, doing a crotch-watcher's special. Most people were quickly driven off by this heavy voyeur scene, but we've seen some really dedicated casual types who withstood it all, either out of complete commitment to the casual ethos or, more likely, out of some secret exhibitionism.

One day we were sitting and talking with a lovely young nude when a hobnail boot-type came stomping along, fully clothed and "eating 'em up." He slowed to a crawl, walked so close to her that he almost stomped on her upturned feet, and nearly broke his neck craning back to get the last beaver-shot as he edged down the beach. We asked her, "Wow, what does that do for you?" We thought we caught just the slighest hint of exasperation, but all she said was, "Eh . . . that's his trip, I guess."

Nude beachers often express a mixture of contempt and pity for straight voyeurs. One guy showed this very well in his description of a heavy CIA type:

"You wouldn't believe this guy. . . . He came strolling up the beach dressed in a tennis outfit . . . with shoes, shorts, jacket, and hat . . . but most important he had on this pair of big sunglasses— on a day when we hadn't seen the sun at all. He walked right up in the sand near the nude bathers and walked at a crawl. After he'd pass the bathers, he'd move out toward the ocean and speed up. The clincher came when he got to the end of the populated beach area. He stopped and surveyed the number of bodies he could look at, figured that there weren't enough to make the effort worthwhile, turned around and spotted a girl in the water, cut a path directly toward her, repeating his slowed pace as he neared the girl and then hastening as he passed. There are a lot of freaks like that at the beach, but he was a classic. I guess you can't help but feel sorry for that kind of person . . . sort of a 'lost soul.' "

As we've said, most nude beachers don't stand up under the strain that well, especially in their early days of "liberation." While we have no definite idea of the population movements on the beach, it's pretty clear from careful observation of who is there, who stays, who returns, and who becomes a regular, that most people who come either don't return or, more often, come only very irregularly. It's especially the

women who don't return, because it's not what they expected. The
heavy pick-up scene (discussed later) may scare some off, but most find
the straight voyeurs and crotch-watchers, whether straight or nude, the
biggest "social pollution" on the beach.

Typical of this view was an amalgam quotation, below, expressed by
three beautiful girls we talked to who were doing the nude thing:

> "I do have trouble with some of the guys down here, but not that
> many. . . . I'd say one or two guys per time I come down. It really
> gets bad on the weekends and holidays. Until last December I
> never got hassled. Since then, just about every time I come down
> I get looked at, but no one really talks to us much. If they do,
> they usually ask if they can lie with us or something. Sometimes
> guys will come up and ask if they can sit with you and when you
> tell them definitely not they say OK and move off and sit only
> six feet away. . . . The first time that happened the man was
> particularly obnoxious and I just picked up my stuff and started
> to leave. Then there were about ten guys that came walking by
> very slow and just gawked and then turned around and left.
> Sometimes I really feel hostile to the lookers. Obviously you
> can't look at people that way even if they are dressed . . . it really
> depends on your attitude in looking. I've even told a couple of
> people to fuck off . . . and some people to leave. I was thinking
> this would be the last time I would come down here . . . there are
> so many sightseers . . . it sort of wrecks your time to have
> somebody *staring* at you."

These girls may have come back again, but we didn't see them. They
seem to have been three more victims of the straight voyeurs.

Contrary to the do-your-own-thing ethos of the beach, some people
have begun to take a more activist approach to dealing with the straight
voyeurs. One of the regulars described the following incident perpetrated by some casual young people who had been driven to a far-out
revenge on a young straight voyeur, an incident that certainly didn't
represent the best of the casual tradition:

> "We were sitting on the beach when we noticed that this guy came
> strutting by fully clothed with his head turned toward the
> beach . . . we all laughed and exchanged stories of the most
> outrageous sightseers we'd seen . . . this one was particularly
> active as he'd been by four times in a short period of time. We
> speculated what would happen if we would invite him over to the

group and Janine [whose first trip was described in Chapter 1], taking up the challenge, went down to ask him. They continued to walk down the beach and disappeared for some time . . . when they returned the guy had his clothes off and they joined us. The guy looked really strange. His hair looked like he cut it himself and short while his clothes were of a vintage that even the Salvation Army wouldn't sell. He was thin and obviously suffering from some skin disorder, so there seemed to be good reason to remain clothed. . . . As the discussion went on we were told that he was a computer programmer, a story which I doubt because he couldn't talk about the basics of computers . . . that he had come by bus to San Diego from Orange County and that he had only been down to the beach three times . . . he was not much to talk to and we soon got bored with his company. I made several attempts to subtly get rid of him, asking 'When does your bus leave?' or 'Don't you think it would be nice to follow that woman down the beach?' He even got to the point that he ignored me altogether . . . there was little doubt that he wanted to have sex with Janine, even asking such questions as, 'Do you read *Playgirl* and get turned on by the pictures?' The other couple had gotten so turned off by the guy that they had stopped talking to us and had begun to carry on a separate conversation. I was getting a little desperate thinking that the guy would never leave so finally I explained to him that we were planning on doing a little sex down on the beach and that we would appreciate his leaving because we wanted the privacy. . . . With that he finally left asking for Janine's home phone number and saying that he would see us around."

The voyeur plague has gone so far on the public nude beaches at times that some of the casual young have reported being driven almost beyond the bounds of casualness, right into the use of force. One young man told us that a camera-voyeur had gotten so heavy, almost taking microscopic close-ups of the girls, that he and some friends told him to fuck off or else. It didn't come to "or else," but someday it might. One normally reliable informant said she had witnessed the stoning of a voyeur on the cliffs in Santa Barbara. That sounded about as logical as Richard Nixon's giving a speech on the greatness of the Washington *Post,* so we didn't believe it. But we knew that on the northern beaches, where privacy is demanded in more unconditional terms, there have been instances where the nude beachers took cameras away from voyeurs and even where they threw cameramen in the sea—no doubt with smirking good humor.

I, myself, came over the years to realize how much the problem of the smirking voyeur is a result of the ambivalence experienced in those creative transitions from one set of shame-enforced rules to another. I could remember my own initial experiences as a clothed voyeur, as I was undoubtedly labelled by the nudes in the early days, when I was merely walking or running by in my suited state. I knew very well the initial excitement, which lasted and mellowed slowly over several years as I became more habituated to the unnatural (for me) state of naturalness. I knew also the way I had protected myself in any situation that might arouse envy or jealousy by the smirk which shows ridicule or shaming of the nudes who threatened us. What I did not at once recognize after I crossed the great divide was that I was for several years highly vulnerable to the ridicule of shaming of the clothed world, either actually observed or merely inferred in paranoid anxiety about being shamed.

In time, I became more mellow not only about being nude, but also about the smirking voyeur, simply because I no longer felt nearly as much shame—the old rules of repressive civilization were losing their force at the same time the erotic excitement of nudity was mellowing. I think I can now once again empathize more with the straight voyeurs, especially by remembering my earlier voyeuristic experiences. It is necessarily exciting for them because they remain ambivalent; and much, but not all, of their "predatory" behavior is due to that, combined with a drastically mistaken belief that most (or all) of the nude women are exhibitionists who are "up for anything." Their ambivalence means that they still easily feel threatened by the nude bodies (sex) and shame at being peeping-toms. Their smirks and their paranoid delusions about exhibitionism protect them from both the threat and the shame.

I also think I can see how my own anger at them grew out of my lingering feelings of shame because I still had the old, shame-enforced rules. When they smirked, or even when my anxiety over shaming made me interpret the slightest distant laugh as a smirking chuckle, I immediately protected myself from the powerful pain of shame, an inherited feeling of man's, by counter-shaming (the filthy voyeurs!) and counter-priding myself and my fellow nude beachers (we alone are really natural!). These moralistic attacks on them and glorifications of us vented my feelings of shame, allowing me to escape with only a feeling of uneasiness, rather than suffering the full onslaught of waves of shame.

(I have even been led to "discover" a natural index of shame feelings that are repressed from consciousness. The more shame one feels at being seen nude, or sexually, the more one's penis contracts to an unnatural or-unrelaxed state; and, conversely, the more relaxed one is, the more it is physically relaxed. One has, thus, an autonomic measure of his unconscious and subconscious feelings even when they are being repressed. One need only know how to read the code of the body to see his deepest feelings, the most important determinants of what he does.)

The fact that even old-time regulars can feel some shame and, thus, counter shame smirking voyeurs can be seen in some of the sly digs I've made in writing about them in the sections above—and which I've left in to show how nude beachers feel—and to get even! Even after all these years, it makes me feel good to counter-attack voyeurs by making fun of them, because as a child and adolescent I learned to feel intense shame about nudity and sex.

NUDE VOYEURISM, BODY DISPLAY AND ORGAN-DISPLAY

We've seen the horror and moralistic anger with which some nude beachers, mainly virgins, look at the straight voyeurs, especially the heavier types. One might expect from this that voyeurism in general would be horrifying to them and that, specifically, they would reject voyeurism for themselves. But this is definitely not the case. All nude beachers are into voyeurism themselves. The feeling they have and the point they make when being very up-front about it is that there is a big difference: The naturalist is a casual, nonsmirking, and appreciative viewer of the beauty of the human body.

As we said earlier, there appear to be three continual motives involved in joining and taking part in the nude beach. Each of these motives seems to be necessary for continued involvement in the nude scene. While there are many other motives for involvement, especially those of casual sex considered in the next chapter, they seem to vary greatly from one individual to another and none seems absolutely necessary for involvement. The most obvious and pervasive motive is that of casual voyeurism (often a bit heavier in the virginal stage). The less obvious, because more "off-color" and, thus, less talked-about and more often repressed, but almost equally pervasive motive is that of displaying one's own body.

Body-display takes the two forms of *sex organ-display* (showing one's sex organs specifically) and *full body-display* (showing one's whole body, with no concentration on the sex organs). Voyeurism is quite easy without joining the nude scene and is most widely practiced by straights, as we have seen, so it seems clear that some form of body-display motive is necessary to lead one to join the nude scene.

The third necessary motive is that of enjoying the naturalism and beauty of the beach scene for itself, without which the nude scene would probably occur in some other, even more isolated spots in the deserts or mountains. (Nude scenes do occur in such spots, but they are very small by comparison.) This love of the natural beauty of the beach is there and is important, but it is weak in comparison to the other motives, since it is obvious that anyone could more easily and with less social risk go to a straight beach. In fact, those who love the natural beauty of unpopulated beaches must now go to other beaches, since the nudity itself has attracted so many people. And many of the most truly mellow of the nude beachers, those most habituated to the nude body, have moved on.

Each of the three motives seems to be shared by almost all the people who join the nude beaches. There are a few exceptions, such as a surfer who hates the whole thing but has been going to the beach for years before it was liberated and refuses to get "shoved off the beach by the nudists," or someone who owns the access to a beach and makes money off it, but is not up for joining the nude scene. But the vast majority are into these three things—especially casual voyeurism and body-display.

While almost all individuals share the three motives, the degrees of each vary greatly. Some individuals are heavy voyeurs and only casual body-display types, while others are heavy exhibitionists or fetishists and only casual voyeurs. And there is a small minority for whom the natural beauty of the beach seems to be very important, while the voyeurism and body-display of the nude scene are relatively less important elements. It is also true that the degree of such motives goes up and down within each individual, varying with his sexual needs and general moods, with the situation on the beach, the particular people present, and the time he has been in the scene. There are probably some times when the heaviest voyeur or body-displayer is overcome with the naturalism of the scene—the warm sun, the beauty of the beach, and the sense of freedom from social constraints. These are times when they all but forget the sexual motives that almost always led them to the beach. But for most people these are rare moments against the background of pervasive voyeurism and body-display.

There is not a lot of talk about one's casual voyeurism among the nude beachers. Because of the heavy straight voyeur scene, and the obvious fact that almost all of those into nudity are against it, they tend to get up-tight when the subject of their own voyeurism is broached. And the "kinky" nature of body display makes them likely to go silent and walk off if you edge around to talking about their own body-display. If you're on really good terms with them, and they can see you're into the nude scene and decide you're being up-front, then some of them will open up some on nude voyeurism, either directly or, more likely, by saying things that make it obvious. They might even say things that allow you to infer they're into casual body-display. But these statements about themselves, what they're into, and why are not the best evidence. We eventually concluded from all of our experience and careful weighing of the evidence that lying is pervasive, almost universal to some degree, about something as emotional and conflictful as public nudity, and especially about sex-organ-display. We came to realize that relying on what people *tell* you as the means of determining the truth about them, their actions, and their motives is based on a terribly misleading bias in our culture in favor of the spoken and written word, a bias that springs ultimately from the Enlightenment Myth of Rationality. Anybody who believes that "in the beginning is the word" is bound to be taken in by the lies, self-deceptions, and put-ons of the nude beachers and all other sides involved in the conflict to control the beaches—and by human beings involved in any highly conflictful situation, which in our society today means most public situations. We quickly learned that on the beach, as in almost any realm of life where human emotions are deeply aroused, where things really count, the body-code and body actions speak far louder than words. We always tried to tie what people told us down to what their bodies said and what we could see them doing. When their bodies and actions consistently told us they were being up-front with us, that their words "checked out," then we began to trust what their words told us—but always circumspectly. (I have presented the complex details of these methods in *Investigative Social Research.*)

Some of the body language on the beach talks loud and plain to everyone. Take, for example, the cliff-dwelling construction worker, Al, whom we've already met. For weeks, Al came down to the beach and walked around with nearly a complete erection. He almost always had a faraway look about him, with a slight distracted smile—a relaxed look of unconcern. His face always said something like, "It sure is a lovely day for a relaxing walk." We never asked him if he thought the nude scene was exciting, but we felt sure he would have said something like, "Exciting? Why? What ya mean? Man, this ain't no sex scene!" But who needed to ask him anything? His body spoke eloquently. It gave external signs of his internal state that no amount of lying verbiage could disprove.

Most of the body-code and body actions are more subtle, and their interpretation poses more problems than this, but they are still much more trustworthy than words. The crucial evidence about nude voyeurism and body-display is of this sort. The strongest evidence comes from carefully comparing the sexual "stares" (the "heavies") on the straight beaches with those on the nude beaches. Almost everyone is something of a voyeur. We all like to see attractive human bodies and will look at them with pleasure even when every part of them is covered except the face or even just a whisp of hair. In this sense, a supermarket is a light voyeur scene. A straight beach is a heavier voyeur scene, where everyone goes around looking at other peoples' bodies, especially the more sexually arousing, beautiful parts—whatever happens to be your thing. The nude beach is much heavier than that, as can easily be seen by watching people watch people. This is most apparent in what we came to call the "sexual promenade."

If you walk behind the promenaders at a nude beach, and especially if you compare them with walkers at a straight beach, a striking fact is obvious. On a straight beach people walking along the water look all over the place—at bandaid-bikinied girls lying on the sand, yes, but also at the birds, the ships at sea, the waves, the surfers, the sky. When you walk behind nude promenaders and, even more, straight voyeurs, you can easily see that almost all of them skew their heads at right angles to their paths most of the time—they're staring intently at the nudes lying up on the beach. When there's a line of people ahead of you, it sometimes looks like a drill team marching by a review stand.

The nude and straight people sitting or lying on the beach do all the things people do on straight beaches: They eat, talk, sleep, read, stare back, and whatnot. But they far more commonly watch the sexual promenade passing in review, sometimes actually engaging the eyes of the promenaders, sometimes pretending to sleep and peeking out through narrow slits, sometimes peek-a-booing from under a hat brim shutting out the sun and searching eyes.

One day we'd just gone up to a group of college students, four guys and three girls, and were talking about the nude beaches they'd been to. One of the guys was talking about how most people see them as heavy sex scenes but they aren't. ("Sex? Who, me!?") While he was talking, one of the other guys started almost whispering and then came on stronger so everyone would be alerted:

"Man, look at that one. Isn't she beautiful—yeah, and she knows it.

Look at her wiggle that lovely ass—uh-uhh! What tits! God, her
nipples have got permanent erections . . . that's exciting."

Women on the beach do the nude voyeur thing, too, but more
covertly, less intently, and generally with less willingness to talk about
it. But some of them are up-front about how they sit there and "size
up" the guys who pass by doing the sexual promenade:

"It's kind of interesting for me to check out the different kinds of
guys—what their bodies are like. I'm interested in them, too. I
think that most of them don't look like much. We size them
up—see what they've got to offer. There're some real weirdos . . .
some with big proportions and all . . . we kind of take note of
their attitudes, like the way . . . if they are strutting their
stuff . . . parading around for hours and hours, walking back and
forth like they really think they are hot shit. What about the guy
that is sitting over there just to the north of us? Seems he can't
take his eyes off us. . . . He's got a hard-on! [laugh] Not too
impressive [laugh]. Under par [laugh]. He rates a number 2 on a
scale of 10."

Looking back over her years at the beach, Carol Ann summed it all
up as we were sitting with her talking about the promenade:

"I don't think anyone would come here unless they enjoyed seeing
the beautiful bodies. It's natural curiosity, sure, but it's also kind
of sexy, but not in a heavy way. It's just a beautiful, natural thing
to enjoy the beauty of nude bodies."

While any kind of voyeurism is potentially a bit off-color and
suspect to the nude beachers, especially since the straight voyeurs have
become such a plague, they will talk about their own voyeurism at
times. The crucial point to them is that their voyeurism is not a heavy
thing, and definitely not a smirking kind, unless someone does too
much exhibitionistic strutting. Their voyeurism is *respectable and
appreciative voyeurism, casual* voyeurism. As Janine put it,

"My voyeurism is more Kosher than other people's . . . mine's more
out of appreciation than out of a filthy mind. . . . You know, I
like to look at nice bodies, but I still respect the people and I
wouldn't walk up to the people and ask if they wanted to
fuck. . . . Why not? They might say no. [laugh]"

Some of the nude beachers are willing to extend the category of casual voyeurism to straights who show proper respect for the nude bodies, especially if they also show appreciation. But most of them, especially after the coming of the plague, insist upon a *reciprocity of nude exposure*. This goes back to the feeling children have about nudity—the most horrifying aspect of it, and that found so commonly in their nightmares, is that they might be the only person nude while everyone else is standing around looking at their genitals, smirking or even making fun, maybe all the while pretending that they have something better. This shame aspect of nudity, which is grounded in our feeling that the nude person is totally *dominated* by the clothed one, and the possibility that smirkers can pretend that they have something better when they aren't up-front for reciprocal observation, leads to a basic demand that anyone who is going to look at your nude body be open for reciprocal observation. The beachers also demand nudity as a symbol of commitment, showing whose side you're on. Some come right out with this demand. For example, one day I was suited-up on the beach photographing some TV-coverage of the scene and shooting some cliff-dwellers with a telephoto lens. A couple of regulars, whom I knew only by sight, came along and asked what I was doing. I told them I was getting a picture of the voyeur on the cliff taking pictures of the beach scene. One of them said very pointedly, "Yeah, the god-damned voyeurs. Anyone wearing clothes on the beach is a voyeur—and we hate voyeurs down here!" They gave me the feeling they were trying to tell me something. As I touched on earlier, I was shamed at the "immorality" of having on my suit—I had done them an injustice, ripped them off, simply by having a suit on. To cover the TV people, I'd stepped across the wavy line, that grey-area of social variability between deviance and respectability, joining the predators.

The distinction between casual (respectable) and heavy (deviant) also applies to the more off-color activity of body-display. The naturalistic attitude is, of course, that the body is a beautiful thing and should be open for appreciation to anyone who is willing to appreciate it, at least on the beach. But, at the same time, all the simple traditional feelings about the evils of "showing off" apply to body-display, and any heavier display—especially that of exhibitionism, which focuses on one's sex organs—takes on some of the same sense of evil that it has for straights. The degree of feeling is very different, far less for the nude beachers, but it still seems off-color to most, or at least a bit embarrassing.

People are much more willing to talk about the body-display of other people on the beach than about their own, probably because the latter would show a lack of humility. (If you're displaying your body to others, it must be because you think it's pretty good.) For example, the group of girls above who were talking about sizing up the men on the beach talked about their ability to tell which guys were proud of their bodies:

"You can really tell the guys that think they have nice bodies . . . especially if they're the muscular type. Take that guy that's walking by. I'm sure he's aware of the fact he's well built . . . he's kind of looking back, thinking it's kind of nice to have four girls looking at him . . . asking, 'Got enough, girls? Want me to come back for a little more?' That's part of the fun coming here—making others aware of what you're thinking . . . and what the others think of you. They don't have to act really overt . . . they just have to show it."

Most of the body-display on the beach is full body-display, rather than organ-display. This is seen, though only very discreetly, in the playing of frisbee or nude jogging by the boys and men. They're displaying their strong young bodies for female appreciation at the same time that they're playing.

Female body-display is generally full body-display, most of it in the way a woman walks or even the grace of body she displays in the way she lies on the beach. But it is most apparent in the case of women doing things such as stretching exercises, in which the full beauty of the body is displayed, often with deliberately sexy motions. A few of the girls even look at themselves as nude models, though we did not find any who had yet done professional work. Two of them were anxious to pose very sexily for pictures.

As one of the regulars, an amateur photographer, told it:

"I first noticed Missy and Donna when a camera crew came down to do a story about the beach. They were hanging around in hopes that they would make it on TV. I went up and started to talk with them. Both claimed to be nude models, and I fed them the line that I was a professional photographer—even had my camera with me, only for scenery shots, of course, but offered to take some shots of them for their portfolios. They both jumped at the chance. We went up the beach and I shot four rolls of film . . . really got some sexy shots. They knew what it was all about, running around trying to get into a sexy pose. My favorite one was of Missy, her head slightly hung to one side and her body set in that all-inviting way. That was one of the few slides that turned out . . . I had screwed up the light exposure . . . sometimes I flash it on my living room wall with the drapes open, blowing the minds of my neighbors. It's not quite like getting an airing on TV, but you have to take it as it comes."

But there is also some female organ-display. We have seen obvious cases where the women deliberately spread their legs in very tantalizing fashions. A few are noteworthy for sunbathing in that fashion, something rarely done. Women are even less willing to talk about their full body-display and organ-display than men, but we came up with one case of female body-display which was really open, all up-front. She'd come down to the beach with one of the regulars, who reported later that he hadn't really wanted to bring her down, but she'd insisted. She'd never been into a nude scene before, so we thought she'd be up-tight about it. But she jumped out of her suit right away, expressing only a slight bit of anxiety about the "strangeness about it all." She had a tremendous build, so she had lots to display, but we were surprised at how up-front she was in doing it. It wasn't any time before she was walking around and saying things like, "Wow, it's really great to have guys staring at me like that. Wow, what an ego trip" When they were about to leave she said, "Wow, if I ever get really bummed out someday, I'm just going to come down here and get a lift—skyhigh!"

We told her we hoped she would and looked forward to seeing her again. It was really refreshing to find someone so up-front about something that most people were into but unwilling to open up about. One of the regulars also told us of some up-front types he'd met:

"Rich and I were sitting with two chicks he had brought down for their first time. They were obviously not concerned with exposing any part of their bodies. Man, they were shooting beaver shots all over . . . laying on the blanket, not seeming to notice which part of their bodies they exposed to view. I was really digging the whole thing and so were most of the other people sitting around us . . . one guy even came over and complimented the girls on their natural sun bathing. . . . He said it was the way it was done in Europe and people would be getting into it here when they got over being self-conscious of their bodies."

Another time Tod told of similar doings.

"There were these three sisters, two of them doing yoga at the water's edge and the third sitting on a blanket watching. A group of about ten guys had formed around them, watching, and commenting about how they had never seen anyone doing yoga exercise and all. . . . One guy was hastily running around with a camera shooting a whole roll of film. You never know why all these people were attracted to the yoga. . . . I sure thought it was a pretty sexy thing and was enjoying the extended muscles that exercise and a young body offer. The girls also seemed to enjoy all the attention and continued with their exercise for at least 15 minutes. After they finished, the girls got applause. All the fanfare had to have something to do with the fact that they were girls. There was a guy not 20 feet away that had been doing yoga for days and had never attracted an audience like that.

"There's just something exciting about a girl's back stretched with her genitals fully exposed and glistening in the sun. . . . Yeah, and there's also this young chick [Wendy] with long flowing blonde hair who runs up and down the beach every day just after 3:00. She's really beautiful and knows it. You can tell when she's coming by because all the guys get up and walk out to the surf to get a close-up of her running by. . . . It's pretty fucking obvious that all those guys didn't get the sudden urge to go for a swim. She really digs it all, flaunting her body, prancing up and down the beach. It's really something to look forward to and even on cold days I'll wait around 'til after three just in hopes that she'll be by. That's something you don't see very often."

Just like nudist women before them, nude beach women keep their legs together; nude beach men do not. Almost all women on a nude beach, especially in the beginning, keep their legs tightly closed. In fact, when they are lying down on their backs they commonly lift one leg (normally the right one) and drape it a bit over the other, thereby more effectively hiding their genitals. As their feeling of shame decreases and, perhaps, their desire to be more erotically interesting increases, they can partially reveal more—so they relax the leg rule. A few women even became organ-displayers, a very rare thing. Sandra was one of them. She would sometimes be in the thick of the crowd, often with some guys who had struck up conversation with her, but at other times she would be off in one of the more isolated spots. (She often looked very "sultry" at these times, a kind of relaxed, "spaced-out" look, but I never saw her smoking or popping pills of any kind.) She would sit on her towel, or sometimes in the sand, with her knees slightly flexed up and out, so that her genitals were quite exposed, but only to passers-by, not to anyone who might be sitting near her. This was a discreet form of organ-display, quite distinct from the far more rare instance when a woman would lie on her back and fully spread her legs with her knees up in the air. Yet, however discreet, it was a powerful sign-trigger to male lust, and she obviously knew it. She also was not upset when the obvious effects became more obvious.

One day I was standing talking with one of the joggers who had been running there for years. A young male virgin with short hair and carrying his street clothes in his hand came along and spotted Sandra doing her thing. He showed the immediate reaction—erection—and went over and sat on a rock 20 feet in front of her and faced her. He then began to masturbate. My friend and I had been watching him, and my friend now turned to me and asked, "Do you see *that?*"

Male body-display far more commonly involves some mixture of full body-display with organ-display, but runs the gamut from all of one to all of the other. The pure full body-displayer can be strikingly found, even on the gay beaches, in the rare muscle-bound types who, when they show up, rarely take off their suits. (This would appear to support the psychiatric idea that muscle-building carried to the extreme is a form of counteraction for fears of organ inferiority.)

Most of the play activity involving body-display by boys and men seems to involve some degree of both. The physical exertion displays the whole body, but the movement also involves a waving around of the genitals. There are a few regular nude joggers who seem to find the activity exciting enough to get an extension, the better and more impressive to wave it around. Male organ-display is not always apparent, since there are probably some men who do not get extended or erect penises when they experience excitement over displaying themselves. But a considerable amount of it is apparent, running the gamut from slight extension of the penis to full erection. Of course, most male exhibitionism is more immediately apparent than that of women.

In the straight world, men, especially very young men, find erections a normal part of life, but generally a secret one. Inevitably, nature runs its course on the nude beach and inevitably some of them are presented for public view. On any day when there are several hundred people on the beach, a visit of a few hours would probably reveal at least a small number of these "events." Most of the time, one would see a number of highly extended organs, stopping just short of the stiff stage constituting an honest erection, and a large number of extensions of various degrees. Probably one honest erection would be visible on such a visit, at least to anyone very observant.

When erections are observed, it is almost always because their sporters have willed it so. There are a few rare cases of guys who lie in wait at certain spots to flash themselves upon unsuspecting women who might come by. This kind of "nude exhibitionism" is very much like conventional exhibitionistic *flashing*. One guy, who was generally quite extended just walking on the beach, was reliably reported to do this near the rocks separating the straight beach from the nude beach, but we never saw him. I started watching for him. One day I saw him come along the water's edge toward three girls going the opposite direction. He had a towel in front of himself. As he came abreast of the girls, he moved the towel. The girls all jumped aside, shrieking giddily. Then they stood wide-eyed and giggling, watching him walk on.

Getting oneself up for the occasion is done far more commonly in a far more discreet manner. We have seen any number of cases where a guy, apparently thinking no one is noticing what he is doing, will pull on his penis, or shake it, or caress it a bit, to "get it up" for presentation to the women. (This strategy apparently works, since Janine was really surprised to learn that this went on—she thought that what she saw was always just the thing in itself, with no front work possible. But even those who present themselves as up-front are often careful to make their up-frontness as impressive as possible.)

But most male exhibitionism organ-display is done without such physical preparation. Men rely on the excitement of being seen by women—or by other men in the case of gays—or else they "get a mental on" by imagining sexy things to get-up for display. There is a common pattern to such display. It is part of the sexual promenade. The sexual promenade itself seems commonly to involve some such display of the promenaders to those sitting or lying on the beach and to those passing in the opposite direction—it is a combination of voyeurism and display of one's own body. But there is also the special pattern we call *nude flashing*, because it is so similar to a conventional flashing (we described it above).

Penis extensions are not very subject to moral condemnation on the beach. They can be passed over as natural, or people may not be aware at all that there is any difference from the penis at rest, that it is in fact an excited state of affairs. Erections are more part of the moral gray area of attitudes and feelings toward sex on the beach, within the range of variability rather than deviance. Some of the nude beachers feel that they should be cooled off, others that they should be appreciated, and most that they should be dealt with discreetly.

As we saw in the last chapter, most people find any actual stiffening disruptive or worse. Commonly, unless a guy is into heavy organ-display, he will act to cool it off. Also commonly, if he doesn't or doesn't succeed, women will take various evasionary tactics. The heavier he is, the more evasive they'll be. We've seen many cases where a guy sitting down will get erect from watching some woman walk down to the water and follow her into the water to present her with his full-scale masculinity. The women almost invariably move away fast but discreetly, sometimes showing displeasure in their facial expression.

One day we saw Ben, a heavy organ-displayer, follow a young girl into the water and get erect as he stood there talking to her. She then came out of the water and started to jog down the beach. Ben jogged along beside her, swinging back and forth violently. She then abruptly turned, with no warning, and ran the opposite direction, leaving him going the other way.

Men are much less apt to notice erections or take them very seriously. For example, one guy used to go around talking to couples while he was erect. We saw him go up to one group of two men and one woman and talk a while, all the time erect. The woman quickly left and went into the water. After he left, we went over and talked to them. We got around delicately to asking what they'd thought of the guy's being erect. The men said they hadn't noticed, maybe because he had sat down not facing them directly. But the woman said, "Well, I did!"

In general, heavy organ-displays are very upsetting to both the men and women on the beach, but the less heavy stuff of erections and, certainly, extensions, are not and may be highly appreciated by the women and the homosexuals. Janine told us she had never seen anybody actually masturbate on the beach, but thought that would really freak her out if she did. But while we were talking with her a middle-aged, heavy-set virgin walked by with a full-sized erection. She watched closely, without embarrassment. In a little while, he came back by, in the same delighted condition. We said it looked like he had a permanent erection, and suggested that from his white body and his heavy approach to the beach he must be virginal and the nude scene was blowing his mind. We asked her what she thought of erections like that on the beach and whether she thought any women there might be offended by it. She said, very quietly but with firm conviction, "I don't think any woman who knows what erections are all about will feel offended about them." This casual attitude is representative of the casual sexual ideals on the nude beaches of all kinds, but the practice is only rarely that casual.

5

Casual Sex

The straight view of the nude beach as a heavy sex scene may be, from the standpoint of their standards, a fair estimate, but they are clearly wrong about the facts of what is going on and definitely misunderstand how the nude beachers see the scene.

From the standpoint of the nude beachers, heavy sex is not where it's at—at least it's not where *they're* at. To them it's the straights who are into heavy sex, not themselves. It's the straights who do the heavy voyeur trip, using the people on whom they spy; it's the straights for whom the beach is a mind-blowing exhibitionist experience involving erections and display, and pretending to be part of the scene; it's the straights for whom the whole scene is a porno show. It's the straights for whom sex is a "social problem." For the nude beachers, the beach is a casual sex scene, ranging from respectful voyeurism to almost every form of consenting sex. To the really casual people into the nude scene, any form of sex between consenting adults, which means just about anyone old enough to have sensual desires, is acceptable and *should* be casual. To them that's the natural thing—on and off the beach. On the beach, as Janine jokingly exaggerated it, it takes the form of "getting 'em off and getting it on!"

From the very casual standpoint, the straight people of this world see sex as a big deal—it's always looked at as a heavy, heartthrob thing. When you get it on with someone it's really important, the beginning and end of the world. When you feel sex for someone, you feel love. When you love, you want to possess. When you don't totally possess someone, you feel jealousy. When you feel jealousy, you hate. When you hate, you want to kill. It's all or nothing; everything now and forever, or nothing at all. Total possession, burning desire. Some sex is beautiful, some evil. All sex is serious, heavy. Approach with caution.

To the casual people, sex that is "consented to" is casual and any act that doesn't use someone else is beautiful, if it's your thing. Sex may be a heartthrobbing thing, but only until it's done. Then it's done. It's here and now, situated, not everywhere and forever. No eternal bliss, no pain. No damnation, no glorification. You have it for now, when it's here. No possession, no jealousy, no hate, no killing. Loving now, as it is, not forever, as it should be in some idealistic, never-never dream-story.

Being casual doesn't mean sex is unimportant. It is very important to the casual, hip people. It's a great pleasure in itself, not something you work toward in the distant future. You enjoy it here and now. Do it. Keep at it. You do it for itself, for the beauty and pleasure of it, not to use or control people, or be controlled by them, the way the straights do. In a world in which making a living is no big problem, in which you can make it by casual work, or living with your parents, or being supported by them, or by welfare, or by unemployment checks, or by handouts, you have the time to be beautiful and sensual. Casual sex can be the focus of your life, and it becomes that for many, and a major focus, if not the only one, for many others. Live casual. Love casual. Get it on with others doing their thing, where you can, when you can, how you can, the best way you can.

That's an extreme, idealized view of both the straight and the casual sex ethos. There is actually a spectrum of casualness to heaviness in the sex activities of the nude beachers, even in those who like to see themselves as super-casual or "really natural." Many of those who come onto the scene are basically straight people who don't know what they're getting into. Some of them suddenly realize what's going on when some of the swingers (discussed below) approach them; then they generally bow out of the whole scene.

At the other extreme, we have the really swinging couples, who show by their actions that they are indeed super-casual. The case of a young couple from a ranch in the mountains can illustrate this. One day we came across Jon, a regular and in some ways a very casual guy on the beach, and very much into sexual hunting, the pickup pattern of behavior. He was lying in the sand warming up a lovely girl about twenty-five, so we just waved as we went by. The next day he described to us the happenings of the day before.

"Man, you wouldn't believe what happened with that blonde chick yesterday. She was really getting friendly and I thought I was about to make it when this guy comes along the beach, looking real casual. She looked at me and said, 'Hey, you'll never guess who that is. That's my husband.' Wow. I didn't know where I was, so I just looked around, my eyes popping out. He came over and sat down, just as nice and casual as you can imagine. Man, he just wanted to talk, saying what a lovely day it was and all. I split that scene, but when I came back by later he came over to me and started talking very friendly like all over again. I don't know."

A few days later she was back down, alone this time. Jon picked up on her again, always feeling a little uncertain, but, while she was very friendly, he never got it on with her. Another day Jon was walking along when he came across this seventeen-year-old girl walking along wearing a football sweatshirt but no pants. He shouted out to her, "Hey, come on, let's play touch football." She walked past and stopped to talk to someone who was obviously her boyfriend, looking over at Jon. The boyfriend *looked* super-casual, with golden locks down to his shoulderblades and mustache hanging down his chin, but he made it clear to Jon that he wouldn't take kindly to anything like Jon was suggesting. You can't tell the casual from the straight by looking at or listening to them. Most are a mixture, and those with the most casual self-images can still get up-tight in concrete situations.

Naturally, most people don't live up to extreme or ideal views. Most casual people have remnants of traditional feelings and ideas about sex and the body more generally which produce important forms of emotional ambivalence. Jon himself was a fine example of this combination of casualness and hang-ups. He was real casual on the beach, except on the weekend when he brought his wife and children. Then he stayed on an isolated part of the beach and refused to introduce his wife to any of the casual men. We talked with him almost daily for months, but he never even told us her name.

Most of the casual types also have sexual relations lasting various lengths of time. Some are super-casual—here, now, this. But sometimes the relationships go on longer, if they're really good.

Jon can be used as a good illustration of the beach "casual sex" type, and, incidentally, of the sort of trouble one incident can cause. When I first met him, he was twenty-eight, six feet tall, powerfully built, intelligent, and attractive, with long, sun-bleached hair. As I noted, I talked with him frequently as we strolled along the beach. It was almost two years before he was willing to *talk* about what he was doing on the beach, because he distrusted everyone. We could, however, easily observe what he was doing. He was one of the most devoted "sexual hunters," always trying to pick up (or hustle) the women on the beach. His entire life, like that of quite a number of the people who came frequently to the beach, revolved around the casual sex scenes at the beach and elsewhere. He lived on a combination of part-time work and unemployment, always making it clear that he did not want to work any more than was necessary. He was not motivated by money or success. Yet, as I eventually learned, he had worked for a number of years as a reasonably successful store manager. He simply did not find work gratifying or fulfilling. It was "boring," especially in comparison to sex.

Those who assume success at business to be the ultimate goal in life would no doubt call him a dropout, but neither he nor anyone who knew him well thought of him in such terms. He wasn't concerned with dropping out of anything and had almost no dislike of society, feelings of resentment against the rest of the world or any of the ordinary feelings of rebels. (I probed for such feelings in various indirect ways and the closest to a response I ever got was, "Well, I guess I kind of wish I had some better place to live than my camper.") Jon was not dropping out, he was simply getting into something more exciting and fulfilling for him—casual sex.

Jon did not start his adult life in pursuit of casual sex. He grew up in a small town in the Midwest. When he was 18, he and his girl friend left their town and eventually wound up in Hawaii. Though they did not get married until years later, they had two children and he supported the family with his managerial work. As his wife later told me, and as he indirectly confirmed in various ways, he was reasonably shy as a teenager and into his early twenties. His wife insisted unequivocally that she had only herself to blame for his getting into casual sex. She tried to convince him that he was really good at sex, at least partly as a simple matter of building his self-confidence, and she insisted that he then started trying out his abilities. He found himself very successful at it and became progressively more devoted to it as an "ego trip."

My own close observation made it seem to me more complex. Certainly there was the ego trip, the thrilling pride of "scoring," especially with the most sought-after women. But there was clearly the highly erotic aspect of it: When he talked about the body of a woman passing by, there was little element of the "social prestige," pride, or ego trip involved. The very possibility of his being successful at it was built on his being erotic. Moreover, though more tied in with the ego trip, there was also the excitement of the hunt. There are millions of men who devote great time and resources to hunting animals. Men like Jon find sexual hunting exciting in the same way, but far more so. Given all three powerful feelings, it is not hard to see how he came to find casual sex consuming.

After I had known him for three years, he introduced me to a sixteen-year-old he had met at the beach a few days earlier. Wendy was one of the most beautiful girls on the beach. Jon soon told me how exciting he found her to be.

> "Man, she's really something. She says she has to make it every day or she just can't sleep—and I can believe her. She had this boyfriend, but he's gone off to college, so now she's out rutting around. She's *really* something all right!"

Since I had never seen him with the same woman, other than his wife, more than once or twice, I was quite surprised to see him with her whenever he came to the beach, for weeks, then months, ultimately for over two years. (He had stopped bringing his wife.) Though there were times when he would come without her and briefly resume his sexual hunting, these got rarer. He was increasingly devoted to her. She became even more devoted to him.

Wendy was much easier to learn about than Jon. She was friendly, extremely intelligent and articulate, liked to talk about her problems, seemed very open, and proved to be honest in everything I was able to check out. When Jon was not there, or when she was looking for him, we would very often talk about what she was doing—school, her life, and Jon. She was a junior in high school. Her father was a very successful professional. Both her mother and father were highly liberal about sexual matters. They had even allowed one of her earlier boy friends to live with her in her home for some time. They knew very well that she came to the nude beach and thought it was fine. (But she felt even then that there were some limits to their "liberality," since she kept some important things secret from them.) She had started coming to the nude beach when she was fifteen, but it had not been easy for her to begin going nude. She had always felt "sort of unattractive, like a black sheep." She wanted to get over this feeling, to gain confidence in her body. When I met her a year later she was one of the few women I knew on the beach who would walk alone totally nude, without any sign of uneasiness, past a hundred teenage male surfers sitting in their suits and slowly turning their heads to watch her as she passed.

When Jon started going to Wendy's home to pick her up, her parents did not protest. He stayed at their house a few times, but only when they were away. They never seemed to like him very much, perhaps because of his too obvious lack of devotion to work. I always thought they disliked him simply because they felt he would hurt their daughter. But Wendy and Jon always seemed not to understand why.

Jon was extremely careful to keep his other life a secret from Wendy, and to keep Wendy a secret from his wife. Wendy began to suspect something was "wrong" after a number of months. Later, she began to suspect specifically that he was married. Then one day, completely by accident, she saw him with his wife in town. She immediately went up to them, asked the woman if she were his wife, and started crying uncontrollably when the woman said yes. Jon's wife, Nancy, was very understanding and sympathetic. She had known that something more than his usual casual sex was going on and was not too surprised by the whole thing. She told Wendy how sorry she was for her and discussed the whole thing with her, telling her how it had been developing for years, that the name by which Wendy had known him for a year was not his name at all, that most of what he told her about himself was false, etc. Jon confirmed it all.

Wendy spent several days in deep depression and crying. As she told me through her tears, she was saddest of all over his lies, since she did not care that he was married. She could not understand why he would lie and build a false life. Sometime during this deep depression, probably because they insisted on knowing what was going on and because she expected consolation, she made the mistake of telling her parents about it. Her father was furious at Jon. He got hold of Nancy (I do not remember how) and she agreed to insist that Jon come for a meeting of the four of them. (I believe it was at this stage that Wendy's father first threatened Jon with legal action, if he did not come. Jon went.)

Jon's own view of the whole thing was mixed and conflictful. He wanted Wendy. But he was unwilling to give his wife up or he would probably have done so much sooner. (In fact, he was extremely possessive about his wife.) He had thought he could protect his family life from his casual life and the other way around by building two identities. As far as I know, he was totally successful for years (except that I and a few others knew he was married), until he was accidentally discovered by Wendy. Because he had so much to lose at home, and because the father's threats were so convincing, Jon and Wendy agreed to separate, to stay away from each other completely, and not to go to the nude beach at all.

A few days later, I ran into Wendy at the beach. She was extremely sad and agitated. She wanted Jon and was looking for him. When she found him, they went back together again. For months, they spent much of their lives together on the beach, managing somehow, with considerable care, to keep it secret from his wife and her father. Jon's conflict was obvious. Whenever I talked with Wendy alone about it, it was clear that she was also suffering. But it was clear that the sexual attraction was too great for either of them to give up the relationship.

Nancy knew Jon very well. She went looking for him and discovered them together on another nude beach. Rather than expressing sympathy this time, she came up from behind and attacked Wendy. She hit her three times very hard and screamed at her. She later got hold of the father, who made further threats. Once again Jon and Wendy agreed to a total separation and to stay away from the beach entirely. The threats were more intense now, the dangers more real. But it was only a few days later that I ran into Wendy at the beach, still nursing her bruises, saying that she understood and could not blame Nancy for attacking her, but tearfully looking for Jon. She found him once again. (As the whole thing got more intense, I never gave any advice, but my expressions of caution and pointing out the dangers increased steadily. I never expected it would have any effect, and I do not believe it did.)

They now took very great care not to be discovered together and came to the beach only occasionally, when they felt safest. One way she got away from her now very watchful father was to tell him she was going to visit a girlfriend's house overnight. Her father discovered one of these lies and confronted her in great anger, demanding fiercely that she either give up Jon, continue living at home and attending college (where she now was), or leave home entirely. She walked out, thinking she had finally resolved her conflict.

The next day Jon and Wendy were working out at the university gymnasium when the police walked in and asked Jon to accompany them outside. He did, and Wendy followed. Her father was there and insisted the police arrest Jon for unlawful sex with a minor, since her eighteenth birthday was still one month away. The police asked Jon if he had had sexual relations with Wendy. He said yes. (Jon and Wendy both knew very well that he not only could but should have said nothing at that point. Jon and Wendy had twice before given false names, addresses, phone numbers, etc., to the police in such situations. But, as they both said, Jon was simply "really scared" this time and could not think of such things.) The police arrested him and started taking him away. Wendy was now screaming, demanding that her father stop them, insisting she would never testify against him, and would never talk to her parents again. The father was also screaming and, for the first time she could remember in her whole life, threatened to hit her. She felt he was "out of his mind." When the police took Jon away, Wendy returned home to plead for his release.

Jon spent a week in the "felony lockup" at county jail, thinking he faced years in prison. Being locked up, being with the people, the violence, the homosexual sex, the drugs all made a profound impression on him. He admitted he was "really scared." He wanted above all to stay out of prison. Wendy agreed to stay at home at least until she was eighteen, only a month away. Her father dropped charges and Jon was released.

About a week later Wendy was back on the beach tearfully looking for Jon. He was not there, but they had established an elaborate way of communicating through a friend. He started coming to the beach again a few days later, doing a little bit of lackluster hunting (and being very cautious because he clearly did not want Wendy to know anything about this). It was unclear whether they could wait a few weeks for her eighteenth birthday. (They did not. I came across them together a few days later.) But it was completely clear to me that there would be no end soon to these profoundly ecstatic and bitterly hateful conflicts.

Sometimes "casual" relations last and last, destroying the possibility of the casual life. Some even turn into the straight life. Some lead to marriages, "for the families." One casual woman who'd been into the pickup scene on the beach for a year astonished us when she told us she was going to get married—formally, with the families there. When we asked for an explanation, she only said softly, "Well, I guess it's the first time I ever felt love." It's a hazard of the lifestyle, and it is guarded against. Even the most casual naturalists have ambivalent feelings they cannot totally escape.

People choose casual sex for various reasons. One of the most common reasons, and certainly the most ideal casual reason, is that casual sex is sex done for its own sake. People into casual sex for this reason believe that it frees sex from all other considerations and allows its ultimate pleasure and beauty. When you're really into casual sex, you *do* sex, you don't *use* sex. Sex is seen as more beautiful because it's freed from "practical" constraints.

Closely related to this reason is the common need to rebel against the "unnatural" constraints of the straight world, especially its painful constraints on sex. Thus, some naturalists cherish the casual sex scene not so much for what it is, but for what it isn't. The casual people hate or fear what they see as the entanglements, the "self-destructive hassles of the straight life." They believe the straight life imposes lifeless, life-stifling demands and symbolic forms upon you from outside, regardless of what your body, your heart, or your mind say. Straight sex is the foundation of the straight life, so escape from the demands, commitments, and hassles of straight sex is the fastest route to rebellion against that system.

Some people are casual because of their lifestyles. To get more serious, more committed, more tied down—straight—would necessitate a total change, and would prevent their being artists, going to school, being radical politicos, or whatnot. They choose the casual route and promote it for everyone else, both because they have moralistic views about the values of casual styles and, sometimes cynically, because promoting it helps get what they want. Like most moral and ideological ideas, it's also a sales pitch, at least for some of those hangers-on who are not really committed to the casual thing.

For some people, like Jon in the early years, casual sex is just an extracurricular activity. They're married and have many of the other characteristics of the straight life, but they find that life partially unsatisfying, without being able to kick the habit, so they practice the casual life on the side, generally covertly. They're not really into the totally casual or natural life, but some of them are half into it, leading double lives. It's not exactly up front, but they manage it. For them casual sex may be just an exciting adventure, the erotic quest for the unknown.

Some of the extracurricularists and some of the casual types are into the casual stuff simply because that's what "turns them on." For some, especially some of the more jaded or sexually weaker old-timers, casual sex is the only attraction left. Like the middle-aged man who wants a young girl because his only excitement is "firm young flesh," some of the young casual types are mainly excited by sex with the stranger. The stranger might—just might—give the ultimate experience.

For some, the excitement of the new, the strange, becomes the focus of their whole lives. Casual sex becomes a compulsion, and draws them further and further beyond the confines of the "straightjacket of the normie-world," into affairs with younger and younger partners, the homosexual scene, swinging, and even more "kinky" preoccupations. These things have always gone on to some extent, especially among the affluent, but today they are far more prevalent and overlap with the casual sex of the naturalist types in places like the nude beach.

TRUE BELIEVERS AND PREDATORS

Even in a really casual scene, there's no clear way to tell the true believers from the predators—those who are really committed to the naturalistic, casual ethos as opposed to those who are merely using the ethos to "score" on the true believers. Those into the scene who are most up-front recognize that they can't even be sure "where their own heads are." Their emotions, beliefs, and the practical needs of the moment are always pulling them in different directions. There's not even any clear-cut agreement over what is casual, what is natural, and what is straight. Everyone agrees there is a vital distinction, like casual sex versus straight sex, but there's no one definition of what is casual that everyone—or maybe even most people—into the nude scene would accept.

Still and all, the distinctions are vital and hold up in most circumstances. The world may not be cut up into two neat pieces, but people do manage to agree roughly on how to cut up any particular situation or event into straight and casual.

There are some light voyeurs over whom there would be a lot of disagreement, but most people manage to agree most of the time on whether any given voyeur is a heavy, straight type or not. When they can get at the facts about what someone says or does in different situations, they can also manage to generally agree about whether he's a true believer or a predator. The trouble here is that preying on others is aided and abetted by the very nature of casualness, especially the very casual nature of the nude beach scene, which prevents the participants from checking out what someone says there with what he *normally* says and does. Consequently, there are a lot of "passers." Our own checking out of people provides some very good examples of the extremes, but there are all degrees and kinds in between.

Pauline was a beautiful example of the casual type. She knew what the scene was all about, was committed to it across the board, and was up-front about it, on and off the beach. She was especially open about her worries about the predator types:

> "I think that even if a man and woman have the ideal relationship they still need to mess around. Even if they both turn on to each other, it's just not human nature. You've got to have something different. I think, a guy in particular sees girls physically, and things might be fine at home, but you still need the variety. It makes the relationship stronger when you're up-front about it. If you're not, the relationship will deteriorate. You hide things from your partner and you cease to communicate. . . . That's what happens with an affair—the secrecy reaches into all areas of your life—covering your ass for this or that reason. The only problem I've had with being honest about all this is that good-looking guys try to score on you. You know the kind of guy that drives around in a sports car and lives in a plush apartment. He puts a notch on his cock every time he balls a different girl. He scores once and

you never see him again. It really makes you feel like you've been used . . . it's those kind of games that can really destroy honesty . . . nobody likes to feel like they have been fucked around by anybody."

One of the regulars on the beach was the very picture of what straights would see as a far-out, casual type, but he turned out to be a predator who was using many different lines about politics and sexual morality to score on the women into the nude scene. Zoroaster would come down to the beach almost every day with his stage props in a knapsack. He'd lay out a big spread, strip down, and start doing yoga exercises, generally standing on his head with his legs crossed. (He was such an interesting sight that the TV people were careful to film him and put him on the air, up-side down.) We'd been watching him for several months, trying to figure out what he was up to. Sometimes he'd walk down the beach, talking to people on the way, and once in a while he'd return with a girl he'd picked up. We asked some of the girls what his story was and learned in general that he'd written some book which was heavy into astrology and mysticism, but was mostly too far-out for them to understand.

One day we were sitting and talking with some friends, two men and a woman, when Zoroaster came over and began complaining about how people he'd tried to help on the beach had "bummed him out." We asked him about his book, and he reached into his knapsack and pulled out a folder that looked like the storybooks kids make in school. It was full of drawings of nude women and men engaged in every kind of sexual practice. Each picture had under it a caption which took a political position on major issues of the day, especially those of feminism, sexual freedom, and equality, but some captions referred to the Arab-Israeli conflict. He said these philosophical positions fit together with the pictures of bodies and sex into a total picture of his world view. While that world view included most of the ideas on astrology and sex, such as you'd see in Zap Comix, he went far beyond that. He had divided the world into the communist conspiracy, the Enden conspiracy and the racist conspiracy.

The commies were people who favored strict control, equality, and feminism, all of which he saw as an infringement on individual freedom. The racists were those from the establishment involved with genocide and exploitation, and, in the process, with developing an anti-matter generator that would feed a psychic bomb which could emit alpha waves so intense that the world would become populated with automatons. The Enden conspiracy was the energy force that would, if all went well, oppose both the racists and the commies. This position, which he favored, was for total liberation, a separatist approach to racial conflict. Most important, it would create the weapon Yab Yum, or the cosmic climax, which would counter all the other forces.

As he explained the details of each of these groups, he kept looking at the girl sitting with us. (She had put a towel over her body and was lying down to rest.) When he finished the presentation, we asked, "Do you score much with this approach?"

Zoroaster immediately took offense at our question and said that he was not putting out a line, but, rather, the truth as he saw it. We pushed him on this: "But you must meet a lot of women down here and you must talk to them about your book. Do many of them get turned on by what you say?" He explained that he met about fifty women a week and would make it with about one a week. Then he kind of opened up. He admitted that he showed the women his book and thought it turned them on a lot of the time. He showed them those pages with the messages he thought would turn on each particular woman, maintaining that the political attack on racists worked best with beautiful women and the commie position best with the plain ones.

The relation between anything like politics and the casual sex scene on the beaches is complex and vague. But the relation between casualness and success within the heterosexual sex scene was neither. Even the appearance of straightness meant almost sure-fire doom. The straight voyeurs were obviously out of it, and there was no more lonely type on Eden Beach than the straight-looking sailors and marines who came down from the nearby training centers. Even when their views were casual, their crew-cut status in life effectively left them cut off from the casual girls. They might occasionally talk with crew-cuts, but that was about it. If the men seemed respectful and got honest by joining the scene, naturalists would feel pity for them, but no love.

Getting honest by going nude was of vital importance. Most of the women would talk to dishonest types in a scornful manner, some almost telling them to "fuck off" or "shine off." And sometimes when the nude men saw a nude woman with a guy who hadn't gotten up-front, they figured it would be easy to cut her out and send the guy packing. One of the regulars told us of an instance in which the dishonest guy simply wouldn't split:

> "It was kind of early in the morning with few people on the beach—especially women. I spotted this cute brunette nude sunbathing. She was talking to this guy who was dressed. He didn't have a towel or anything that would indicate that he belonged

with her so I figured I would go over and try to cut him out. . . . I walked up and asked her if she would mind some company . . . she was friendly enough so we exchanged the usual questions— how long she has been coming down to the beach, what she thought of the scene and so on. She was really coming down hard on the other guy. While she didn't say anything to him directly she turned the discussion to the heavy pick-up scene and the clothed voyeurs. She said that she had picked the south end of the beach where there were more families to avoid the creeps. She had been so pissed off with them at times that she wasn't sure she would return. She felt the clothed voyeurs were into a sex trip and she didn't like the idea of their using her body to turn on to. Throughout the whole thing the [dressed] guy had that shit-eating look on his face, not saying a word, confirming his guilt by his long silence. He got real restless and kept changing his seating arrangement. Normally one would take her comments as an insult and move on, but I guess that his turn-on to a beautiful body made the insults bearable. He just sat it out and kept looking."

This same horny regular teamed up with Jon one day in a more successful attempt to cut out a dishonest type:

"Jon and I were out surveying the scene, hoping to meet some new chicks we could get something going with. The weather was pretty shitty so there weren't very many chicks around. We saw three chicks nude sunbathing, talking to a guy. The guy had short hair, a tattoo on his arm, and the dumb fucker hadn't taken off his trunks . . . he hadn't joined the girls on the blanket so we figured he hadn't come down with them. Things looked pretty bad elsewhere, so we figured we'd move in on him. We walked right up and asked if we could join them, sat down and began to talk. We got on the guy's case about not getting nude, carping on the guys that come down and just look at the nude girls and all. Within a half-hour, he was totally excluded from the conversation and within an hour he sort of wandered off. He even had a six-pack of beer, which is usually golden down on the beach, but he really had blown it. It's so fucking obvious, the guy was in the military, really starved for sex, and he was down drooling over the nude chicks. He didn't stand a chance with all that going against him, especially when he wouldn't get up-front."

THE NUDE THERAPY TRIP:
DE-INHIBITING YOURSELF

There is one common form of "using the nude scene" which isn't really seen as predatory. In fact, most of the people on the beaches are not aware of its existence; and most of those doing it don't realize there are many others there doing the same thing. The people "using" the nude scene this way are respectful and up-front and almost never tell people what they're into because it would be embarrassing to do so. They look like anyone else into the scene, except that they are commonly somewhat older. These are the people into a *nude therapy trip.*

Because nudity and sex are so inextricably intertwined in the minds of most people, the repression of one seems to them to involve the repression of the other. When people get highly concerned about escaping their sexual inhibitions, especially frigidity and impotence, many of them decide that escaping their hangups over nudity would rid them of their hangups over sex. They think this especially because they believe the fear of having sex organs seen is a major cause of frigidity and impotence. So, if they got into the nude scene and learned that people didn't laugh at their genitals, then they could better manage their sexual problems. There's a lot of dispute about this, since other people insist that it is possible to be unashamed about sex organs and still sexually inhibited. Regardless of that, a lot of people at the beach believe that they can de-inhibit their sex lives by dis-robing in public.

A lot of people got into traditional nudism for the nude therapy trip, a kind of commonsense, self-help therapy. But since that implied something sexy about nudism and went contrary to the nudist argument about "health-and-naturalness-in-the-sunshine," it was rarely admitted until recently. The big public push for nude therapy came from the professionals—psychologists, psychiatrists, and various others who professed expert knowledge about the condition of the human soul. Esalen Institute, at Big Sur, California, was the most famous center for nude therapy. They developed and marketed nude encounter group therapy to get people back into touch with themselves and into touch with everyone else. They became famous for their nude tubs and the nude "group-gropes" that grew out of their ideas about nude therapy, but the nude beaches soon became a setting for their nude therapy. The only legal nude beach between Santa Barbara and the Monterey area is a private beach near Big Sur. But the ideas have now spread throughout the state. Some of the people into the nude scenes on faraway beaches started at Esalen.

One man at a nude beach just south of San Francisco told us he had started his nude therapy trip at Esalen as part of his job training for counseling rehabilitated alcoholics. He told us that his therapist was trying to reorient him from the cerebral distortion common among Western people to the realization of the body's wants and needs. Western man, he said, has centered his attention on the mind to the neglect of the body, and needs to get back to nature and realize the place that the body plays in the "total being." One of the ways his group leader suggested involved getting out to nude beaches, where the body was very much the center of attention. So he went to the nude beach to get in touch with his body.

The idea has caught on with professional therapists all over the state. In San Diego, one of the regular girls told us about a middle-aged man who admitted that he was there because his doctor had suggested he go to a nude beach to get over his body hang-ups:

> "He kind of stood out among the regulars. He was sitting on this huge blanket, drinking a bottle of expensive wine out of a wine glass. Upon further investigation, it turned out that he was a high school teacher down on the beach to get over a low opinion of his body. His analyst had suggested he go to Eden to compare his body with the others. By doing this he would come to realize he was no different than anyone else and hence gain a better self-image. While his body was not perfect, no one else's was either."

Most of the people on the nude therapy trips, however, are doing a commonsense thing. It's like a kid who decides to get over (i.e., "extinguish") his terror of snakes (or anything else) by slowly working into it, starting with a little green snake, and working up to a six-foot diamond back. We've literally seen a few middle-aged, timid types take months to work into the nude beach scene. One pleasant-looking guy crossed the rocks every day for months and walked along the water's edge, tightly suited, but respectful in casting side glances at the nudes on the beach. After months of this demure behavior, one day he went up on the beach, sat down, proceeded to quickly tear off his walking shorts and slip on a pair of swimming trunks: "You can see, I'm just changing into my suit so I can dash into the water. Anyone can see I'm not *going nude*—not that, my God!" After many more anguished days, we even saw him sunning, face down, in the nude. I tried talking to him many times. I'd wave, but it was some time before he'd even wave back. Then I started saying hello. So far he has only nodded in response. I felt certain that, unless he was the most demure and timid voyeur on the beach, he must be into a secret nude therapy trip, slowly working up to touching that first little green snake.

There's also a common variation on the nude therapy theme. Many of the parents who bring their children down on the beach and *throw them into* the scene do so to prevent their developing hangups about their bodies. As has been found with traditional nudism, this idea seems to work if kids are thrown into the scene at a very young age. Up to four or five, the kids really do not think about being nude; they're the most natural people on the beach. After about five, they commonly have deep fears of public nudity, and there are very few preteen or early teen types into the nude scene.

There are also a few parents who use the nude scene to get their young teenagers used to the opposite sex, purportedly so it won't come as a shock some night. But our own feeling has been that parents who take their kids on a sex-education tour of the nude beaches haven't been instilling hang-ups anyhow, and any parents who *have* been instilling hang-ups would freak out their teenagers by doing such a thing.

It's impossible to say whether the nude beach therapy trip really works. There's no doubt that if you get into the nude scene at all you begin to feel more at ease about being nude in public. But even that is largely restricted to a situation in which the whole thing is accepted by the people there and is reciprocated. Except for a few heavy exhibitionists, the nude beachers wouldn't feel much more comfortable about being nude on a straight beach and no one, to our knowledge, has started feeling relaxed about being nude in the local supermarkets, in spite of what some atrocity stories might lead one to expect.

But even that kind of totally relaxed attitude about public nudity wouldn't mean the nude therapy was successful, since the therapy is aimed at moving from uninhibiting nudity to uninhibiting sexual feelings and behavior. *If* someone has a hang-up over sex because they're afraid of what a partner will think about their sex organs, then *maybe* such progressive de-inhibition will work. But what if a person gets onto the beach and finds that, especially in comparison with the exhibitionists, he or she *doesn't* measure up? Might that not have the opposite effect from what was intended?

More importantly, while sex and nudity are linked in our cultural thinking, the emotional and behavioral links seem much more tenuous and complex. Like most other things in life, the relations between nudity and sex are very individual and should be treated that way. Regardless, we figure that baring kneecaps didn't eliminate hang-ups and baring buttocks won't either. There's no easy road to sexual paradise. In fact, there may be no road at all. Certainly the nude beach doesn't qualify as that road. (On the other hand, we've never heard a suggestion that the nude beach leads to more inhibitions. Any effect it has must be uninhibiting, except for some small minority who may feel more inferior.)

SEXING 'EM UP

As we've already seen, regardless of whether the nude scene de-inhibits people, the sight of nudity is sexy to anyone who isn't extremely inhibited about it. This is especially true of the *public* nude scene. As almost anyone would imagine, a bunch of nude strangers running around, especially when most of them are young and many more or less beautiful, is a turn-on—more or less. As almost anyone would also imagine, this is especially true of men and is a major reason why there are so many more men on most nude beaches than women. But the reasonably uninhibited woman is also turned on by the scene, if she isn't put off by the straight voyeurs, the rare exhibitionism, or some infrequent glimpse of heavy sex. Regardless of how much women are in fact turned on by the scene, men expect them to be, and thus many use the nude beach to *sex up* their women. A bit like the straights, many men suspect that if a woman is up for the beach, she's probably up for anything.

One of the horny regulars, Tod, told us of a typical case:

"I'd met Margo off the beach and had told her I went to Eden Beach. She asked all sorts of questions about what went on down there, so I suggested she come down and see for herself. I picked her up and we went down. She had some problem deciding whether to take a suit or not. . . . I said I would go nude or with a suit whichever she felt best with. She took her suit, and when we got down on the beach and I asked her which way we should do it she said she was not up-tight about being nude but was worried about what I'd think. . . . We both ripped off our clothes and went for a walk along the beach. Things were really looking good. . . . She came up close to my body as I pointed out the different things on the beach . . . she played footsie games as we lay on our blanket. . . . I suggested we move on to her place and perhaps do some body massage. . . . We went on to her place and both of us got nude for the massage. She did my whole body and then I began on her. . . . It wasn't long before we were making love."

Sara, a regular, told us she had begun going to the beach under similar circumstances:

> "I'd met Bill at work and he seemed to be a nice enough sort of guy except his reputation around work was sort of wild. He mentioned he went down to the nude beach a lot, and I must admit I was sort of curious. After a few such talks, I agreed to go down to find out what it was all about. We spent the day on the beach and after I got over the initial shock we really enjoyed it. We went back to my place, and took off our clothes. Our trek up the cliff had been a long hot one. It seemed kind of natural enough after all, we'd been sitting nude on the beach together all day. Nothing happened that day. We talked some, but that's all. He did ask if we could get together later and I agreed. We met at his place, down on the beach, took a walk, and then went back and made love—finally."

There are plenty of times when the scenario doesn't work out that way. These failures show the misconceptions that even many of those into the nude scene have about the people on the beach. Many of these misconceptions are direct results of male bravado.

Kevin used the nude scene once in a while to test girls and sex them up. He told us about a girl he put the make on at the beach, and she later told us about the same events, not knowing he'd told us his view of it. We couldn't be sure, but his account, while agreeing in general, seemed just *slightly* tinged with bravado and hers sounded more like the way things happen on the beach.

As Kevin told it, he met Linda at school and took her down to the beach to see if she was into sex enough to handle it. He said he wanted to turn her on so that he could later get it on with her. He reported that when she got down to the beach, she jumped out of her suit and played around at getting it on, but never went all the way. He said he could have easily done so, but he lost interest and simply stopped calling to ask her out.

Linda's account of the same experience was different. She agreed that they had met at school and had gone down to the beach. But she claimed that she only took off her top, and even that with some reluctance, not really knowing him that well. She felt he had "attacked" her on the beach and said he'd "scared the hell out of me." Kevin had called several times since their trip to the beach, and she had refused to go out with him because she feared she knew exactly what to expect, and was not up for it.

Gary, one of the other regular guys, told us about a truly disastrous experience he'd had in using the beach for sexing up. He'd been married about a year, and his wife had never developed any real interest in sex. They'd gone from the excitement of newness to the dutiful wife stage, and finally into the "dead fish." It didn't seem to be anything personal, since he was sure she wasn't involved with anyone else, so he decided to bring her down to the beach to sex her up and save their faltering marriage. She bought the idea, but when they got to the beach it didn't seem to be what she had expected. She froze up, and while he de-suited, no amount of pleading would get her to do the same. They sunned for a couple of hours next to two nude couples lying on the sand. The couples were drinking some wine and, as the day grew warmer, they started getting all steamed up.

> "Man, they started really making out, rolling around on the ground, grabbing all over the place, and giggling. Then this one chick really got turned on. She started working this guy up, but she just couldn't wait, so she just popped him right into her mouth. . . . Wow, I tried not to notice what was going on and my wife never said anything. But she must have seen it. She just seemed to get colder all the time, maybe thinking I knew what was going to happen. Anyhow, she never would fuck after that. It didn't work out the way I expected."

Though less common, there are also cases where it's the man who has to be sexed up. There are probably men who come down to the beach alone so they can get sexed up, go home, and make it with their wives. No one confessed to this obvious ploy, but we did find at least one case in which a young couple we'd known for years had conspired to use the beach to sex up the husband. This was one of those cases of the overly cerebral husband, Hal. Hal had spent the first thirty years of his life developing his mind, picking up several degrees along the way, and subordinating his body, especially the sexual parts of it. At thirty, he hooked up with an experienced woman, Cheryl, who decided to turn him on to the world of sensual pleasure. For whatever reasons, she married him and proceeded to try to de-inhibit and sex him up. The de-inhibiting went along okay, but sex remained a once-a-week addition. Cheryl went on making it with a lot of the guys at a nudist camp she'd joined and, when Hal found this out and took exception to it, they decided the situation called for drastic measures. They started coming down to the nude beach to try to get him sexed up enough so that their sex life could provide Cheryl with the frequency she desired.

The beach, however, didn't do that much for Hal, so they began swinging instead. The beach hadn't worked as a sexer-upper for them, but, then, nothing after that seemed to work either. Some months later, Cheryl met a guy on the beach, went home with him, started living with him, became a masseuse, and divorced Hal. Janine moved in with Hal to try her therapy on him. She liked Hal, but soon surrendered to his disinterest.

A higher percentage of couples probably use the beach for sexing up both of them. We found a fortyish couple from Los Angeles on one of the nude beaches in Santa Barbara for this specific purpose. At first, they gave us a lot of other reasons for coming to the nude beach, but as we got to know them better, they began to open up:

> "Before we started coming to the beach things were pretty dull at home, we had really gotten into a rut. I'd come home from work, flip on the TV, sit there until it was time to go to bed and then I'd wake up and start another day of the same thing. The nude beach really changed all that. Now we come up here for the weekend, drink a little wine and just unwind . . . and it's really done great things for our sex life. . . . That was in a rut, too, but not any more. We wait around until late afternoon when everyone has gone home and get under my wife's grandmother's blanket and make love. Maybe we'll even get it on in the car on the way home and then again when we get there. I don't know if it's the nude bodies that make us horny or what. All I know is that it works."

Sexing up is an ancient strategy of seducers, both of self-seducers and of other-seducers, with a vast number of specific ploys, everything from "turning on the heavies" and "whispering sexy" to "slipping them a magic-potion aphrodisiac." In the new age of sexual liberation, when both men and women are commonly turned on by the sight of nude bodies, there has been a vast explosion of ploys using nudity for sexing up. Some men use porno "nudist magazines," in much the same way a nineteenth-century Lothario might have used his "art prints"—both to test a woman's morals and to turn her on. But these days this is too crude for most, and nude movies are used more than anything else. However, as we pointed out in the beginning, nude films are still unreal for most people, especially those who have been through it all and have become jaded. The films are also somewhat crude, with little of the "naturalist ethos" enveloping them to ward off the feelings of guilt or "being dirty" that still seize the newly liberated, especially women. The nude beach is both enveloped with the ethos of naturalness and more directly sexy—and it's secretly sexy, with an ideology and a front that allows each person involved to deceive himself into thinking of it as a family social in which he or she just happens "unintentionally" to get turned on. It's useful both for those who are ready for sex straight on, nothing hidden, and for those who still need a front behind which they can let their sexual desires percolate until they become "uncontrollable."

This is a powerful combination. If the forces of sexual freedom continue to succeed, the nude beach should keep developing as one of the focal scenes in which those forces can be given full play.

HETEROSEXUAL HUNTING

Those who use the beach for sexing-up already have partners or prefer to bring one on a date. But a large percentage of heterosexuals into the nude scene use the beach for a pick-up scene. Some of these people simply don't have dates at the moment, feel horny, and want to try to find someone to get it on with. Others find dating too dangerous because of outside commitments (like marriage), so they need a place where they can be completely anonymous. But many are simply sexual hunters. Most could easily get dates, but they crave the excitement of the hunt, the thrill of going out into the risky scene and bagging the beautiful prey—or being bagged—with nothing but sexual charm. For them, the nude beach is the ultimate test of the hunter's mettle, far more of a test than most hunters realize.

Sexual hunting is rampant throughout our society. Affluence and leisure time make it possible, and the liberation of libidinal forces, both male and female, make it probable. Casualness is the crucial feature of sexual hunting, remaining casual to stay free to hunt again. There is also the excitement, the "mind-blowing" exhilaration of the hunt. For sexual hunters, the unknown (the stranger) and the ego-risk ("putting all your shit on the line") are the strongest attraction. Added to the excitement of the unknown, the ever-present hope for the ultimate sexual thrill, is the pride of the conquest, the score, which sends the ego soaring.

The hunting scene, more commonly called the pick-up scene, is a vital aspect of sexual hunting. As the practice of hunting has prolifer-ated, so have the hunting scenes. Hunting can be and is done anywhere, but hunting in an undesignated scene, especially one which has unseen "no trespassing" signs posted all over it, is very difficult, frustrating, and dangerous. Pick-up restaurants and bars, body shops, open parties, and many other scenes have increased rapidly, and straight beaches are increasingly used as pick-up scenes for the young. In colleges, even libraries have become clearly designated hunting areas.

The nude beach is a very heavy hunting scene. Hunters of all kinds abound. The gay hunters are the most prevalent and the heaviest, as we'll see below. But the heterosexual hunters are also numerous and devoted. In some ways, the nude beach is the hunter's dream come true, and some of the regulars on the beach, discovering this, devote their lives to beach hunting. The quarry is right there, in all her glory, and surely she knows it's a hunting scene and has chosen to be hunted. That's not true, for a few don't know or aren't at that moment up for the hunt, as any hunter soon discovers. But, even if she is up for it, will she be up for a specific hunter, will she turn onto him? The hunter, of course, is also revealed in all his glory, or lack of it, and the fear of not "measuring up" haunts would-be hunters. Trying to make it with a naked stranger demands tremendous confidence or foolhardiness. A little experience reveals that even the best hunter doesn't score on many of the women he stalks.

He can sometimes spend a whole day courting, making every expert move, calling forth all his sexual charm, cautiously doing his casual body-display as he saunters by, trying to sex her up, only to find at the end of the day that she doesn't feel this is the place or the time or one of a thousand other things a woman can think of if everything hasn't gone just the way she wants. The successful hunter has to accept these defeats and come back the next day to stalk again, undaunted by yesterday's failure. The truly successful have tremendous confidence, generally built on years of relative success.

Most would-be hunters don't have this confidence, and they become the pitied stake-out artists, the *vulture* of the nude beach. Unless they do get some success, they generally soon leave for less-challenging hunting scenes. The stake-out is easy to spot, at least to those who have developed an eye for the nude scene. He's almost always dishonest, or a virgin, or a recent immigrant who doesn't yet know the ropes of the beach. If you look closely, you can sometimes see his nervousness, revealing his intense excitement, when he stalks his "prey." If he's joined the scene, he often has an extension or, on rare occasions, even an erection. He carefully tries to hide his intentions, to look casual or even unconcerned (however difficult that might be). He stalks his prey stealthily, not looking at her directly. The beach may be all but deserted, yet he just happens to find it necessary to sit near her. (As one young regular, Barbie, put it, "He just *happened* to discover that

pile of decaying seaweed over there is the ideal spot for sunbathing.")
He doesn't go up to her; he circles, sometimes almost moving backward.
His courage carries him only so far, no more. He generally parks about
twenty feet away, but, if there are other people around to keep him
from being too conspicuous, he may get up close, especially if his
excitement is intense.

One day we were sitting near the cliffs talking with Gary when two
lovely young women came along the beach, disrobed, and sat down a
short distance away. Almost immediately, we saw the vultures begin to
circle, and we watched their progress, recognizing each move as one
that had been rehearsed thousands of times before on the beach, even
when each guy was thinking he'd discovered a whole new way of
"playing it cool." The flow-chart below shows how clearly their intentions were written in their paths, though none of them ever spoke a
word.

Generally, the vulture just sits and sits. He may begin to eye the
woman. If he gets excited, he may "turn on the heavies," hoping this
will turn her on so much she'll give him a come-on. Many of the girls,
especially the beach virgins, get uncomfortable over being stalked. As
Janine said, "Who wants to be treated like a wild animal?" The more
experienced girls will sometimes be driven to un-casual extremes, especially if the vulture is dishonest, and taunt him: "Hey, fellow, you got
something to hide over there?" Generally, the girls just walk away
down the beach, or roll over and pretend to sleep until the would-be
hunter gives.

Barbie, who has large breasts and is very often vulched, described
what this felt like:

"I'd been to the beach before with my boyfriend and decided to
make it down on my own. It was in the middle of the week and
there weren't many people. I went up to the north end of the
beach anyway to really make sure I wouldn't be bothered by
anyone. First an older guy with his dog came along and he placed
his stuff just to my south. Then a younger guy came along,
looked up the beach to see if there was any action, and there
wasn't, so he sat down to my north. Before long I was completely
surrounded with guys, all of them faced toward me. The two guys
that got there first began playing frisbee, but they both kept
making 'mistakes' and throwing the thing right near me, always
complaining about the wind or the bad toss. I knew what they
were up to. I really felt kind of funny. There couldn't have been
more than a hundred people on the whole beach and here I sat in

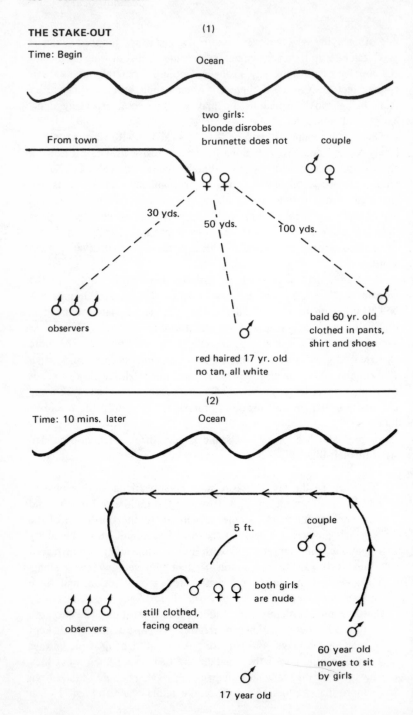

THE STAKE-OUT

(1)

Time: Begin

Ocean

From town

two girls:
blonde disrobes
brunnette does not

couple

♂ ♀

♀ ♀

30 yds.

50 yds.

100 yds.

♂ ♂ ♂

observers

♂

red haired 17 yr. old
no tan, all white

♂

bald 60 yr. old
clothed in pants,
shirt and shoes

(2)

Time: 10 mins. later

Ocean

couple

♂ ♀

5 ft.

♂ ♀ ♀

both girls
are nude

♂ ♂ ♂

observers

still clothed,
facing ocean

♂

60 year old
moves to sit
by girls

♂

17 year old

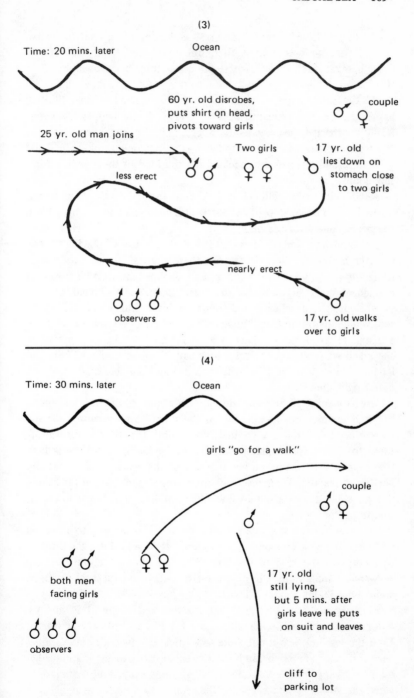

the middle of them all. The rest of the beach was really deserted. I tried to ignore it at first, but couldn't. I finally moved my blanket up the beach, where the whole thing began again."

At the other extreme from the vultures, at least in their hunting approach, are the *yawannafuckchick types.* Some people think this heavy approach is peculiar to the nude beach, but that's far from true. It's really happening all over. And everywhere people think it's peculiar to their situation—probably because it's the kind of thing people don't talk about.

Kevin delighted in telling how he'd done this in Hawaii. When he felt horny he'd go down to the beach at Waikiki and greet every "broad" on the beach, one after the other, with "Hey, yawannafuck?" He insisted that he'd always find one and that it was all a matter of playing the law of large numbers: "Somewhere out there there's a chick up for any-thing, *anything*, you name it, man, and all you have to do is turn over enough of 'em and you'll find that one." Kevin had also plied his trade on the straight beaches in California; we even found one girl who'd received an invitation from him and "freaked out." We saw Kevin (from a distance!) go up to a strange woman's apartment, knock, and, when she asked what she could do for him, say, "Wannafuckchick?" She did let him in and later he told us it took her an hour to explain why she *didn't* right then.

It's happening all around, adding a little spice to life here and there, but it happens more commonly on the nude beach because so many men, especially the heavy virginal types, think the girls are just waiting there for them. We've already seen at the beginning of this book how this happened to Janine on her first day on the beach and how she and her friend reacted. Their reactions were pretty much par for the beach, though a few do freak out. A few might also like it, but wouldn't want that to be known.

For example, we saw a case where Jon and Tod went up to a woman and, after a few preliminaries, suggested, "Hey, why don't the three of us go up on the cliff and get it on?" She thought about it, then answered, "Well, I don't think I want to today, but I'll think about it, and if I do, I'll let you guys know."

Most women just take an "ohjeezezwhatnext" view of it, and we never found a verified case of success for this super-heavy approach. Even the less heavy, but not quite sophisticated," heyyawannagoupthe-beachwithme" approach rarely seems to succeed, unless it's preceded by a lot of softening up, so it's normally done only as a joke and only when the guy isn't that eager for the woman he's joking with, because that direct approach almost always fails. As in warfare, success in sexual hunting depends on indirection, on all the management of uncertainty and deceit common to any form of seduction, not on a direct assault.

The experienced and successful hunter is a different type entirely. He knows that stalking doesn't fool many of the prey, and that it gets them up-tight. And he knows the wannafuckchick types are more likely to freak women out than to score on them. He knows the important thing is to be casual, natural. He doesn't circle around and make a big deal out of it. He comes up and starts talking about the things everyone talks about—the need for a drink of water, a cigarette, maybe a joint, the sun, whatever seems most up-front at the time. But, while he doesn't appear to be stalking, he is. The point is to *set it up* far in advance. Know the prey so well that you know how to act, how to move in for the score, in a totally planned manner that appears totally casual, unplanned, spontaneous. Planned spontaneity is the only path to success.

Jon was the supreme master of hunting on Eden Beach, at least until his fateful encounter with Wendy, described earlier. He worked at it day after day, month after month, year after year. When he didn't have to work and the sun was out, he'd arrive about ten or eleven in the morning. He knew position is vital. He wanted to be in the right place, on station, when the girls started arriving. And he wanted "to have first crack" at the best of them before any other hunter could pick up on her and before the vultures could freak her out.

Just in case any girls had come down earlier, as sometimes happened, he'd make the rounds quickly, jogging as far as the beginning of the gay beach, then back down to his favorite station at the foot of the road which most people used for access. There he would lie in wait, casually, almost where they'd have to step on him to get by. Most of the girls—especially the new ones, who were the ultimate prize—would sit on the beach near the road because they were still too uncertain to go further. It was then easy to sidle up and start talking. If action there was slow, he'd move down the beach under the cliffs to detect any telltale sign of a lone young woman.

Jon didn't "move in" on every attractive woman. He wasn't some "dumb heavy" who figured every woman would go into paroxysms of delight at the sight of his nude torso. He knew the body-code of women in general and of the beach specifically. He could detect the slightest down-turn of a mouth, giving the danger sign of cold disdain, an indication of, "You think I'm that kind, huh!?" He knew they were *that* kind, especially in the early days when almost everyone was pretty casual, but he also knew that with almost every woman everything hinged on the right entree, the feeling of the initial approach. Most approaches on the beach would give the nude woman the feeling that she was being preyed upon, that a man was trying to use her, and really looked at her as "cheap." So Jon watched and waited for just the right moment, searching for a come-on sign, the look of relaxed warmth, maybe a slight hint of a distracted, dreamy smile, maybe an ever-so-slightly sensuous movement of her body. As he always said, "Ya gotta have the touch, man."

He was an attractive man, and he kept his body in the lithe, muscular shape most women appreciate, but he knew that all of that would come to nothing if he didn't have the "touch." After all, there were a lot of men on the beach with physical merits, and quite a few with better builds than his own. But *no one* made it as often as he did, because he did have the touch.

There were days when he'd work his ass off trying to pick up on someone, only to go home in the evening with nothing to show for it. On those days he was a forlorn sight, hanging around the bottom of the path at the cliff, hoping against hope that someone, almost anyone female, would come along at the last moment to save the day. When no one did, he would slowly scale the cliff, probably consoling himself with the thought that things would go better tomorrow. And they generally did. Most days he did pick up on someone and take her down the beach for a little more privacy. When he did that, as far as we could tell from our research voyeurism, he generally had to settle for some mutual masturbation or less. More commonly, if his depth readings told him she was up for the real thing, he'd take her to the cliff path and back to his van.

It was obvious that most of the women were open for consideration, especially in the early days of the beach. If the approach was done right—up-front and natural—it was easy to start negotiations. It was also obvious that the vast majority of the women who went, especially those who came alone or with a girlfriend, knew the score and were up for it in general. It was also reasonably clear that most of them appeared on the beach frequently, though by no means always, with some anticipation that something really worthwhile *might* come up. This is a major reason for being open to negotiations and, as Janine put it, "It's kind of fantastic the way any discussion down here always turns to sex." The negotiations are always partly sexual negotiations. If everything went right, you scored, generally later in your van or apartment, but sometimes either right on the beach, which is very rare (except for the hand jobs), or a bit more commonly up one of the convenient canyons.

But scoring was extremely hard for most people; though it looked so easy, it proved so elusive. This was the considered opinion of one of the more experienced hunters on the beach, Tod, who had specialized for several years in hunting on the nearby straight beach, where he'd found the hunting pretty good, especially among the tourists who were always looking for some fun and games away from home.

As I learned soon after meeting him:

"I'd heard about the nude beach from some friends and came down to find out if it was really a good place to pick up on some chicks. In the three weeks that I've been coming down here I've scored one piece of ass and got into the pants of two others. You cruise along the beach until you spot a chick alone, then you go up to her and talk. As quickly as possible, you bring up the topic of sex and find out where she is coming from. If she is up for sex, she will come off pretty free sexually and then you suggest a walk up the beach or a climb up the cliffs. There are problems with the scene. First, to get the girl in a place where sex is possible you have to break the continuity of the seduction. Like, if you are in an apartment it's pretty easy to shoot off to the bedroom, but that long hike up the beach is really awkward . . . there's a lot that can happen along the way that can blow the whole thing. And, since it is so hard to have sex on the beach, you've got to assume that the kind of chick that's up for it must have really hot pants and I think that means she's more likely to have VD or the clap. Who wants to come home with more than a sun tan? But probably the hardest thing about pick-ups at the beach is simply keeping it up. Chicks that want to ball with a stranger are a rare bird. You've got to go thru a lot of them before you score. All the others shut you down in one way or another and that's a tremendous blow to the male ego. It sure as hell hurts me—where it counts, man! I really think that there are better places to go. Bars, schools, even the local grocery store. If you can offer a reason to be there, it's pretty easy to move on to your apartment from there. That way you don't have to be so up-front about your interest in sex, so you don't have to lay all your shit on the line."

This same point of view was echoed, even more strongly, by Anne, a young woman who had been on the beach off and on for some sime, even though she had been up for it the first time she went there.

"Most people, under these kinds of circumstances, you know, if they're cool at all, they realize that these aren't the best kind of circumstances to meet people, you know, friendliness can be easily misconstrued. The first time I ever came down here, about four years ago, and people were nude, I met this really nice guy down here, and I was talking to him and he said, why don't you take your clothes off? So I did and we sat around for a couple of hours and really had a nice time. But that was before this beach got so popular and crowded. Then there were really friendly people; now you don't know what you'll get. That was the only guy I've met down here. I've never met anyone else. This just isn't the place to meet people."

But, regardless of the difficulties, we have to remember that there are successes, and even one success can be terrific, because the situation—the naked proposition—is so demanding that even a single success can be a monumental ego-builder.

Men are certainly the obvious hunters on the beach. But, as in all other realms of life, the women are on their own hunting trips, hunting in ways intended to serve their own purposes, and all the time seeming to be against the whole idea of hunting. Janine was an excellent example of this. After she'd been a regular on the beach for about a year, and we'd been watching her, we asked her to write up an account of how she picked up on guys at the nude beach. She told it the way it is, including the problems that even a woman hunter faces:

"A woman's very existence on the free beach, especially if she is nude, is taken by males generally as a come-on. A woman merely has to present herself to make the first move. Usually the wait is not a long one. Men on the beach seem ever ready to try a lone nude lady out. But if a woman really wants to be picked up, there are a few things she can do beyond passively existing and waiting. Most important is to be situated in the midst of the crowd—but being careful it is not the gay crowd. This seems to allow more exposure and lesser distances for the hunter-males to cover. Body language is vital. Open legs invite. Sensuously covering oneself with suntan lotion (paying careful attention to one's breasts) is inviting. Generally posing—showing off one's most glamorous features—is contrived and generally understood by both sides as a sign of approachability. The most aggressive move a woman need do is to make eye contact with a male and smile warmly. It almost always works.

"Beyond this body-oriented stuff, women also have costume consid-erations. In most areas of life, a woman can let others know she is ripe for the picking by wearing sexy or revealing clothes. This form of self-expression is not completely lost on the nude beach. Floppy sun hats, jewelry, and makeup are devices which women can still use to attract males. A necklace against nude flesh can be very effective in conveying a woman's awareness of her feminin-ity beyond her natural female-ness.

"A woman can also advertise herself by movement. Stretching or exercising, frisbee-playing or running along the beach all show off the body. Promenading or walking by the water's edge allows one to move sensuously rather than merely look sensuous. Water's-edging and even swimming are also important because they offer a mobile place where men can approach more easily than having to make a special effort to come to a woman's blanket or towel. The water's edge allows for more casual, noncontrived reasons for a man to talk to a woman.

"Mostly I've met men down by the water. You can stay by the water and really attract attention. Guys come up and say, 'How's the water?' or 'Any jellyfish today?' or something dumb like that. Honestly, the men make the stupidest comments. But then you answer and the guys come into the ocean with you. I've managed to 'pick up' about ten or so guys this way. Mostly after playing in the waves together for a while (sometimes touching—more often not), the guys have been reluctant to leave. Usually what happens is they follow me to my towel and then go get their stuff and bring it over.

"I like the water's edge trip because it is also easier to get away from an undesirable person. You can say you want to be alone, then walk away. It's really more graceful than telling a guy to leave. Another advantage is you can talk for a while friendly-like before committing yourself one way or the other. On the blanket trip, you kind of have to say "stay or go" right away; you don't have a decent time interval to decide. If you say "go"—that's it. If you say "stay," you are stuck—no graceful way out—it gets messy to have to tell a guy to leave 'cause you don't like him after all. It is hard for me to tell a fellow human being to fuck off—even if he is a creep. There is no really polite or easy way to do it. So I take the water's-edge trip. . . .

"Only one time have I made a super-aggressive move toward a guy on the nude beach. It was an early summer, super-nice day. There weren't too many people around yet. It was early in the day and I'd come down by myself as usual. And here was this really foxy-looking dude going around picking up trash. He was a regular—I'd seen him before, dark tan all over. He had a good thing going with the garbage trip. There was a lot of trash on the beach. I said 'Hi,' and he said 'Hi.' He made some comment about the people keeping their own beach clean and went on about his business. He was right. So I started to collect some of the cans and bottles and papers also. We talked a little and it turned out he lived about three blocks from me. He was pleasant—not a come-on artist like most of the dudes there seem to be. I asked him if he would mind if I moved my stuff over beside his stuff so that I wouldn't be bothered by any creeps. He said O.K. Well, we both just read and after a little while he left. He just left and that was all. I saw him on the beach a couple of times later. We always said, 'Hi neighbor,' but that's as far as it ever got. Too bad—he was sexy and seemed considerate. I wonder now if the roles weren't reversed for a bit—the male being passive and the female aggressive. I'll bet he thought I was a "creep"; the way I think of most come-on guys at the beach as creeps. It was an interesting experience. It's hard for a woman to pick up on a guy anyway except to just make herself open for it. I mean, you know, I think most dudes, even a nude dude, just aren't up for anything more aggressive yet."

The women are cool hunters, but every now and then we'd come across some women who were so horny or else simply so heavy in their approaches that none of the guys would believe them. We came across a couple of these one day, who were so heavy we found it hard to believe. Some mutual friends introduced us to them, one an attractive brunette of about thirty-five (a school teacher on vacation before getting married), the other a cute, bleached blonde of about twenty-five, slightly plump in an appealing, feminine way. They were with a short, stocky man about thirty. The brunette sized us up, running her eyes over us, and really bore into us with her eyes when she talked. The three of them walked up the beach, but when they came back we went over, sat down with them, and struck up a conversation. Three other guys soon dropped by, obviously thinking they'd pick up the two women, who immediately started teasing them, telling them how horny they (the women) were.

The brunette started off with, "Wow, am I horny today." She grabbed her crotch, rubbed it slowly and moaned with only a little smile, "Hey, can't one of you dudes help me out a bit?" The two of them went on like that, talking about how great it'd be, weaving sex into almost every subject that was discussed. When no one seemed to want to help them out, they started coming on heavier, then getting hostile. They poured it on their "friend" first, intimating that he was gay and couldn't do a damned thing for them. Then they turned on all the rest of us, charging that no one was man enough to get it on with them. We all just sat there shifting around, gawking, and not knowing what to do with two women who talked like some "wannafuckfellow" types.

After a while, the three other men split, perhaps giving up hunting for good! The girls came back a few times, the blonde finally picking up on a guy who seemed to be what she was looking for. The brunette, for some reason, never seemed to score on the beach, so she decided to go home to her school teaching job and marry her fiance.

THE SWINGING SCENE

The sexual hunting we've been considering so far has been one male or more hunting one female or more, or, in some cases, females hunting males. But there's another form of heterosexual hunting that goes on on some of the beaches, varying in intensity from one time to another, like almost everything else.

The nude beaches are hunting scenes for the swinging hunters, the couples or teams who hunt for other couples or teams with whom they can swap partners. From the early days of the late 1960s to the present, the swinging crowd has found the nude beach an important hunting scene. Though the extent varies greatly from one beach to another, swingers seem to be into all the beaches. And the sexual freedom groups, with a heavy concentration on freedom to swing, are very active in supporting and extending the nude beach scenes. All forms of swinging go on, from the conversion of novices to swinging all the way to "group gropes."

Sometimes, though not very often, you find a couple in which one of the partners is using the beach to sex up and turn out the other. This is somewhere between individual hunting and swinging. It involves finding a partner for one of them, without a swap, but with the help of the other one. Since we felt that most couples into swinging are using their partners to get at other people and are often on a selfish trip, we weren't prepared for this kind of single swinging, but we found some.

The first couple we encountered was young, about twenty, glee-fully submitting to the attentions of three straight camera-voyeurs, who were shooting the couple from every angle, with lots of close-up beaver shots. The couple was posing for them, bending over backwards, strik-ing erotic poses, and laughing. This in itself was uncommon, but not unheard of. People have been known to agree to almost any nude photo blitz, and sometimes camera types even come down on the beaches with paid models, using the scene to pose some shots for porno magazines which use nudism as a front. But this scene was not like that. The camera-voyeurs were "pawing all over the woman," and she and the man were both enjoying it. We had met the couple before and knew they were married, but had not seen anything like this happen to them before out on the beach.

After the voyeurs split, we talked with both of them a while. They just acted as if nothing had happened, as if it was just all natural. The next day we came across the woman on the beach alone and worked around to discussing the camera scene. She opened up right away.

"Well, it's not strange at all when you know what's been going on with us. We've been married just two years and a little. About a month ago, I discovered that my husband was balling my best friend. We had a big battle and it almost split us up. But Joe said he was really sorry about it, really guilty as hell, and wanted to make it up to me. Then he just seemed to get over feelings of jealousy. He brought me down here and started trying to turn me on to other guys, saying this would loosen up my sexual inhibi-tions and then maybe we'd have a better thing together."

She didn't really seem too enthused about the whole idea, and when guys would try to pick her up, she would try to get them to stick around to meet her husband (which they never seemed to have time for). The man seemed to really like his wife when they were together, so we figured he was just on another amateur nude therapy trip, trying to turn his wife out to turn her on so they could enjoy sex more together—or trying to inhibit his (or her) feelings of jealousy, or escape them, as many casual types are convinced they can do if they just keep trying long enough. But she didn't seem to like being turned out, and it must not have worked because they quickly disappeared from the scene.

Most couples who come to the beach come alone and pretty much stay to themselves, except at the small cove beaches where the press of humanity forces them into a greater sense of community. Sometimes they'd talk to others, but they were generally involved with each other and didn't want to merge into a swarm of humanity. But there are an increasing number of groups of two or three and, rarely, more couples who come down together, and there are some couples who seem anxious to get more involved with other couples. Today, these couple groups will often have their children with them. The groups—especially those with children—make the whole scene look a bit like a family social or a church picnic. Now that nudity is spreading to people who are less casual about sex, that is more and more common and is more often the whole truth.

But in earlier years that was almost always only the surface, the appearance of normalcy. Almost any time we looked below the façade in those days we found there was more than normalcy. As a rule of thumb, we concluded that friends who go nude together commonly swing together—not always, but commonly.

The typical thing was for a couple of us (a male-female pair) to approach a nude couple on the beach and strike up a conversation. It was especially easy if they were sitting near us and hadn't brought down anything to drink. "Hey, would you like to join us in a beer?" never failed, since beer is precious on the isolated beaches. One topic would lead to another, and that would generally end in a discussion of parties-and-sex, in which we talked about parties and meant sex. They'd say they had these lovely parties. We'd say, how neat. They'd say, why don't you come by sometime? We'd say, how interesting. They'd say we didn't have to worry about getting home because we could stay over all night. We'd say, how convenient.

People rarely talked about what everyone meant, but everyone meant what almost everyone knew they meant. As with so much else on the beach, talking was done mainly not to be understood by those who didn't already understand what the scene was all about. If you weren't in, you were really out—and you could look at a group grope and see a family social. ("Isn't that cute, Harry, a group of neighbors coming down to be friendly the natural way.")

This misunderstanding of the obvious by outsiders always reminds me of the middle-aged couple who brought their young son down to the beach and, told us how delighted they were to find there weren't a bunch of nude gay guys running around like everyone told them there was, while they were sitting in the middle of one of the biggest gay nude scenes ever. "But they look like normal men anywhere." Indeed they did. They very often look straighter than any straight on the beach, and that's often what first tells you they aren't straight. It always seemed strange to us that there were so many people who seemed surprised to learn that people often aren't what they want you to think they are and that talking can be a major way of making yourself out to be what you know you aren't.

A beautiful example of the most common swinging types on the beach were three couples, with kids, to whom we talked one day. They were all sitting nude on the beach, but rigged out in CIA outfits—tennis hats, bulbous glasses. They were quite nervous at our approach, but, once we got them calmed down, it turned out the three husbands were in the Navy, probably officers scared to death some of the enlisted voyeurs patrolling the beach would spot them and pass the word in the barracks. (An officer nicknamed Captain Nudist wouldn't go very far in the Pacific Command.) They were all from different parts of the South, but stationed at the Navy's facility in San Diego. They had met each other down on the beach, became friendly enough to get together off the beach, and now spent each Saturday night partying at one of their homes, coming together to the beach on Sunday. We suspected they might be more than just friends by the way they talked; our suspicions were confirmed when one of the husbands grabbed and fondled someone else's wife.

The swinging couples on the beach normally swing only heterosexually. But the trendy swing of many casual people to bisexuality has also had an effect on the beach, and it is not uncommon to find the swinging couple moving into group sex of some sort or other. There are even instances in which the tendency to not talk about what is meant led to a great deal of confusion because of these blurring lines in swinging.

Tod told me of such an event one day when he was with a girl:

"We were sitting by this really foxy couple, exchanging glances of appreciation and a knowing nod. I went over to ask the time and to strike up a conversation. They invited us to join them. They had learned about the beach through a swinging magazine and figured they'd come down and meet some people, but they had been there for several hours and no one had even said so much as hi. We made it clear we were interested and they let it be known they were too, but we couldn't figure out just which way. It seemed that both the girls were bisexual and it never became clear if they were after a threesome or a foursome and in just what combination. Nothing ever happened that day and we even wrote a letter asking what they wanted, even laying out all the possible options, all the things we were up for, but they never wrote back. It's one of those things, if it doesn't happen at the time, it probably never will. It's too bad, too, 'cause we were all really interested but we couldn't put it all together. I don't know what happened."

The swinging couples we've been looking at have all been freelancers, the unorganized swingers. But the American genius for organization has also produced organized swinging, some of which looks suspiciously like bureaucratic sex to some of the casual people on the beach.

Some of the sexual liberty organizations are still quite active on a few of the beaches. Their main interest is in highly organized swinging parties. There have been some people who got into these by first getting into the beach and then getting propositioned by someone in organized swinging, but that seems rare. The movement has been mainly from the organizations to the beach, not the other way around. The beach people don't normally like that much organization of their swinging—they're freelancers. Janine pretty well summed up most of the naturalists' views when she told about her one visit to such an organized league party: "Uh, well, you go there and they take you in the bedroom and fuck you and that's that. Wow, like big deal."

But there are some much more successful semi-organizers of the nude swinging scene. These are people who have no formal organization, but have dedicated much of their lives to the swinging scene. They create their own personal organizations of swinging couples out of sheer lust and dedication. On Eden Beach, there was an especially well recognized group of hard-core swingers who largely revolved around one fifty-year-old guy who had literally dedicated his whole life to swinging. This guy, whom we sometimes referred to as the Dirty Old Man of the Nude Beach, had been heavy into nudist-camp swinging for a while, but found the camp rules too constricting. For him and many others, the openness of the nude beach was a sexual Eden. The beach became their recruiting ground.

They staked out a specific area on the beach, just below a path down from the cliffs and right in the center of the heterosexual beach. They'd come down in a small group, so they'd have a nucleus around which new individuals and couples could coagulate. Then they'd start in with their games and shows, meant to attract people and to lead to laying their hands on the "firm (hard) young flesh," the beginning of a whole sexing-up process they'd developed.

One of their big shows was hypnotism, practiced by the Dirty Old Man. He'd almost always choose a very young, lovely girl (apparently he didn't consider men and older people very good subjects for hypnotism). If the girl wasn't nude already, the group pressure to get honest would mount, going from joking to more serious seductions and even nude beach rapes. Then he'd take the lovely young nude by the hands, turn on the heavies, put her under, and then tell her he was going to count to ten, at which time she'd experience erotic excitement inside but not give any outside sign of it. We'd often see him take a girl he'd hypnotized back into the canyon, and we assumed they were "getting it on," though there was no way to tell for certain. The Dirty Old Man was so successful with this ploy that he soon became the envy of many men on the beach half his age.

He and others in the group also would sex 'em up by a laying on of hands, doing massage. A few of the girls were from massage parlors, so this was a natural for them. And the others were generally tuned into the natural massage practices that were floating around, so it was easy to move from talk to "getting hold of the firm young flesh." Janine described the Dirty Old Man's massage techniques, which would have gone over very well in a massage parlor for women:

> "First he'd tell you to lie down, face down. Then he'd take hold of your legs and spread them apart. Then he'd move in on you, putting one knee between your legs and pressing firmly up against your crotch. . . . Then he'd move his hands all over you, down your back and all over your ass—*sexy.*"

It really turned on most of women he did it to, and even the guys watching would get turned on. As Janine said, "Yeah, one day Gary got so turned on by it he got an erection, and with him that's really impressive. . . . He had to go plunge it in the water to cool it off." Anybody walking by could just see a family circle practicing some outmoded artificial respiration techniques.

For days in advance, the Dirty Old Man of the Nude Beach would prowl the beach looking for "firm young flesh," as he liked to call it. As soon as he spotted some likely young buttocks roasting in the sun, he'd swagger over and say, "Howdy, y'all look like the kinda really sensuous women that'd like to come to our party this Sataday . . . we c'n promise y'all the best we got . . . how's about it?" (The Dirty Old Man was real down-country, just plain folks on the nude beach. But note that he was not "casual." He swaggered, rather than sauntering. That is an important difference in body language.) His chosen targets would usually hem and haw about it and then a few would make their way over on Saturday night. They could come alone (firm young flesh was welcome anytime), but more often the group would scurry around and get people paired up on the beach before the big event. One young aficionado, Tod, picked up on Janine for this event and gave an account that checked out with all other accounts:

"I'd been going to the beach since early in the summer. It all began when my wife, who I had been married to for some five years, cut me off sexually. I guess it had been getting worse all along and finally one day I said fuck it and started going to the beach in hopes of finding some chick to get it on with. I must admit that I didn't find much on the beach either until I met this guy who was promoting some young chicks to make it to one of his swinging parties. This old guy had a real groupy thing going. He'd get these young chicks, then hypnotize them and tell 'em they were having orgasm, and then do deep-body massage, and then turn them on to his swinging parties. Anyhow, through a mutual friend I was able to get invited, but I was told that I had to bring a date with me. There were six or so guys in the same boat, definitely willing, but no one to take. . . . Luckily, I found Janine.

"Things were all set, I had the necessary date and she was even good looking. I could tell my wife that I was called in to work the late shift. Shit, just think, I could make up for all that sex I'd been missing with my wife. I drove over to check out the pad where the party would be and it looked really nice. I also grabbed some Z's and made a firm resolution not to drink anything that would hinder my performance.

"Date in hand, the first thing that I did when I got to the party was to rip off my clothes, saying that we really have to get into the program of things. Not many of the people were nude, and most of them were sitting around the living room soaking up its mod cocktail lounge decor, watching some porno films of a couple of girls doing sex with a dildo. There were people there of all ages, ranging from as young as fifteen to as old as sixty-five. There was also as wide a range in physical appearance, some really foxy chicks and some definite dogs. I recognized about a dozen or so people from the beach and later was to learn that some more were there from a neighboring nude beach. All in all, there must have been a total of 60 or 70 people. I figured that I had better get the ball rolling, surveying the room for my first sex partner, and finally zeroing in on the host's wife. She was in her late thirties and beyond her prime, so I figured that she would dig getting laid by a younger stud. Humping the hostess also made sense because I knew her better than anyone else. I suggested that we retire to a vacant bedroom, she agreed, we got it on and I must admit that for an older woman she really knew her shit.

"It didn't take long to realize that the party was segregated both by age and location. The young hip types hung together smoking dope and exchanging mates. They were new at the scene, and some left crying, upset that their boyfriend or girlfriend would get it on with someone else. The twenty- to thirty-year olds formed much the same kind of group, but they were more likely to drink liquor than smoke dope. The over-forty group were the hard-core type, drunk on their asses and obviously very familiar with the scene. The house was divided up into areas for different forms of sex, so that the living room became the place for exhibitionist sex, the master bedroom accommodated the group-gropes, and the single bedrooms were for single-partner sex.

"During the course of the evening I made it with four different women and struck out with two. Of the four that I balled, one was a foxy married woman from up the coast, one a very nice-looking masseuse, and one was, of course, the hostess, with the last one totally nondescript. Of the two that I struck out with, one, a cute middle-aged blonde, said that she wasn't up for it right then—the other I did get into the bedroom, but we somehow didn't get along. She kept talking about some motor-cycle gang friends with chains and everything. I couldn't help but think that she was into S-M and that was not a turn-on for me. The party went on until early in the morning."

THE GAY SCENE

To the gay guys, the nude beach is a dream come true, paradise on sand. In the clothed world, gay cruising is the heaviest form of sexual hunting, since straight males can rarely score on women with such heavy tactics. And on the gay beaches, the same is true. As in the clothed world, the gay forms of voyeurism, body-display, and hunting follow patterns similar to those of the straights, but they are much heavier, more open, and more successful. The gay beach is the super-casual scene.

All the big nude beaches have gay scenes, though some of the smaller wildcat beaches certainly don't. As we saw earlier, the gay beaches are probably the oldest nude beach scenes. A few of them, as at Eden, go back twenty or thirty years. In the old days, homosexual men simply sunned and cruised in the tall grasses or canyons, or sometimes built windbreaks on the beach to hide from both the winter on-shore breezes and the police telephoto lenses. When the scenes were legalized, the gays simply came out of the bushes and started doing their thing more openly—which later became a short-lived problem for the nude beaches in general, as we shall see in the next chapter.

On the bigger beaches, the gay scenes are generally clearly demarcated socially and often physically. On a beach like Eden, you can point to where the gay beach starts and ends, though at each end of the three-quarter-mile stretch of gay beach there are a hundred yards or more that is mixed on most days. This sort of demarcation is very affected by police or other official action. For example, in the fall of 1973, when officials temporarily put up "Nudity prohibited" signs at the north end of Eden Beach, most of the gays quickly started moving down to the heterosexual beach, where there were no signs. On the smaller, cove beaches, the lack of space and physical boundaries makes it harder for the gays to stake out and hold a distinct area. Even there, however, they tend to congregate at one end of the beach. At Cliff Beach, for example, they congregated at the south end, where there was a little more shielding from the voyeurs above and, thus, more chance to do sex.

But the gays and the heterosexuals (or straights) greatly prefer sexual segregation. Gays can almost always spot the gay beach, and generally only go to a straight beach if they don't realize there's a gay section further on. The heterosexuals, on the other hand, often aren't very aware of the gay beach areas, partly because those sections are more remote and partly because the preponderance of males on the beaches generally makes the gay sections appear much like the rest without close inspection. The straights wind up in their own areas mainly because they are more accessible, because if they do get into the gay areas they come to realize it's not for them, and because they definitely gravitate to that area where there is more heterosexual action. A few women have jokingly said maybe they should go to the gay beach to be let alone by the hunters, but they almost never did that because, however much they didn't want it publicly known, they didn't want to be on a beach surrounded by a bunch of guys who had no interest in them.

In recent years, as the nude scene has changed, many of the gays at Eden have become more integrated by quietly staking out a hundred-yard section of the straight beach as a congregating area for themselves. But on a big gay beach like the north end of Eden was in the summer of 1973 you could literally walk three-quarters of a mile, seeing several hundred gay males, perhaps a few gay girls, and only a few misdirected female or male tourists who didn't know where they were.

There are only a few gay girls on the beaches. Every now and then you'll see an obvious pair, a butch and femme, who have come over for the day and once in a while a pair of the more discreet (and far more common) lesbians, who look heterosexual but show furtive signs of a physical relationship with one another. There is thus no gay girl scene, only a few isolated pairs. The gay scene is overwhelmingly male. I do not know why, and the gays themselves aren't clear about it. It's probably partly because gay women are less involved in casual cruising. This may be the reason there are always fewer gay bars for women than for men, so it makes sense to see it as part of the reason for fewer gay women on the beaches. But the disproportion is so vast that there's probably more to it. After all, there are still many gay girls who cruise wildly, using the powder rooms, if less frequently, for their "tearoom trade" much the way men do use men's rooms. Some more of the reason would seem to be the greater desire of the men for sexual display and voyeurism. But even all that hardly explains the total disproportion. Some people on the beach have speculated that it's because the gay girls have much greater hang-ups about their sex organs than straight women, which remains to be substantiated.

Just like the heteros, the gays are overwhelmingly into voyeurism and display, with fewer taking part in the cruising scene. Voyeurism, body-display and organ-display are all much more open than on hetero beaches—and "heavier" by hetero-casual standards. The gay guys are always obsessed with "doing the gorgeous trip"—both being seen as gorgeous by the other gay guys and seeing the gorgeous bodies of others. And on the beach the gorgeous trip reaches its ultimate expression. (Probably the only places that match them, and may supersede them because of the greater ease of performing sex acts, are the many private gay clubs in the big cities which have nude scenes around the indoor swimming pools or baths. In many ways, the nude beaches are just the free alternative to the private clubs, but they also offer more chance of picking up strangers—something highly prized in all gay cruising.)

Gay voyeurism is unconcealed. They'll often sit in a group of from two to about ten and just size up all the guys who pass by. But they also do a lot more walking than the heteros, so much so that the "gay promenade" is a distinct part of the gay areas. As they walk, they do a travelling voyeur trip. Most of this is confined to the gay areas, but there are some gays who like to go to the straight areas to look at the hetero guys, especially at what one of them called "the pretty surfing boys." But most of this is pretty discreet.

We found only one case where a heterosexual guy felt he'd been heavily voyeurized by the gay guys. He said he was sitting on the straight beach when three or four couples of gay guys started sitting near him, giving him the heavies. But when he left, no one followed him. Most of the heteros really don't seem very aware of the gays, and many reacted with surprise when we mentioned something about the gay beach area.

The other side of the gay voyeur trip, of course, is the gay display trip. Some of this is strictly body display. These types often keep their suits on, presumably because they figure their body in general is more gorgeous than just their sexual parts. With only one or two exceptions, we've almost never seen any of the proverbial muscle-bound gays doing the gay display. They do once in a while, but almost always in their tight, tiny-suits, which are increasingly the order of the day on the gay beaches. Maybe this is because muscle development is the result of fears of organ inferiority, as some people maintain. For whatever reason, their display trip is whole-body display, not organ-display.

But there's a lot of the organ-display, commonly combined with body display. The ultimate display scene was for a long time the gay display on the north end of Eden Beach. There's a low hill, about fifty feet high, that juts out from the two hundred foot cliffs. A road leads up this hill, covered with the scrub trees that can exist in California's eight months of dry, hot weather. It thus provides good cover for the private gay life. There are some rocks and clearings at the edge of the hill facing the beach, and these form the gay display area. On bright summer days as many as ten to twenty gay guys would sit, lie and stand in this area, both suited and nude, displaying themselves to those below. Other guys would then climb the road and discuss the amenities of the surf and sun and so on. The gay display has been a bit more discreet in recent years, but it goes on.

The gays, with their intense concern for being well-endowed, or "really hung," are the ones most anxious to display themselves to best advantage. They are, then, much more likely to use the caressing techniques of getting up for display purposes. We've seen the most open instances of guys who, when they get their suits off or stand up to take a walk, will "tweak a little" to get started right. It's generally the most obviously homosexual who do this heavy stuff, much to the disapproval of the gay community generally, and especially to that of the many secret gays who prefer the isolated beaches to more dangerous bar cruising. As more of the openly gay types poured into the gay area at Eden Beach at the end of the summer of 1973, we saw much more of the wide-open display stuff, which has also cooled a great deal in recent months.

Some of the gays just come for the sun and surf and a chance to sit around and be gorgeous and see gorgeous guys. These are especially the settled guys who come down with their lovers and, therefore, are generally unable to get involved in the gay beach cruising, unless they're a rare breed of gay swingers. But most are up for some cruising and even those who come with their lovers are often up for open sky sex, especially once the sun, wine and gay display excite them.

One young hetero type told us what the gay hunting scene looked and felt like to a hetero prey:

> "My girlfriend and I had been to several nude beaches before and decided to give this new one we'd heard about a try. We started to put our things down but before we could this really drunk guy came along telling us we really needed to go for a swim. He sat down with us and mumbled stuff about the military, what the different ships did and all that. But it became increasingly obvious that he wanted more than to talk—he wanted my girlfriend. I got kind of pissed off—I mean what kind of guy did he think I was to let him walk off with my girl? We tried to get rid of him, but he just kept talking. My girlfriend really got tired of the whole thing and got up for a walk. He jumped up and followed her down the beach. It wasn't very long after that when these guys started walking by, trying to get me to talk to them and all. I didn't know what to do, so I pretended to fall asleep. One really fat dumb guy came over and sat down talking about his motorcycle. I kept it at yes and no and finally got rid of him. Another guy kept walking back and forth in front of me. It really gave me a sense about how girls feel. We pieced the whole thing together afterward. . . . We had sat in the gay area of the beach and everyone figured we both were looking for a guy. It's really a funny feeling to have guys lurking about, giving you the heavies, really hot for your body."

Gay hunting on the beaches involves the full gamut of hunting strategies. The gay display devices make you available for the hunters. There are also all the ways of putting yourself in position to spot the prey. One of the more interesting devices of this sort is "hawking," which we found near Santa Barbara. The beach had a lot of small sand dunes just at its perimeter. Anyone, gay or hetero, could sit there, with just his head showing, and watch for some likely newcomers. If they looked likely, the hunter could swoop down on them, but in the meantime the dunes provided some good cover from the eyes of those who strolled by on the beach.

The gays generally choose a beach area that has good cover and, especially, a handy canyon or two. A canyon is best and immensely preferred, since no one can get into it without giving plenty of chance for those outside or near the entrance to warn everyone else. Probably the ultimate example of this is Gay Canyon on Eden Beach. This is a canyon immediately south of the road leading up to the gay display area. The mouth and path leading up into it are shielded by some high bushes, so that the path is invisible from the beach itself. The path leads up into the canyon, each level or tier being more difficult to get to. The gay guys distinguish "five tiers" or levels, the highest being the safest one for sex.

Gay Canyon has been used for sex for many years, some say for twenty or thirty. Whitey, who was the most regular of all regulars on the gay beach, had been coming to the gay area at Eden almost every warm day, and many cool ones, for ten years. (I'd seen him there on my runs almost every warm day for five years, always on the same little rise of sand on the beach. He knew all the regulars and was a gossip, so he quickly picked up on newcomers. He was the ultimate insider and was pretty up-front about the gay scene. Moreover, everything he told us checked out with what other gay guys told us and with what we could see going on.)

Whitey said that the canyon was invaded once by the police, who heard about it from someone and wanted to shut it down. They went in in force to "clean it out," but didn't realize there were five tiers. "Yeah, they thought they'd really cleaned it up, but all the time they were hunting around on the first tier there were guys doing sex in the higher tiers." A number of years ago, there was apparently a cave (called the Ballroom) higher up in the canyon where many of the guys would go to do sex, but it's gone now. Whitey thought the cops had come in, before his time, and blown it up with dynamite, but some other people thought there had simply been a cave-in.

At one big beach near Santa Barbara, there is also a canyon, as usual in an isolated part of the beach. But it's not as safe as Gay Canyon at Eden. One day we were talking to a gay guy, George, when a young muscular gay, Tim, went by, suited up. George mentioned that he'd met Tim earlier up the canyon. Tim was friendly enough and was really up for it, but afraid even the canyon wasn't safe enough. He wanted to do sex through his tiny bikini, but George didn't go for that, so they didn't get it on.

The big beaches also have other forms of cover. At Eden, for example, the scrub trees on the road provide excellent cover, almost as good as Gay Canyon, and some guys prefer it—maybe because it's so convenient to those using the gay display. The small cove beaches are bereft of most amenities such as canyons or any other major cover, so only the desperate get it on there. At Cliff Beach they used some indentations in the cliffs, but this left them open to passers-by.

When the nude scene was illegal, the gay guys would keep out of sight, especially when doing sex. But once the nude scene became legal, they came more out into the open with their sex as well as nudity, even beginning to integrate with heteros as the social stigma waned. Some of the openly homosexual discovered the fun of the gay scene on the beaches and started using them for their sex thing. As Whitey put it,

> "These screamers started coming down from L.A. And one weekend there was a whole bunch of them. Yeah, and they were just doing sex all over the place, right out in the open where the straights going by could see them and the rangers too. Oh, man, it just blew my mind. . . . My God, don't they know it's going to ruin the whole thing for us all if they do that sort of thing?"

It did get kind of heavy, though we ourselves thought this sort of thing was really visible mainly to people up on the gay beach, like Whitey, rather than to those passing by. Still, there's no doubt the gay scene is a major reason straights in general attack the nude beach—they are often afraid of what might happen "with all those queers running around." They're right about there being a lot of gays into the nude scenes, but wrong about what effects this has on heterosexuals. The heterosexuals have to be pretty knowledgeable to know anything about the gay scene. We ourselves had a lot of trouble getting all the necessary information.

THE FUTURE OF THE CASUAL SEX SCENE

It is already apparent that the casual sex scene, especially the heavier forms of hunting and swinging, is no longer as prominent on the nude beaches as it was in the beginning. It's still there and is just as intense, but the arrival of new types into the nude scene has diluted the sex scene, at least in its heavier forms. The first nude beachers were the most casual, often even communal, types, for whom casual sex was a way of life. They were up for almost anything, from swinging parties to bisexuality. It was a simple matter of self-selection, and they were the people willing to take the risks involved. But as more straight types have hit the beaches, types less up for casual sex, or, at least, demanding more "respectable fronts" for their casual sex, the sex scene has diminished in visibility. It's still a focal scene, but other foci are growing.

It seems likely that if secure affluence continues in our society, then sexual liberation of all types will continue to grow, and the nude beach will serve as one of the many different forms of casual sex scenes where people can pick up on those of a like, casual inclination. It will probably remain the most demanding and exciting sex scene, unless we suddenly get a new form, like "Totally Nude Pick-Up Bars," where people have to go up-front even more in their sexual hunting. But the sex scene on the beaches will be less obvious, more thinly spread, and less a deterrent to those who want to do the respectful voyeur and body display trip without getting into heavier casual sex.

6

Politics and the Future
of Nude Beaches

Most nude beachers want to escape from it all, to find sex, peace, and freedom on the beach. But in our age of social conflicts, such escape is generally short-lived. Politics has become almost a seasonal happening on the nude beaches. Since increasing thousands have joyfully thrown themselves into the nude beach scene, only political and police repression can stop their spread. Politics is where the future of the beaches lies.

All beaches have become a big political issue in California and other coastal states. Americans have been fleeing most of the cold hinterlands, with beautiful exceptions like Colorado, heading for the warm suburbs that sprawl along the South Atlantic, Gulf, and Pacific Coasts. Abundance and leisure have led to vast increases in the number of people congregating on the beaches, while the amount of beach space has remained the same or even shrunk because of private development.

In California, the press of humanity toward the coastal regions has become intense. The population has continued to grow, though at a decreasing rate, and almost everyone wants to live as near the coast as economically feasible, because the heat and smog increase rapidly inland. Real estate values within a mile or so of the coast have soared in recent years, so these areas have been developed almost exclusively as home and recreation sites for the well-to-do. This, in turn, has produced a political counter-attack from the not-so-well-off, who swelter in the inland valleys, met by static from the coast-dwelling well-to-do, who want to preserve what they have. They have created "ecological politics," demanded and gotten ever greater constraints on private developments along the coast. The development of nude beaches thus comes at a time when beaches are already the object of hot political contention around the state.

But, of course, there is a special emotional flavor to the political conflicts over nude beaches because of the deep feelings over public nudity and the revolutionary implications of nude beaches—especially public nude beaches. In a state of twenty million people, there is hardly a single voice raised against private developments of the beaches as a violation of the word of God, but there are no doubt several million fundamentalists who believe the nudity on the beaches is a vile act against God and humanity.

We have found repeatedly that many of the "liberal" people who start out complaining quietly about the parking problems caused by nude bathing wind up screaming about the evils of the nude scene. We have found that these feelings drive some people, including a few politicians and law enforcement officials, to go to extremes to stop the public nudity. But we have also found that the political forces support-ing the nude beaches have grown, partly because so many thousands of people have now sampled the nude scene and partly because there is a widespread view among influential libertarian groups that nude beachers should be allowed to do their own thing as long as they don't interfere with the rights of others.

As with military battles, the outcomes of political battles are always uncertain. But the nude beaches have a lot going for them politically. Law enforcement could not *eliminate* nude beaching now, but it could greatly restrict its size. Moreover, the forms beach nudity will take depend on the outcomes of the political battles. And the outcomes of the battles depend largely on what people think and see is happening on the beaches, and above all on how they feel about them.

Since most people, especially the influential, have not yet been to the beaches, the mass media become their eyes and ears on the nude scene, their only source of perceptions of the concrete situation. The impressions the media give of the nude scene thus become one crucial factor in determining its future.

THE NEWS ON THE NUDE SCENE

Most of the people who go to the nude beaches, including the heavy straight voyeurs, who are taking more of a porno view of the beach than anyone else, see nothing wrong with the casual sex scene there or anywhere else. While even some of the casual types aren't happy about sex done out in the open for public consumption, most of them can manage that on the unusual occasions when they are called upon to do so.

One young man recounted, probably with a secret sense of awe, his experience with the super-casual scene. He and his girlfriend were walking up into the hills above a beach in Santa Barbara to do some nude sunbathing when they came across a nude couple making love right in their path. As they passed by, the girl looked up at him, so he said "Hi!." She smiled back and said, "Hi there." Most people on the beach aren't ready for that kind of super-casualness, but they manage such happenings by tunnel vision—they sense something intimate is going on nearby and manage not to see it—or, rather, they look at it "casually," not pantingly, and are careful not to be seen looking excited. Their casual observation and looking away turn what most straight outsiders would see as a public show into a *social fiction of privacy.*

The nude beachers feel, as one woman on the beach put it eloquently, "If anyone sees sex on the beach as a problem, then that's their problem, not ours." Up-tightness about casual sex, even publicly visible casual sex, is a personal and social problem, but the *doing* of casual sex is not. The nude beachers, then, would like the whole society to be concerned with solving the problem of up-tightness, rather than being concerned with "solving" the problems of casual sex.

At the same time, almost all of them are realistic enough to recognize that this view is a not terribly popular one and that presenting it as the public defense of the nude beaches would not wash. In the same way that each of them almost instinctively pulls the mantle of the naturalistic ethos around his or her sexual activity on the beach when dealing with most other nude beachers, so do they even more instinctively pull this mantle over their public appearances. When they make public pronouncements about the beach, by writing letters to the editor, going on TV, or confronting political officials, they don't say, "Hey, man, what's wrong with *you* that you don't accept the casual sex scene?" Rather, they immediately, persistently, and almost universally say, "Hey, man, what do you mean sex? There isn't any sex on this beach. How could you have gotten your head so screwed around as to suspect that *we* would do sex, of all things, on *this* beach? Oh, man, this is a natural, mellow, cool scene—not a sex scene."

They take this same stance toward any form of social research, of course. The only person we know who had attempted any systematic study of the nude beaches before us had passed out a questionnaire to several hundred people at random on Eden Beach. Among his many questions was one concerning reasons for going nude on the beach. He found that only a minority mentioned sex of any kind as a reason, and these mentioned only "sexual curiosity" and "show off body." The results of this whole study are presented in Table 1.

Almost all the reasons given were those which could be seen as "naturalistic" or some more mundane thing such as satisfying the curiosity of one's mate. The researcher became a part of the scene and, while he never penetrated the heavier sex scenes, like the hard-core swingers, he knew a lot about the casual sex scene on the beach and knew the results of his questionnaire study were erroneous. But he didn't think sex should be dealt with in any report on the beach scene because it would be bad public relations. One student heatedly tried to convince me and my colleagues that there wasn't any significant sex on the beach at all, even though he was with some people we knew to be into super-casual stuff, and he insisted against all arguments that we were trying to close the beaches down by dealing with the sex scene. (Our own feeling was definitely that the enemies of the beach already believed all kinds of groundless atrocity stories about the beach, so it couldn't hurt much to be up-front, and, regardless, we weren't about to do it any other way.)

But the social researchers weren't of much concern to most people. They were all part of the scene, and few people ever thought they might be trying to close it down. As soon as we let them know we already knew what was going on, most people were surprisingly up-front. The people who got the nude beachers up-tight were the news people. The beachers knew that thousands of others would form their ideas of the beach through what they saw in the papers and on TV. They knew that the news people didn't know what was going on. And they could see that the news people could never be part of the scene. It's hard to fit into the nude scene when you don't know anything about it before you get there, you have two hours to discover the whole, complex scene, and you're standing there amid several thousand nude beachers with your coat and tie on, your street shoes, and your camera crew swirling around you waiting for instructions on what to shoot. It's especially hard when the nude beachers are all ready for you, organized and waiting to show you just the right things. But all of this was really fortunate for the nude beachers. The beachers got a terrific TV image, from the standpoint of the straights.

The private beach owners in the north have always been very much against news coverage of the beaches. They enforce their no-cameras-on-the-beaches rule against the newsmen and threaten them with lawsuits as well. (One of them threatened us and was highly uncooperative, while the others were friendly and helpful, probably in part because

TABLE 1

Questionnaire Data on the Nude Beach

248 questionnaires: 168 males/80 females

Ages: 12 to 64, with 24 year average

55% single/33% married/8% divorced

Occupations: 1/4 students, rest include artists, professors, engineers, business managers, architects, etc. Majority of professions indicate a high level of education.

Moral values: 57% liberal/23% moderate/7% conservative/10% radical

Political outlook: 47% liberal/30% moderate/9% conservative/11% radical

72% don't consider themselves nudists/36% would like to visit a nudist park/40% no desire/19% already have

Sinful exhibitionist? 4% yes/87% no

Reasons for going nude:		
	Freedom from clothes	92%
	Swim nude in ocean	85%
	Relaxation	81%
	All-over tan	80%
	Sense of well being	72%
	Closer to nature	62%
	Esthetic totality	58%
	More honest soc. int.	48%
	Sexual curiosity	40%
	Exercise	32%
	Rebelling	26%
	Show off body	21%
	Others	21%
	Spouses interest	16%

54% said they would volunteer time to work for preserving nudity/do nothing 19%/try to find another beach 36%/other 18%

94% favor setting aside areas/2% no/2% no opinion

What don't you like?		
	Hard to get to	38%
	Peeping toms	22%
	Too many men	23%
	Litter	48%
	Men trying . . .	6%
	Too many dogs	11%
	Other	25%

Printed by permission of the author.

they could see we weren't newsmen.) Their general view is "out of sight, out of the public mind, hence, let alone." There's a lot to be said in favor of that view, since the politicos normally leave the beaches alone when there are no influential complaints against them—and no publicity to be gotten by attacking them.

In the winter, when there are few people involved in the nude scene, the politicos are quiet, but they start making noise and threats when summer brings the people—and the media—back to the beaches, The nude beachers in San Diego might have chosen the same tack, but they didn't get that chance.

The TV newsmen started covering the nude scenes as "human interest" or "feature" stories. The first couple of stories came across as tongue-in-cheek, about people doing "no-no things." Only as the political conflict heated up did the media begin to cover the nude scene as a serious issue.

After a few local feature TV stories on the beaches, one of the networks came down from L.A. to find out the truth about the growing political controversy. As usually happens on these two-hours-to-get-at-the-truth junkets, this one had to go to the organizational leaders of the two sides. These leaders, being highly political and thus conversant with duplicity, quietly set up "on-the-spot impromptu interviews" for them. One of the property owners who was very much against the nude scene for financial and personal reasons, but who wanted very much to come off as "liberal about it all," was presented in his role as local scientist "telling it like it is." Needless to say, he didn't stress his concern with property values. Nor did he mention that he and other property owners had fought for years to keep access to this beach difficult for the public by preventing the construction of access paths and by keeping a locked gate at the head of the only access road to the beach. (He also didn't mention that when surfers managed to get keys made for the lock, the property owners immediately put on new locks.) Instead, he stressed the need for "all the people" to enjoy this beach. As the Great Egalitarian, he believed that everyone should be able to enjoy nature's beauty, instead of these several thousand nudes, so he and the other property owners were all in favor of building a public access path to the beach, opening it up (and only incidentally making it a nonisolated beach so that the courts might not allow nudity there). It was obvious that anyone who opposed this ideal was against democracy and the rights of all the people to natural beauty. (This same man later helped finance the placing of piles of dirt along the road in front of vacant lots to prevent people from parking near the beach.)

But the nude beachers outdid the property owners. When the network TV newspeople came down to shoot them, the interviews were pretty much arranged by the grandaddy of swingers—the Dirty Old Man of the Nude Beach. He brought out really sympathetic, natural types to tell the media, "You know, people who've never been down here think this beach is some heavy sex scene, but I've been coming to this beach for years and I've never seen any sex here." This became Standard Scenario No. 1 in the interviews on the nude beach.

Then the interviewees would talk about how natural it all is. They'd never mention that they themselves were into this kind or that kind of casual sex, for which the beach was a staging area, if not the scene for actually doing sex, or that they knew all about the big swinging scene staged on the beach by the guy standing just behind the cameras, or any of the other sexy things they knew about on the beach. As the Dirty Old Man pointed out at the end of the first interview, "Man, we really fed 'em a line of shit." The nude beachers would then go on to point out that they too were great protectors of the common man's rights, since anyone was free to come to the beach, clothed or nude, and that they were simply protecting the "civil right to go nude." Then they'd put it all together under the great umbrella of natural ecology: They were against opening up access paths to the beach because that would destroy the natural ecology of the beach—and, also only incidentally, might make it appear unisolated to the California Supreme Court.

The nude beachers got a great press, especially great TV coverage, partly because they carefully controlled what was presented, making sure no super-casual type told it the way it really was, and partly because almost all of the newsmen and women who covered the beach were favorable to its existence before and after coverage. We had previously studied the newsrooms of the local television stations and knew, to varying degrees, just about all the TV news people who were assigned to the beach. All of these people developed the opinion, "Well, it isn't something I myself would care to do, but I'm in favor of letting other people have a beach to go nude on if they want." They essentially bought the naturalistic argument, and took a libertarian view of it, before they ever began the interviews. (As far as we knew from our observations, only one newsman ever really got involved in the Eden Beach nude scene. He was with a local rock radio station, became good friends with a couple of the beach organizers, and wound up giving a powerful editorial on the radio in favor of the scene. Most of the other news people never seemed particularly at ease with the whole scene. In fact, one woman TV reporter who covered the beach two different times in several months, both times completely dressed, had one ot the most intense cases of tunnel vision we ever saw.) When they got down on the beach, they'd shoot their film and do their interviews in line with their expectations that it was a natural, mellow scene.

Most of the feature news coverage of the nude beach can be seen in the major filming and airing done by one of the network affiliates. The well-known reporter in charge of this programming had done a small program on Cliff Beach earlier, so it was known by the beach organizers that he was basically sympathetic or, at least, libertarian about the whole thing. They had decided at one of their meetings that they should try to get some more favorable coverage on the beach and that this reporter was the man to approach. They got hold of him and arranged to let him have an exclusive on their side of the story if he'd do it. He came down the next Saturday to do the shooting, but it was cool and cloudy, as much of that summer had been. He and the nude beachers both wanted a big crowd to show how the scene had expanded, to make it more significant to viewers, and to get some more action into the film. The taping was postponed, and the reporter came back the next Saturday, which was beautiful and sunny. About five thousand people turned out, as many as on any other day that summer.

The reporter and his camera crew of three were met by the nude beachers and escorted onto the beach. Just before they got there, one of the organizers enlisted us to help pick up the trash strewn around the beach and put it in big plastic bags. One of the first things the reporters were shown when they got to the beach was the carefully bagged trash, an indication of how clean the people kept the place. The bags of trash were dutifully filmed and later aired. (What wasn't aired was the fact that the organizers and we researchers had to do the picking up because the nudes who'd done the littering had only one response when we asked them to help us: "Naw, forget it." We felt that we should have been given a credit line for the production of trash sacks. Actually, there is a small minority of the nude beachers who take ecology seriously and go around picking up the cans and paper with diligent frequency. As elsewhere, most people on the nude beach have no sense of common decency.)

As the TV crew worked its way down the beach, they were surrounded by the beach organizers and an entourage of the regulars. Just as they hit the beach, a guy with an erection walked by at the water's edge. He was probably a heavy organ-displayer making a bid for stardom, but the regulars saw to it that he didn't get filmed.

We walked down the beach about a hundred yards, past hundreds of casual young couples, and finally came to a couple of toddlers making sand castles. Here, at last, the cameras rolled. The attractive young mother of one shouted out, "Hey Aaron, smile for the man," then asked when the film would be aired. A short distance further on, we came to a lovely young nude mother with long, flowing blonde hair, bending over her toddler in the shallow water, with the sun a little behind her to produce a sparkling halo effect on film. It was a cameraman's dream shot, and contained no pubis shot to get it banned by the censor. It, too, was recorded on film.

We wandered on, shooting the cliffs to show how isolated the beach was. Then we came to one of the "Save Eden Beach" petition tables, taking signatures to oppose opening up the beach with the new access road. This was a major reason the TV people were brought here. The political activity was also filmed.

About this time, three of us researchers spotted Al, the ex-voyeur turned organ-displayer, wandering around the periphery of the TV crowd of about twenty-five people. He was obviously on a fantasy trip this day, because he had an almost full erection, and was strolling by looking at the young women with an inviting little smile on his face. The camera operators had discovered a few more toddlers among the masses, and were not paying attention to Al. We then followed the crew over to some people the organizers were getting together for the reporter to interview. They pulled a doctor they knew out of the sand (they might have encountered him by accident, but he was more likely a "plant"). He told the reporter how healthy and natural nudism is, medically speaking.

We wandered over to some more people anxious to go up-front on the air-waves, and about this time the camera crew got independent and began choosing their own people for interviews. But they chose from among those around them, so they got about four beach regulars and two lovely girls, irregulars, who happened to be lying with their boy-friends on the sand nearby. They all spoke about how natural and beautiful the scene is.

One old-timer, a retired regular living partly on unemployment, went up-front to tell how most people think the beach folk are a bunch of radicals, but he was really pro-Nixon. (The organizers smiled and encouraged mock applause from the rest of us.) He *also* told how natural the scene is and insisted it was no sex orgy either.

(This reminded us that we had long wondered just what this guy was up to on the beach in addition to really enjoying its beauty, which he did. He was very nice, and we always enjoyed talking with him, but we also knew that he went around photographing nude little girls and lying around looking at them. We knew he'd never been married or had any kids, so he could be just a would-be fatherly type. But we also worried that his "thing" might be little girls. We found him very articulate about everyone else's sex trip on the beach, but he would never open up about his own feelings.)

Then the girls spoke before the cameras about how safe everyone is from sex on the beach.

We were standing at the back of a crowd of about fifteen or twenty people watching all this filming, when Al came up from behind. We were joking with each other about how, "You know, sometimes it gets a little steamy down here, maybe even heavy." Then we saw him moving in for a score and we'd never seen anything like it on the beach before. He moved in, casual and steady, on a young redhead. Then, with that same little smile on his face, he rubbed his hard against the young woman's buttocks, looking at himself the whole time, probably to be sure it was really happening to him, out here in broad daylight, with the cameras ten feet away. We couldn't think of anything to do in this crisis except struggle to get our own cameras in focus to record this event for posterity (which we never did).

There was no beach rule for this. If he went ahead and tried to actually rape her, then we'd know what to do, depending on how she reacted to the whole thing. But as long as he was just doing a kind of *organ-display rape,* a totally creative and unique event, we didn't know what to do. The woman didn't seem to know just what was happening to her. She waved her hand behind her, not touching him, then moved forward slowly toward the camera crew, with him keeping in close contact. We kept thinking that here was history being made, a wholly new kind of rape in a really new kind of human situation, with totally unknowable implications. The camera crews went on filming, just ten feet away, *in the opposite direction,* recording the political activity.

The redheaded woman moved away with the camera crew, leaving Al, the creator of a new kind of sexual scoring, savoring his triumph for the day. We walked off down the beach toward the access road, a little ahead of the TV crew, wondering about man's future and about the nature of TV truth.

We made our way slowly and when we got to the access road, about a half-mile away, the woman was there with a guy who seemed to be her husband. They were dressed, putting on their shoes for the rocky climb ahead. We went up with our tape recorder in hand and told them we'd been studying the TV filming and saw her watching it. She said she'd been interested in it. Then we worked around to asking if they thought that seeing the beach on film would make most people oppose it; would it make them think of the whole thing as a sex scene?

The man chuckled at this, "I don't think there's any sex on the beach at all . . . that's ridiculous." Then we talked about the legal situation and such and came back to sex again, trying to see if she knew about the organ-display rape that had been committed on her fifteen minutes before. We asked, "Do you think maybe nudity on the beach leads some people into creepy sex?" She came right back with, "No, never . . . if anyone has feelings like that they'll get over it in five minutes. . . . I don't see any sex scene here. . . . I mean, frankly, maybe I'm missing it, but I don't see any." We couldn't argue with that. A lot of people miss it.

We started up the road, musing on the complexities of reality. The TV reporter came along and gave us a ride up. All the way up we kept thinking about what we'd seen and heard, wondering what it meant. We talked about how inaccessible the beach is, with blisters and all, and listened to one of the organizers say how people need to change their minds about the beach because it isn't what they think, and it doesn't hurt others. And this made us think about this guy and his wife, who seemed to us to be into the nude scene to find another guy to make it with. Maybe we were wrong about what seemed obvious. Maybe the man didn't see what seemed obvious. Maybe he and the redhead both knew what was happening all along but thought that was all right, if that was Al's thing or his wife's thing.

We knew there were many things we'd never know about the scene, but we knew most people couldn't believe the things we did know. And we knew that most people never would know what we knew to be obvious because they hadn't been able to see what was going on *behind* the TV cameras all the time they were recording the grand, idealistic front. But, while we were interested in getting at the truth, we wondered if presenting the truth about the beach on TV would lead people to want the police to repress everyone. The TV reporter seemed to be a pretty casual guy, and maybe he knew all that and thought the truth would produce more injustice and evil than would the presenting of false fronts. If so, maybe he was right.

In any event, the TV programs and the local newspaper accounts saved all the people from the truth, and the beaches got good public relations in the eyes of the straights. That made it more difficult, if not impossible, for the politicos to start shouting about the evils and inequities of the nude beaches and the need to save civilization from the barbarians by using guns on them or putting them in prison.

The beach property owners, who were the only organized force opposing the nude beach scenes until church groups organized, quickly became aware that they were looking bad in the press. Most of the time they hardly had a chance to tell it the way they saw it, since property owners didn't have the sexy human interest aspect the nude beachers did. And when the owners did get to tell their story, they came out looking like landlords trying to control the beaches (not a very popular position in California these days) and like arch-conservatives trying to repress the young, which does not accord with the upper-middle- and upper-class liberal image they hold everywhere except when their own interests are directly involved. They felt it was "very unfair" of the nude beachers to carry their case to the news media and decided not to take part at all in such programs because they didn't want to make it look like the argument was between property owners and nude beachers (which it was). This left the news media almost completely to the organizers of the nude beaches, which gave them a boost at a time when they needed it. That and the courts were their only major political weapons, since the property owners were able to go behind the scenes, without media coverage, and try to get the politicians to pass new laws banning nudity on beaches. (We never could figure out why this was more "fair." In fact, we found it rather difficult to figure out how anyone could decide what was fair or unfair in this jungle of conflicting interests, fears, joys, morals, and differing views of realities.) The attempt to pass anti-nudity laws has become the main thrust of the political action against nude beaches. It is an effort supported by most, though not all, police officials and by many political leaders.

THE POLICE AND THE NUDE BEACHES

A minority of the police are the front-line troopers guarding the ramparts of civilization against the savage hordes on the nude beaches. That statement may be biased, but anyone who has watched these few police at work knows that's roughly the way *they* see it, and may even be a milder rendition. And by acting with the dedication demanded of those entrusted with such a noble goal, they create a lot of "pig haters" on the beaches. By acting on the belief that they are the guardians of morality, this minority of police also throw their weight behind the forces out to stop beach nudity. Their attitudes and actions on the nude beaches are grounded in their general attitudes about the casual young and, in some areas, their long-standing dealings with nude beachers.

The police all over California have definite feelings about the casual young, feelings formed largely in the 1960s, the heyday of their struggles with hippies and student activists. These feelings are summed up beautifully in their terminology for them. Most commonly they refer to the casual young as "assholes," but sometimes they call them "pukes," which is a little more specific and separates the casual young from other forms of "assholes" with whom the police are locked in combat. What isn't said by the words is said by the tone of voice, which contains varying degrees of contempt. Like most hatred, this is reciprocated. Many casual people refer to the police as "pigs" almost all the time. As with the police, it's the tone that tells you how intense the feelings of contempt are. Even in those rare instances when someone has a personal friend among the police, he's apt to refer to him as a "pig."

These general feelings have been intensified toward nude beachers by two earlier forms of experience the police had with those who joined the nude scene. In some areas, especially in San Diego, the beach patrols have considerable experience with the casual types on clothed beaches, and have had near riots on their hands at times when they tried to close down parties on the beach. They've also developed hate relations over the years by harassing the casual types there in the same ways they do on the nude beaches. (In Santa Barbara, many of the casual types on the nude beaches have been into the casual scene in nearby Isla Vista, and the conflicts between the police and the Isla Vista young have been even more intense.)

The police who patrol the beaches have also derived some of their feelings about the nude scenes from the contacts they had with the gay nude beaches over the years. This was especially true in San Diego. As we've seen, the gay nude scene on Eden Beach went back twenty or thirty years. The police used to survey this scene from the cliffs, try to get telephoto shots of the gay nudes (and a few skinny dippers) to use as evidence in court, and send beach vans flying down the beach to catch the culprits in the act. Because many of the police, especially the older ones, have such moralistic hatred for the gay scene in general, their attitudes toward the nude beach scene have probably been more contemptuous than they might have been without this history of gay beaches.

The historic Chad Merrill Smith case, as detailed earlier, grew out of this beach patrol policy of the San Diego Police Department. Smith was arrested for "indecent exposure," which both he and the police stipulated involved lying on the beach nude and falling asleep. As we saw earlier, unlike all the previous cases, he fought the case up to the California State Supreme Court and won a reversal of his conviction on the grounds that his behavior did not involve any lewdness. Subsequent to that decision, approximately fifty cases of arrest on lesser charges for nude bathing at other Santa Barbara beaches were thrown out at the local court level.

At that point the local police forces and prosecuting attorneys could have decided to try to circumvent the Court decision's effect by interpreting it very narrowly—that is, by interpreting any behavior other than lying nude as "lewd." Since the Court's decision had been unanimous and had stressed the need for clear evidence of lewd intent, that narrow interpretation would probably have been overturned eventually. As we shall soon see, that possibility does not always dissuade officials from making and enforcing laws in order to achieve immediate personal goals, but while we were never able to determine how or why the decision was made, in this case the local officials decided not to take this path. Based on what we do know, we expect they did not do so because of fears that the new legal challenges would allow nude bathing to go even further than it could go with a more "lenient" police and prosecution policy. All subsequent official actions seem to have been based largely on that fear, and the fear seems to have been well founded.

The San Diego police and the Santa Barbara police decided to allow any behavior other than clearly "lewd" sexual behavior on those beaches which are "isolated." "Isolation" has come to be defined in working terms by the police largely as any area where there are few complaints about nude bathing and, specifically, as an area where nearby residents cannot see the nudity from their homes.

Citizen complaints are very important for a number of reasons. First, complaints obviously can create political problems for the police. Second, however much the police may dislike nudity and "pukes" for personal reasons, they clearly have more important things to do than chase around after nude sunbathers, so they generally do so only when there is pressure on them. This is quite important in San Diego, where the complaints about nudity on beaches is handled by the Homicide and Sex Crimes division, which has limited manpower to deal with very serious crimes and hardly any manpower to devote to nude beaches. (Even the most fervent hater of nudity would hardly compare it as a crime to murder or rape.) And, third, public complaints are vital in getting convictions for charges of "disturbing the peace" or, rarely, for "creating a public nuisance." There obviously can't be disturbing the peace without someone disturbed.

The police now rarely charge anyone with "indecent exposure" for nudity on any beach, even nudity on a big public beach in Los Angeles. The best reason for this is simply that prosecuting attorneys realize that the Supreme Court decision makes it likely that any case taken to it without clear evidence of "lewd" intent will be overturned, even if the beach is not isolated. If this happens even once, the now straight public beaches could be opened up for nude bathing, obviously a contingency they want to avoid. Lawyers representing the casual interests in the state have been searching for the ideal test case for years to break open all public playgrounds to nudity.

Even on highly unisolated city beaches in Los Angeles, such as those near the casual and gay scenes in Venice, almost all recent arrests for beach nudity have been on charges of "disturbing the peace." This does not mean, however, that the police and prosecuting attorneys do not use the indecent exposure laws; they do indeed use them in almost all cases prosecuted for beach nudity, *as a threat*. They can point out to the arrested nude, or assume that any defense attorney will do so, that if he is charged with indecent exposure he is officially labelled a sex offender. Besides, any individual arrested for public nudity knows without being told that the mere fact of being arrested for such a "sex crime" might stigmatize him for life. Even if he fights it to the Supreme Court and they decide that he can't legally be listed as a sex offender, the general public, through the totally irresponsible reporting of the news media, already knows he's been arrested for public nudity. The news media would rarely report that he was later found innocent.

So the police and prosecuting attorneys play on this deep fear, and almost everyone cooperates by pleading guilty to something of which they are not, from their own standpoint, guilty. They may also be innocent of the specific charge in the eyes of the legal officials, who are afraid to charge them with any greater offenses because they expect they would be found innocent. The great thing about plea-bargaining for the prosecuting attorneys and police is that, so far, it *works*.

Much of the time, this is the way the system of "justice" works in our conflictful society, but rarely does anyone involved in doing this sort of thing open up about it. Remarkably enough, one city attorney in San Diego did confront the subject in a campaign speech. As reported in a local newspaper, he told a college audience that

> nude sunbathing, per se, is not illegal under present law and court cases. It is illegal, however, if accompanied by "lewd" conduct . . . but there are no good legal definitions as to what "lewd" means in connection with sunbathing. Technically . . . someone could go to a big public beach and take off his or her clothes "but I wouldn't advise it."

And rightly so. He knows that the police and his office would legally prosecute a person for doing something he himself believes is technically legal and that he would almost certainly get the victim to cop a plea to disturbing the peace.

The fact is, however, that this situation does not normally arise today. Hardly anyone is anxious to offer himself up for public sacrifice as a test case, and hardly anyone is interested in doing the nude thing on straight beaches when he can go to one of the nude beaches, where the police won't arrest him. (I saw only one man deliberately walk nude across the rocks into civilization. He only went several hundred yards, but nude beachers still thought him "crazy.") Moreover, when anyone begins a wildcat nude scene, he almost always does so on one of the more physically isolated beaches. Rather than jumping to a big public beach, the nude scene spreads from the most isolated beaches to those which are somewhat less so. Consequently, there is a slow encroachment upon the straight domain, giving the straight public time to adjust to each new spread so that there is not an outburst of anxiety, threat, and stigmatic rage.

And this adjustment by small stages is what seems to be happening. As long as the police don't get a lot of complaints, they generally attend to what everyone, and definitely they themselves, see as more important business. Today some of the wildcat scenes involve beaches that are just barely isolated. (Of course, even Eden Beach, where the one closed access road is long and steep, can be reached by wheelchair if someone helps. Once, we saw a group of a half-dozen physically handicapped teenagers down on the beach, with one of them in a wheelchair. One of the boys could barely walk with two crutches, but he had managed to get his clothes off and was wandering around nude in an excited state. There is also a very old man who comes down frequently. He can hardly walk but manages to creep along for hours on his cane, just to get nude.)

The legality of the public nude beach scenes is uncertain, actually fuzzy, to most of the participants, to the property owners, and to most of the local officials. Each side has been feeling its way to see what it can get away with without running any big risks of losing everything. The people into the wildcat scenes are in the most uncertain situation, but most of them seem to be quite young and hence more willing to risk legal stigmatization. But even here their sense of risk is greater than commonly proves to be the case, because the police feeling of uncertainty leads them to leave even the wildcatters alone unless there are serious complaints. If they do anything, they normally just tell people to put their clothes on. The people so warned almost always do. In fact, most of them keep a wary eye out for the police and scramble to get their clothes on at the first sign of them.

This same sense of uncertainty, though in lesser degrees, afflicts many of the irregulars in the bigger, more stable nude scenes. Most of the people on the beach for the first time or so are oblivious to the legal situation. Seeing so many hundreds or thousands of nude people running around, they simply assume that, since somehow or other people go nude without getting arrested, it must be legal . . . *or something.* Even people who have been on the beach many times will sometimes say things like, "Well, gee, I don't know, is it legal or what?" or "Yeah, I guess it's legal. . . . I don't know." Some people doing it say they think it's illegal, but the police don't do anything about it. Even some of those who know much more about the situation and have seen the police beach vans go peacefully by for months remain jittery. As one guy said, "Man, I keep my bathing suit rolled up in my hand at all times, or certainly no more than a few feet away from me. . . . You never know what the cops are going to do. That suit's my lifeline back to civilization and I don't want it cut." As Paul Rasmussen said in the early years, "Yeah, I suppose it's legal, but when I see the pig van coming I head for the water."

There are a few counter-culture types on every beach who are willing to fight down the line for rights as they see them. These people have threatened to have nude-ins if the police try to close down the beach or, on rare occasions, to go further, including tearing down any access roads built in an attempt to end nudity. One lifeguard doing patrol on Eden said he thought "there'll be shooting and murders if they try to end nudity over here." But that kind of view is born of a straight's misconceptions of the casual types. Clashes with the "pigs" show the naturalists to be on an escape trip, not a rebellion trip.

The three major clashes with the police since the Chad Merrill Smith case have been in Los Angeles County, in Santa Barbara, and in a beach adjoining the legally nude beach in San Diego. In August of 1972, two months after the Smith decision, the Sheriff's substation in Los Angeles County, under some pressure from property owners and wanting to express their own feelings, decided to shut down the nude scene at a cove. They suddenly appeared over the cove in a helicopter and announced over loudspeakers that people had twenty minutes to get dressed and disperse. There was an immediate scramble to suit-up and disappear. Only a half-dozen out of several hundred remained to be manacled and marched off across the rocks back to prison. Similar mass arrests have occurred by horseback round-up as recently as 1976 in Santa Barbara County and generally lead to small fines for "disturbing the peace."

The situation at Eden has been very complex. Actually, it isn't even legally clear who owns the beach, let alone who has what rights to do what about nudity on it. The property owners and some others always thought the nearby university owned it, and they put up signs saying so. But then during the nudity conflicts, the university administrators, probably desperate to avoid falling out with their casual student body, but equally desperate as property owners to "get the nudity out of there," "discovered" by title search that the city owned the beach. We always suspected that the university title specified ownership down to the "mean high tide line," but, since no one knows where that is, they could easily *claim* they didn't know if they owned the beach—who knows where the beach is and where the ocean is, since it varies greatly every twelve hours, and from one part to another. It's equally unclear whether the city or even the state could legally do anything about nudity below the mean high tide line, wherever it was. One official said he thought that, if they did ever try to enforce the ban on nudity in the park, they could only do so down to the mean high tide line.

The police who patrol Eden know perfectly well that there isn't much they can do to catch people in lewd acts with the limited manpower they have. Unless people on the beach are completely strung out or out of their minds in an unlikely sexual frenzy, they can see the beach van coming a mile away, so they just cease and desist until the police leave. But, if the police can't get them for something the nude beachers know to be illegal, they can get them for something they don't know is illegal and can keep them off-balance with petty hassling. Thereby, they believe, they help to "keep the lid on" by just showing up. So they ride around looking for kids with dogs. There is a city law against having dogs on city beaches, and this law is apparently even enforced on the straight beaches where there are a lot of "pukes," but we found the law is rarely enforced on straight beaches nearby. The nude beaches never had any idea such a law applied to this isolated beach, so the police would get them with $35.00 tickets, no mean sum to the casual young, and quite a blow to the dog lovers. Eventually the dog lovers started warning each other and learned they could go for a swim until the "pigs" left. (The police never wanted to take a dog in the van, so everyone was safe if no one admitted to being the owner.)

There were also isolated charges that the police would arrest anyone with a dog, or drinking, who couldn't show any ID on demand and drive them off the beach, only to release them after scaring the hell out of them. (As one guy said, "Who carries an ID on the nude beach? Man, I couldn't even prove I'm a human being, if they demanded it.") We could only conclude these were just ways the police expressed their personal feelings and, maybe, "helped to keep the lid on by reminding them we're here." They would also jump out of their vans and swoop down on some group of unsuspecting nude beachers if they looked like anyone might be drinking a beer a smoking a short cigarette. This was a specialty of "Super-Pig," a big, burly thirty-fivish cop who seemed to really have a thing on for the nude scene. He'd jump out of his van with a snarl on his face, point an accusing finger at some kid half-dozing in the sun with a suspicious beverage can nearby and shout, "Hey, you! Get up here! Where's your ID?!"

Sometimes they'd search people or their things. Over many months, we saw only one arrest—a dog-walking criminal who was probably let out at the top of the cliffs. No doubt they arrested some people when we weren't there to see it, but we were surprised with how many people were submitted by "Super-Pig" to often harsh questioning and, sometimes, searches, without any "reasonable grounds" for suspicion that a crime had been committed. Had these people gotten witnesses and fought the cases in the courts, at great expense and time, they could often have proven false arrest, but, as in most other realms of our society, neither the time nor the money was usually available. "Super-Pig" was later assigned elsewhere and for the past few years at Eden the police have been "mellow" by comparison, relying mainly on warnings and not noticing minor violations, even in the peak summer months when the van comes two to three times a day.

Whenever the police respond to political pressures by using harsh tactics, they have the effect of keeping nude beachers off balance and mad, but not clothed. If the police are very diligent, nude beachers go where they aren't. Some police have consistently pursued other tactics as well to try to discourage people from taking part in the scene. Very importantly, they have systematically refused to take any steps that would specify for people just what their legal rights are in these nude scenes—they "keep them uncertain." While it is true that the police aren't themselves clear on this, it is certainly true that they know they do not intend at this time to arrest people for nudity on the well-established beaches unless there is some lewd behavior associated with it. But they never make this known publicly. Very importantly, as we noted earlier, some of the police and other enemies of the nude scenes have long insisted that one of the grave dangers of the nude beach scenes is that some unsuspecting tourist might come along and be shocked out of his or her mind by the barbaric sight. But all have refused to allow the posting of signs by the police departments or anyone else specifying that a nude beach is ahead. For example, a simple sign at each end of these recognized nude beaches would warn people: "Beware! Nude Bathers May Be Found on this Beach." Such a sign would not prevent a change of legal status in the future. But the police and their supporters no doubt believe it would also encourage people who are now afraid to take part in the scene, and might tend to stop the few complaints they are able at present to encourage. It might also commit the police to accepting publicly the court decision on the legality of nude bathing on such beaches, thereby removing their option to change their minds and start arresting people.

Some of the police officials have intermittently gone further in joining the fight against the nude scene. They have taken an active part in trying to arouse public sentiment against nude bathing by helping people to see it exists and, thus, mobilizing popular support for laws against it. Many people have long contended that some police officials try to "legislate the morality" of the whole society by passing and enforcing laws against behavior not considered immoral or injurious by most people.

A key part of this police activity is arousing public moral feelings against the behavior the police want to ban by showing people things the police know will make them feel threatened. In the case of nude bathing, this is done in two ways: First, by insisting that the nude bathers are all some kind of sexual perverts, especially homosexuals, and that all nude bathing should be banned because of this. This has certainly been the public stance of many property owners in their complaints to the police and politicians, and some police have supported this view.

The second way in which at least one police department has tried to create public views of nude bathing is by photographing the nude scene to show people, especially politicians, what the "social problem" is. One of the Sheriffs, who was a keen foe of nude bathing and a strong supporter of new laws to ban the whole thing, was reported to have sent sheriff's deputies down to the nude beaches to photograph the activities so they could make people aware of the "problem." This was just another of what we now know to be massive instances of police and other officials photographing people involved in legal activities with the hope of making their activities illegal and of trying to stigmatize them. It may not be quite as horrendous as the Pentagon keeping files and photos of "dissidents" not known to be involved in any illegal activities, but it is an unsettling reminder of the prevalence of the police-state mentality of so many officials.

Not all police take this kind of activist approach to law enforcement. In one county, where there was a great deal of wildcatting going on, the sheriff specifically asked the board of supervisors not to pass a new law banning nudity on the beaches. He contended that there were already laws and that the problem was how to enforce them, presumably referring to the court decisions and the resulting uncertainties. He probably did this because of the general fear that new legislation might be overturned and, thus, make it more difficult than ever to contain the nude phenomenon. But, regardless of the reason, he was not taking any simple approach to making everyone conform to his views of nude bathing.

PROPERTY OWNERS, POLITICIANS, AND NUDE POWER

While, as we have seen, there are some moralists dedicated to ridding the world of nude beaches, they are few and, thus far, insignificant. Most of them just decide it's all the devil's doing and stay home. But there is a hardier and more powerful breed of nude beach hater—the local activist property owner. While constituting only a small minority of property owners, the activists have considerable support from other owners and considerable political impact. They work behind the scenes to bring pressure to bear on the politicos and police to end nudity on the beaches.

We should make it clear that in one sense their position is one which we would expect almost anyone in their situation to take. This position involves two points which are about the only things the property owners near nude beaches almost universally agree on. (Obviously, this does not include the few property owners of private nude beaches in the North, who charge entry fees.) The first point is the dislike of the traffic and growth in transient population brought on by the nude beaches. All of the nude beaches were originally isolated, and few people went to them, so the property owners had none of the usual urban traffic problems. The beach areas are commonly suburban, with big, expensive homes and yards and once nearly empty streets.

Now, at least during the summer and on any warm day throughout the rest of the year, they suddenly have hundreds of cars streaming noisily through their neighborhoods and hundreds or thousands of "nudists" tromping around, some of them walking on grass near the street, and some shouting out to friends and wandering offspring. No one, of course, wants that, and anyone whose suburban peace was suddenly shattered by noisy and dirty cars would be anxious to get rid of them. The second point is the widespread, but not universal, feeling that the beaches once belonged to the property owners, even if they never really owned them, and that they have now been seized by a wholly different group whom they are not willing to join on the beach. These property owners feel dispossessed, and just as any gang kid might fight for his turf if a neighboring gang started moving in on his sidewalks, so the property owners fight back against the invaders.

All of that is understandable, but even these positions cannot be accepted by most other people. After all, the invasions of traffic the property owners are now suffering are less than the traffic invasions suffered in almost all other beach areas at an earlier stage. And, if the nude beachers don't destroy their suburban peace now, some other hordes of beach-hungry Californians will do so very soon. (As most nude beachers see it, what *right* have the property owners got to special parking rights to keep people away from a public beach? Other rich people and all the non-rich have long endured this traffic invasion near the beaches. Some are even less understanding, insisting, "With their palatial homes costing from $100,000 to $2,500,000, they should be unhappy with a few cars?" Some people just don't understand that in America today everybody from the janitor to the bank president is convinced that everyone else is ripping him off all the time in all ways.)

There is a third point to this position that many property owners share, but which is not universal. While the nude beach invasion has been going on, there has also apparently been an increase in burglaries and vandalism. This sort of thing is very subject to changes in reporting of such crimes, and it is common for neighborhoods being "invaded" by any group seen as somehow foreign and frightening to suddenly start reporting everything suspicious or the least bit damaging—the natives are just mad and frightened and want to use police power to strike out at these invaders. But in this case there are some very reliable witnesses who give balanced, detailed accounts indicating that there have been such increases in banditry. The people who give these reliable accounts also argue that it doesn't seem to be nude beachers doing the ripping off. Rather, they know that there has been a general increase in such crimes in all suburban neighborhoods, that the influx of any group of people will attract many others not into the scene but drifting through with them, and that the crowds provide a natural cover for all kinds of criminal activities which before would have been immediately spotted. (Universities experienced the same kind of drastic increase in vandalism and burglary in the same period.)

This assessment squares with our own knowledge of the non-ripping-off character of the nude beach types. The same kind of thing seems always to happen when a beachside community becomes the parking area for a large beach crowd and probably would remain so even if the beachgoers wore formal dress.

But in assessing the property owners' feelings and complaints against the nude beachers we have to keep continually in mind the fact that, with the activists, this "reasonable" rap against the "nudists" is largely a cover, a front for much deeper, more gut-level, "nonreasoned" feelings against the "nudists." Certainly there are some property owners who are really only concerned with the neighborhood problems augmented by the nude scene on the sands below. But these are not often the leaders of the movement against the nude beach. The leaders, those willing to devote long and tedious hours to the bitter struggle, are commonly inspired by deep fears of or hatred for the "nudists." (I use the property owners' term, "nudists," for the nude beachers here, because it is one of the clearest bits of evidence indicating they don't know very much about nude beachers. Calling them "nudists" is a lot like a college president negotiating with some black militants and referring to them as "colored people.") We eventually concluded as a rule of thumb that if you "scratch a reasonable property owner leading the fight against nudity, underneath you'll find a hater of nudity, a stigmatizer who feels threatened."

Time and again, people would start out being so sweetly reasonable in their opposition to the nude scene and wind up *screaming* against the "nudists." And a few of them started out screaming and escalated from there. (As we saw earlier, the property owners were the main creators and disseminators of the most lurid atrocity stories about the nude beaches.) It became clear to us that nudity was *the* issue for the core of the opposition. Nudity was also inextricably bound up in their minds with the whole casual sex scene on the beach, so that those who didn't fear or hate the nudity for itself feared or hated the sexuality, nudity on the beaches and they demanded a *total* ban on nudity, sexy or not! It also became clear that their emotional opposition was so intense and unswerving that this hard core was not willing to compromise on anything. They insisted on a fight to the death—presumably either the death of "nudism" or the death of what they saw as "common decency."

The property owners have always been small in number by comparison with their opposition and, as we saw, they have a big tactical problem with the hostile mass media, which makes it almost impossible for them to gain the sympathy of the mass public, most of whom would almost certainly oppose the "nudists" if they were aroused and felt threatened. So, like Arabs using the oil weapon, they've fallen back on the one big stick they have—wealth, social position, and political influence. The property owners near these beaches are very, very upper-class types. They have the money politicians need to finance their mass media PR-politics and the personal contacts with the politicos that come with that and with their managerial positions in the business, professional, and academic worlds. The nude beach organizers never have friends in high places. But the property owners can go directly to politicos. They meet with the mayors, supervisors, city council men and women, police officials, city attorneys, assistant city managers *et alia,* in their homes and offices and tell them of their woes and how it would be to their benefit to do something about all this "nudism." If they don't "understand," the property owners turn up the heat. One city attorney was reported by a police expert to have gained "understanding" when threatened with a recall petition. He started giving speeches against the beach and vaguely promising anti-nudity ordinances, even though he had already given a public speech saying he thought non-lewd nudity might be technically legal on any beach, not merely on isolated beaches.

There's little doubt that most of the politicos, like the police, would like to pass some new city or county ordinances to ban nudity or, at the least, to make it easier to push it into the most isolated of isolated beaches. But they are the ones, rather than the police, who would bear the burden if the courts overturned their ordinances. They would then be failures in the eyes of the property owners and in the eyes of their legal and political colleagues.

In fact, passing a new ordinance poses the perfectly obvious danger of having a court injunction issued against its enforcement immediately and having the courts eventually overturn it. The reason for this is that California is not a home rule state. In California, the state government has preempted the legal authority to legislate the laws concerning sexual violations. This authority was upheld in the famous Carol Lane case, in which a young woman's conviction for prostitution (sexual solicitation) under a local ordinance was overturned on the grounds the state alone has such authority. This is the legal ground on which courts issue quick injunctions against local ordinances aimed at controlling the controversial massage parlors. Unless some legal fiction can be created to circumvent this situation, the local areas cannot pass laws concerning nudity—which could only be aimed at sexually "lewd" conduct, since anything else would be a violation of all kinds of basic rights, such as the right to submit to medical examinations.

The greatest hope of the politicians would be to get a new state law passed banning nudity on all beaches—or at least on all public beaches. This would involve all kinds of conflicts and likely court tests all over the state, any one of which could overturn the whole thing, so one state legislator decided to try to pass a bill that would give authority to govern nudity on beaches to the local areas. (At one point, the nude beach organization in San Diego was convinced by the city attorney to support this legislation in the hope it might make it possible to legalize beach nudity at the local level, but it would really be suicidal for them.) Since the U.S. Supreme Court has decided that local areas can set standards of pornography, there might be some chance for such a law. However, in California, it would probably have to be general, allowing local areas to set standards for all sexual behavior, and that would be very difficult politically, especially since the whole hefty sex industry of California would probably fight it down the line. It seems unlikely this line of attack will work—but the anti-nudity types will no doubt keep trying to find some legal means to repress beach nudity.

As usually happens in America, attempts to repress any large group's behavior leads to opposing political organization. Most grass-roots political organizations, including the property owner organizations, are really largely fictions, big fronts with nothing much behind them. They generally have gigantic and idealistic names, like Citizens for the Preservation and Enhancement of the Earth for All the Peoples. But lying behind the names is generally one person or at most a small band with a hot typewriter and a fluent mouth. This one person or a few people, the red hots, put a lot of effort into getting everyone out for one meeting at the beginning, or to sign one petition, and then they assume that their actions represent everyone who agreed to the initial vague proclamation of group intent. Meanwhile, most people have gone off to watch the football games or something. On the nude beach it's especially like that, because most of the people aren't there for political action or any kind of work, and many of them are not anxious to take a public stand telling how beautiful it is to bare their all in the California sunshine.

The first nude beach "organization," as far as we could determine, was pretty much a one-man job, by an ex-traditional-nudist who decided to try to open up some of the beaches for nudists. He had minimal effect because his effort was aimed at getting support from traditional nudist groups, but these were largely controlled by the nudist camp owners, who didn't quite relish the idea of having their nudists traipsing off to beaches for free. He later worked with Nude Beach, an organization created largely by one man to fight the arrests for trespassing in the cove near Los Angeles. Nude Beach took very radical positions of all sorts, being whatever the one leader said they were. He created a neo-Marxist rationale for nude beaches, which scared the straights by confirming the fears of some of them that nude beaches are a "conspiracy of the commies" and which alienated the nude beachers also because most of them want a nude beach, not a political fight. He also alienated nude beachers because he proposed to the police that they regulate the nude beaches by giving out police I.D.'s to nude beachers so that they could keep out the perverts and whatnot. The idea of carrying around a police I.D. on the nude beach "freaks out" most nude beachers. When that group later proposed amalgamating with an earlier San Diego group, the San Diegans politely ran away.

The most effective nude beach power organization by far has been the Committee To Save Eden Beach. It consisted of a handful of people willing to help get petitions signed and such at various times, but at its core were just two people who appointed themselves as *the* committee at the beginning and then proceeded to present their positions as if they somehow represented the beach people. They did actually represent the public front most people wanted to have presented about the beach, and they were out to save nudity on the beach, so most people would probably have supported them, if there were ever an occasion when they might do so. The one occasion when they did seek some such support was at their inception, when they needed petitions signed to show officials they were talking about a lot of nude beachers, not just themselves and a few others. About twelve thousand people signed it in a few weeks, both on and off the beach. This gave some democratic validity to their self-appointed roles as leaders of the Committee.

But petitions and other political moves of the Eden Beach Committee were not the reason for their success. The politicos could pretty well assume that most of the people who signed the petition didn't vote anyhow and, if they did, they weren't about to vote for them regardless of what they did. That number did show that there was a lot of growing libertarian support for the right to do nude bathing somewhere and indicated that attempts to suppress it might prove costly.

But that also wasn't the source of the relative success of the Committee. The Committee was successful mainly because of the great press it got, especially TV coverage, and this was more the result of the reporters being libertarian about such things before they ever heard of the nude beach. The Committee's real plus was just being willing to get up and say what the TV people themselves would have said if there weren't professional ethics to be considered.

The Committee To Save Eden Beach was born literally overnight, when a group of several regulars (one of them the Dirty Old Man of the Nude Beach) learned from the local newspapers that the property owners had pulled a fast one. The Recreation and Parks Commission had gotten the city to approve a bond issue to be placed on the upcoming ballot, which would support a large number of park projects, almost all of which the naturalist types on the beaches would have ecstatically embraced. But buried in a long list was a small item of money to be used to build an access path down one of the canyons to Eden Beach.

The nude beachers figured this was a ploy to present the beach to the courts as no longer isolated, hence no longer legally nude. It was a ploy engineered by the property owners, who had quietly got the parks department and then the city officials to just slip it in with all the other park improvements. The item would also have built a parking lot at the head of the access path for all the cars clogging their streets, but the real aim was definitely to get a court ban on nudity, as further events proved.

(In a way, this was just one of those ideas born of ignorance of the other nude beaches. Actually, even with a paved access path Eden would have remained the most physically difficult of the nude beaches to get to. All three nude beaches in Santa Barbara are almost on the freeway, and they are no more isolated than the immediately surrounding straight beaches. As one supervisor said, "What is 'isolated'?" It's always *possible* some court would have seized on this new development as a legal fiction and thereby banned nudity. But it doesn't seem likely.)

The Committee got totally idealistic and moralistic right away. They contended the access road would bring so many people it would ruin the natural ecology of the beach. (Actually, we thought that if it did end nudity the beach would largely revert to its unused status for a few more years, since the path would still require very steep climbing. It was the nudity that brought the great population explosion.) Hence the word "save" in the committee name.

But, of course, the word was meant to have a double, secret meaning for the nude beachers—Save Nudity on Eden Beach. Both sides were continually using Aesopian language to communicate with their adherents, while hiding from their enemies. And each side really understood this. They were always saying about the other side, "Yeah, but what they really mean is. . . ." But, of course, there were probably some relatively unconcerned voters who didn't have any idea what it was all about who might be taken in by the doubletalk, the idealistic frontwork.

The campaign of the Committee consisted largely of putting out bright bumper stickers—"Save Eden Beach," "Vote No On Proposition A"—and a lot of media presentations. The anti-nudity politicians must have gotten concerned, since all the major political groups in the city wanted the new park funds, and feared the Committee might be able to tip the balance against the bond issue because of its good media coverage. So they started intimating compromises in private discussions, not really promising to leave nudity alone on Eden, but talking as if that might be what they meant. Anyhow, the heat was pretty bad for the two leaders, especially since they wanted the rest of the bond issue. Finally, they changed their position in anticipation of a private deal— which would probably never have stuck, but probably also would never have mattered.

The bond issue lost, but it had nothing to do with the Committee, since it lost by a great majority, mainly older people who systematically turn out to vote against any bond issue in sight.

Meanwhile, the property owners started hatching a scheme to get the city to spend money to open up the beach "To All the People," as they liked to say. The Eden Beach Committee decided that the property owners might be put off and kept quiet if they accepted a compromise. So a big meeting was set up between the adversaries. The Committee proposed that the northern two miles (including the State Park) be opened to nudity officially, with signs and all, and closed to straight voyeur types, and that the southern half (somewhat less) be banned to nudity—a safe haven for the propertied class. They really thought this was a benevolent compromise and had great expectations of ending the dispute. But as soon as it was proposed, an elderly propertied woman got up, very agitated, and put all the property owners' feelings up front: "Never! Never! Never! No compromise! All the nudity must go! Out with nudity! Out! O-U-T!!" They weren't the least bit interested in compromise. This was their beach forever, and no "pervert nudists" were going to romp around on it. It was to be a fight to the death—at least, the legal death. The lines were drawn as they had always been.

Since the initial political battles among the Committee To Save Eden Beach, the journalists, the property owners and the politicians on various sides, there have been numerous smaller battles. Most of these have been initiated by the property owners' group, which is headed by several women who work almost full time in city politics and who, for this reason, are quite influential with the politicians who depend on such free intelligence and energy for election. Each time the property owners' group launches an attack on the legal status of Eden, some nude beachers coalesce to meet the threat. These nude beach groups are generally very much like the first one at Eden. They are small, made up of the few people who take an active interest in politics and who rarely spend much time on the beach because their thing is politics more than nude beaching. The original organizers of the Committee To Save Eden Beach almost completely stopped coming to the beach once their battle subsided. In fact, we thought they were glad to have an end to the battle because it proved more demanding on their time and emotional energy than they had expected. Grass-roots politics is very consuming.

A similar pattern seems to be followed by each succeeding group of nude politicos. They come often during the time the battles are raging, set up tables to get petitions signed, pass out leaflets on the latest beach news locally and around the nation, make news media pronouncements, confront the city council (in front of TV-news cameras) over the urgent need for more honesty and naturalness in the city, and disappear more or less as soon as the publicity subsides. The interesting thing about this is that those people who are potentially to be denied legal status, the nude beachers, are responding politically to would-be labellers of them as deviants. That is more or less what the so-called labelling theory of deviance in sociology would predict, except that the potential deviants mobilize politically, and they are not "oppressed minorities," but, rather, are *victorious minorities.*

None of the regulars we have talked with believes that the general public would support the legal status of the beach if they had to vote on it. In fact, when one of the ad hoc political groups tried to force a public vote on the issue (see below), most of the regulars thought they were out of their minds and tried to stop them.

The city council stopped that and voted to allow the nudity to continue being legal. The minority had won. One could even argue in this case that the minority was oppressing the majority, except, of course, they have no real intention of doing such things. As far as we could ascertain, it seemed to be a classic case of interest group politics in our society today. There are so many people involved in the nude beach that it is politically (vote-wise) inexpedient for most of the politicians to oppose them until the majority is aroused by the beach issue and votes against those politicians who vote for it. Thus far, the majority of people are not aroused because it is an isolated issue, literally out of sight, but more are becoming aware of it.

The most interesting thing of all is that the instance in which the beach came closest to being labelled illegal was the one time the ad hoc nude politicos started the attack, or, rather, decided to broaden the counter-attack. The three or four most activist beach politicos this time were much more radical types than any of the earlier groups at Eden had been. The nude beach was for them a symbol that could be used to attack the "oppressors," so, rather than taking the always before successful strategy of presenting a mellow, conciliatory program and otherwise maintaining a low profile, they decided to "get idealistic." They counterattacked in strength, demanding that more straight beaches be nudified, including some nonisolated ones in the heart of suburbia, and demanding a vote of the whole city to "show how strongly people support public nudity." This led almost immediately to the formation of three church groups to counter-attack the counter-attackers. The organized fundamentalists were now aroused; the battles grew more intense. The city council's vote not to go to the public for a vote stopped much of the battle and in the next vote on the beach legality, the nudes won by only one vote, whereas previously they had normally won by three votes. It seemed quite clear to the regulars that these "nude crazies" had completely misunderstood the political situation and, by acting as *moral provocateurs,* they had deeply threatened fundamentalists who previously had hardly heard of nude beaches, and who then became legal battlers trying to stigmatize the nude beachers and brand them as illegal. The politicians, acting in terms of their cunning assessment of how many votes could be won and lost in the concrete situation they faced, were the ones who saved the minority potential-deviants from themselves—and, rather than labelling them as criminals, continued to de-label them.

We have no doubt that new political battles will be launched by one side or the other, and we suspect the new battles will be lost or won largely on the basis of the political strategies followed by the two sides, rather than in terms of who might be right or wrong.

7

The Limits of Naturalness and the Future of the Nude Beach

Like so much of life, the nude beach naturalness and casualness appear to have limiting conditions, which they themselves produce directly or indirectly, and which then serve to limit their further development. The most obvious limiting condition was discussed in the last chapter on the politics of the nude beach. Much of our society remains quite ambivalent about sex and body freedom, and an important minority obviously still sees public nudity and sex as highly threatening and, thus, continues to stigmatize it. It is clearly to be expected that, as the nudity spreads and becomes better known, it will generate counter-pressure, backlash, counter-reformation, or whatever one wishes to call it. It has done that in recent years, most especially when any casual politicians have tried to press the public nudity beyond the cliff confines of the original situation which was very effectively cut off from civilization. But there are more important, more inherent limitations.

We have argued all along that, on the basis of what we know from the beach and surrounding evidence, as well as from all the other evidence about human sex, erotic feelings are greatest when there is ambivalence—a desire both for and against, a yes and no. As we argued, it is the ambivalence of clothing that makes it so effective in titillating erotic feelings: clothing first covers up (makes unknown), then partially reveals, sometimes by only showing the form of the unseen (like a bustle exaggerating the female buttocks), thereby exciting, titillating erotic feelings. What happens, then, when one becomes "really natural" about the body and sex organs—that is, completely uncovers them? We have seen that the initial feeling is excitement—the unseen exposed is exciting. But then one becomes mellow, especially in a public situation in which one cannot consummate the erotic desire and where even erotic responses like erections are still shamed. One comes to have less erotic feeling for nude scenes—one mellows. What then?

The main thing that seems to happen is that people become less motivated to go to all the trouble to get to the beach. So we get high rates of turnover in membership in the scene, even among the old-timer regulars. Part of this is because they move away, but there is also just a lower rate of visiting the beach even when there are no practical problems. At the same time that these people are becoming less natural (clothed), some people become less natural in the scene by covering up in other ways so that they once again become more erotic and more dominance(status)-displaying, thereby doing by other means precisely what clothes do.

It seems likely from what we know of primitive people today who are nude that the earliest forms of covering up and symbol-displays for erotic and dominance-display purposes were body decorations, such as styling the hair and painting and adorning the body. All of these seem to be increasingly used by nude beachers. Even body painting, which for so long made little appearance on the beaches, is becoming pretty common—just as it did to a far greater degree among the nudists. In addition, people, especially the fashion conscious female, have used necklaces, waistbands, and ankle bands to attract attention and titillate feelings. Hats are sometimes worn by women, or a shirt by men which hides all but tufts of hair.

Janine gave us an extreme example of this which well illustrates the general phenomenon. We were walking along the water's edge in the gay area of Eden one day when a gay guy came along. Janine started staring at his genitals, so we looked. Our attention was riveted to something around his penis. Janine, who had gone over the years from her first-day's jitters to being very up-front on the beach, went up close to him and, pointing down at it, said, "Hey, what in the world is that?"

He smiled slightly and said, "That's a prick."

Regaining her composure, Janine then asked, "I mean what's *on* your prick!?"

"Oh, that's just my prick-ring." We had never before that moment heard of a "prick-ring."

It was a tiny thing, an inanimate, by all reason insignificant object, yet it riveted attention on the penis with the intensity of a trumpet blast. The adornment of the human body is a powerful attention-getter and lust-arouser. In the absence of the full panoply of clothing sex-displays, an otherwise insignificant thing can become a sex-display—and the ever sexy and cunning human being makes do with anything at his or her creative disposal.

But, far more importantly, the body itself in its natural state is used for the supposedly nonnatural purposes of titillating erotic feeling and displaying personal and group-dominance (pride in superiority). We have seen throughout our visit to the nude beach that one of the most pervasive forms of sex-display and dominance (status) display is the simple presentation of the nude body—especially the beautiful nude body. It is precisely because the nude body is extremely sexually exciting to people in a civilization which has been covered up for millennia that people want to uncover it in the first place. But even from the very beginning, the "natural uncovering" people, especially women, very carefully present their bodies in the most alluring way. They let their hair grow long if it is beautiful and cut it if it is not. They comb it and let it flow in the wind. They walk in beautiful and alluring ways. But, far more important, they also develop socially shared symbols of dominance or status. The nude body versus the clothed body is from the beginning presented as superior, not as a sign of your equality to everyone else.

Very importantly, within the nude scene itself, those with "all-over golden-brown tans" use their skin color as a status symbol. The tourist-white is a sign of the outcaste, while the all-over tan is the sign of the brahmin. And the very way of walking comes to symbolize group membership in a hierarchy of groups. The casual person *saunters* (or may even dance on tiptoe when running) to communicate his casual-dominance, whereas the virgin with the tourist-white *swaggers* (even commonly flexing his chest muscles and holding his arms slightly akimbo to show his torso). This is not something that people do consciously—it's just natural.

And that's what I mean. To strive for social dominance, to create and transmit status systems and ways of life, and the symbols that communicate them—that *is* natural in human life. And so is the use of adornment, clothing, and partial concealment of any type whatsoever that works to elicit attention and sexual arousal—readiness for negotiation. Those things are found throughout all of human history and in all currently existing societies. They are also found in the subcultures where people strive consciously to become totally "natural" and equal. Even the striving for equality becomes a symbol of your superiority, as is especially obvious in the bitter recriminations against those who explicitly favor inequality of some sort.

What the naturalists are really doing, largely unrecognized by themselves, is proposing and creating a new form of naturalness in which they are the dominant people. And an important part of their new dominance is their sex-success. The young person with the beautiful body, or some variant thereon, was the most common type in the early days—a majority of the most casual people have been like that. In a society of unclothed dominance, they obviously have the advantage, as any perceptive middle-aged person soon realizes in the scene. As *we* always realized, the nude scene provides everyone with a profound incentive to stay in top form—obviously for reasons of body-display and dominance-display, the two being intimately linked in that setting. This is the kind of status war they can easily win.

But, of course, it isn't exactly a war. It only feels that way to the tourist-white middle-aged when they first enter the scene, because they feel inferior. The casual people really aren't paying them much atten- tion—just being quietly dominant in an aloof way, the way an old, rich person feels and acts driving by in his limousine, without concern for the clods on the sidewalk. The rich have confidence in their dominance; the others have confidence in their inferiority. If the whole world were to uncover, then these people would be the sexually dominant group insofar as body sex-displays go, and they surely know it. That is an ultimate reason most people are unlikely to uncover easily.

The same natural limitation, of course, is roughly true of casualness. In our traditional, sexually repressive society, sex life is non-free, noncompetitive. What would a really sexually casual society be like? Presumably, everyone would be competing for everyone else. Casual people, of course, would be shocked at the idea of sexual competition; but all of our study has shown that, regardless of their words, that is what happens. The most casual people we know experience jealousy when someone takes their sex partner(s), and the most casual is com- monly striving to be sexually attractive to get other people's partners— they're "on the make." As anyone can guess, in an uncovered (natural) state, the beautiful bodies get the most attention and create the most sexual excitement.

Competition. Status. Dominance. Success and failure. Just like eco- nomic life, only here it's body and sex. Most people from the clothed world are apt to say, "Hell, sure, that's natural." And that's my point. They are natural, regardless of whether you are covered from head to foot or nude in front of the world.

On the other hand, we must not let this confusion and rhetoric of "naturalness" and "casualness" obscure a real difference. When they get tied in with the rhetoric of political ideologies, or merely used as front work and self-deceptions under threat, then they wind up doing the same things that similar ideas do in the "repressive society"—repressing natural human instincts.

But there is a real core, a true sense in which it is more natural to go nude. This is the sense of body-freedom. If the person wants to be nude, given all he knows about the situation, his body, and so on, then it is freer, less repressive, to do so. The true message of body-freedom, like sex-freedom, is "Let the individuals decide for themselves what their things are." That is the libertarian message of the nude beachers when they aren't doing front work and rhetoric. And the wisest of them recognize it. As the wise old-timer, Pete, used to say:

> "If they want to go clothed, let 'em. If that's their thing, who cares? But why can't they take the same point of view toward us? That's all we want—a place to do our thing, not theirs. They can have a beach—why can't we? Look how many thousands of us there are on this beach alone."

Of course, when straights would come down on the beach all covered up, Pete would seem less free-spirited. I've even seen him berate straights, a bit heatedly, for not being "honest." ("Who cares what they do in *their* territory, but in our territory they should not do what shames us and prides themselves.") Well, that doesn't surprise me. That's natural enough—human natural.

It seems clear enough from our moral wanderings down on the beach that human beings are not about to give up adornment as sex-display and dominance-display, nor are they about to give up trying to create status systems and stable ways of life enforced by moral rules. We have simply seen old ways of doing those things cast (slowly) aside and new ones created. It is important that the nude ones have not become repressive ones. There is still a relatively greater degree of natural casualness in that sense—letting others be more free to do their things as long as they don't try to repress or subordinate you. There are also some regulars, like Big Don, who have become naturalists in a total sense. Don even seems to feel almost religious about the body, a nascent sense of pantheism, a merging of his body with nature. In this way, the nude beach scene merges with the rapidly growing natural food, natural exercise, natural religion movements in our society. Most of these movements tend to be libertarian.

We cannot say whether that would grow if the whole world uncovered or whether nude-morality would become absolutist. Since there is no immediate prospect of that, for the obvious reasons of continuing feelings of failure by the body-unbeautiful types, we are not very concerned with nude repressiveness. Instead, we are concerned with whether this relatively greater body-freedom will be able to continue existing and, perhaps, continue to grow as it has done.

THE FUTURE OF THE NUDE BEACH

It's hard enough to predict anything about most social trends under the best, most stable conditions. Human beings are simply too insistent upon acting like the creative and sometimes free beings they are—or can become by trying—to allow any simple predictability. Humans also resent being treated like robots, so if you try to predict their actions as if they were robots, they're likely to do the opposite just to prove you wrong. The tumultuous changes swirling about and within us today make it even harder to say with any reliability what's going to happen. But the hardest events of all to predict are the outcomes of the truly revolutionary conflicts—those which involve vast ambivalence in our feelings.

We think there's little doubt that nude beaches, especially the public nude beaches, unprotected by the ancient private property laws, are truly revolutionary. If they become an accepted part of our social world, fundamental parts of ourselves, our very body feelings, images, and sexual expression will change in important ways. Nude beaches won't usher in any Utopian end to repression or any fulfillment of longings for ecstasy, nor will they mean Armageddon for traditionalists. But their widespread acceptance and enjoyment would mean basic changes in the rules of our civilization, so deep emotions and powerful political forces are being martialled to do battle for traditional ways. The battles for the body and the beaches will go on for many years, and we won't know the outcomes with any reliability until the sand settles. But a few things do seem very likely to come out of it all.

We feel most convinced from all that we've seen that the general public is by no means ready for nude beaches. Nude beaches are, as we argued in the beginning, partially an outgrowth of a basic trend toward free body expression in our society—if we hadn't already come a good way, we could never have taken the giant leap into public nude beaches. There are still tremendous conflicts within us as individuals and between us as members of a society over lesser forms of body freedom— nude films, for instance. And nude beaches are too giant a step for most people right now. If it were to become a choice between all or nothing, between having all beaches nude or none, we have little doubt that the general public would recoil and choose none—body freedom be damned.

Fortunately for the cause of body freedom, most of the nude beachers understand this and are not pressing to liberate all the beaches, or even many of them. They are willing to take a few here and there, just a sunny place where they can do their thing freely. In fact, they are often anxious to keep their place isolated to get rid of the straight predators who demean their natural dignity by doing a "porno" trip of their own. We expect the legal situation will eventually be stabilized in such a way that some beaches will be designated as nude beaches, for nudes only, and some as straight beaches.

But we also clearly expect a slow spreading of the nude scene through wildcatting, with more people joining up and the movement developing in stages. It's happening now and there is no great outcry or terrible repression being brought down on those who dare to demand such body freedom, even in some very "conservative" communities in Southern California. There will no doubt be considerable upset but, barring catastrophic developments, such as do occur at times in our society, it will spread, and the upsets will die down. We also expect a continual growth in the numbers of people, primarily in the major nude scenes already established. This has certainly been the pattern thus far—and most people so far have heard only rumors that they exist!

Most of the people who are ready for nude beaches have not yet had the opportunity to join. When they know where they are and know they won't get arrested or stigmatized for life by joining up, they'll do so by even more hundreds of thousands. This development will come as no comfort to most of the pioneer nude beachers. One of the last things they want is urban congestion on their beaches. It's already hard to feel that wonderful sense of freedom and escape which was so strong in the beginning of the nude beach scene. Most people who were into it in the beginning wish the scene now had fewer people and no publicity. But there are millions who crave the new body freedom, the new feeling of openness and natural beauty, which can be found on the nude beaches, if only at their best. We've seen that there's a lot of cover-up of the nude scene itself by the people trying to protect their casual sex scene from stigmatization and repression (and from a lot of compulsive sex as well). But there's also a lot to the naturalistic ethos. It's not the reason most people will join, however much they pretend to themselves or the TV audiences, but it's something that grows on people once they are into the scene. What starts as a self-deception and a front to prevent shame and repression becomes increasingly true.

And on those beautiful summer days in California, it's almost impossible not to be seized by the sense of natural openness and freedom that comes on those miles of isolated, sandy beaches that stretch out of sight under the towering cliffs. The people will come for sexy reasons, sometimes for compulsive reasons, but, if they stay and the nude scene grows on them, they will do so because of the sense of natural beauty and body freedom. This will be even more so as the casual types, the only ones with the deep motivations and courage to face the possible stigmatization in the early days of the movement, are joined by others, more straight types who find they can get up-front about their bodies without destroying their lives. If it spreads far enough, the nude beaches will be no more casual sex scenes than straight beaches are today (which is a lot more so than most people know or are willing to say). That, too, will be a disappointment to the more casual types into the scene today, but it probably means the nude beaches will just become more heterogeneous than they already are— gays and heteros already have their partially separate scenes on the same beaches; casual types and straight types will probably do the same.

A lot of uncertainty and conflict remain for the years immediately ahead. Most obviously, the body-freedom and sex-freedom scenes can only continue to open-up if the secure affluence of our society con- tinues—and that is always a very uncertain thing in civilization, espe- cially because such leisured nude cavorting about in the waves contributes nothing to our wealth or military preparedness. If our presently secure affluence remains secure, then we expect the beach scene will slowly spread—unless other catastrophes befall our human condition. But even the slow spread will involve considerable political conflict. That's a tragic fact of our excitingly heterogeneous society. Maybe the property owners, the fundamentalists, the politicians, and the police will repress it all with the guns and prisons of their civiliza- tion. But, on balance and necessarily cautiously, we don't think so.

Jon put it all together one sunny day as he looked down the endless miles of golden sand and foamy-white blue-green ocean: "Man, this is a beautiful scene. Too many people love it. If they close down this scene, we'll find someplace else. They can't stop us now."

Appendix

Getting the Nude Beach in Perspective

Poverty has been the natural condition of mankind. It was only 5000 years ago—a tiny fraction of man's million years or so—of existence, that certain social and technological changes allowed human beings to save enough of the necessities of life to allow the huge investment in creative talent necessary to produce civilization. Until the nineteenth century, only a small percentage of human beings were able to take part in the freedoms made possible by the abundance of civilization; and even the small leisured classes were commonly constrained by the fact that they were surrounded by masses of relatively more impoverished peasants who supported them and who would deeply resent the "corruption" of "profligate living." Only in absolute tyrannies, such as Rome became by the third century A.D., were the leisured so unconcerned about their political legitimacy that they could freely indulge the feelings of their bodies.

All civilizations were created by the rationally efficient use of terror, oppression, and repression. The tragedy of civilized man has always been that he has never found an effective means of maintaining civilization for long without the use of a great deal of the force used to create it in the first place. For over 5000 years now, since the dawn of civilization, we civilized human beings, we citizens of those vast empires of intellectual and military power, have dreamed of those lovely lands of Erewhon, those Utopias of past golden ages, of Edens, Shangri-Las, or of future heavens, where we could live in blissful pleasure or simply in peace—without the terror, oppression, and repression of the imperial powers that created and still guard civilization.

There have always been some secret moments and secret places to which we haunted people of these civilizations have escaped to dream, to play out our dreams, or even briefly to live those dreams of utopian peace and pleasure. There have often been élites, leisured classes, who could do so to some degree for long periods by using police terror to oppress and repress those who produced their secure affluence. And there have been a few golden ages of human history in which a whole society was able for brief periods to be civilized without the normally severe uses of terror, oppression, and repression.

These ages have been periods of economic affluence which seemed secure because superior military ability and luck kept the envious "barbarians" beyond the ramparts, but in which the internal relaxation of oppression had not yet allowed the growth of the inevitable fragmentation and conflict which undermines the affluence and the military strength, thus leading either to renewed internal repression or conquest by invaders—or, commonly, both. In all long periods of affluence and social order which seem secure, civilized people have partially thrown off the repression of civilized life and created or expanded patterns of personal freedom and pleasure-seeking, especially those of sex, drugs, adventure, art, science, and magic—all things which produce that sense of ecstasy which we seem to crave as soon as we are not frightened by our life situation. But these very pursuits, these "diversions" from the work of civilization, lead to less production of wealth, less military vigor, and more internal fragmentation and conflict. As the competitive position of the society declines, it must either once again successfully clamp on its iron rules or it must suffer the far worse terror—oppression and repression of foreign conquerors.

Ancient Greece as we know it, especially Athens in that brief time called the Golden Age of Pericles (a mere 50 years in fifth century B.C.), has always had a very emotional allure for us Western peoples precisely because it was highly civilized with a minimum of internal terror, oppression, or repression. The Greeks we know were so lacking in repression that they took the pleasures of the body for granted, including not only the pleasures of the various sex acts, but also the playful ones of displaying and enjoying the beauties of the nude human body in certain concrete public situations such as the Olympic Games. But, of course, those Greeks we know through the literature which has come down to us were all members of an affluent élite who lived by the use of a minimal but very real terror to oppress and hold in slavery people about three times their number. And that brief 50 years that made up the Athenian Golden Age did breed internal fragmentation and weakness that soon made easier their conquest by the military terror of one of the most repressive of civilized peoples—the Spartans. But after conquering, the Spartan citizens themselves then suffered the ravages of luxury, gave up their ancient discipline and were, in their turn, defeated. Following their defeats, they were forced by a tyrant to return to harsh discipline and they alone were able to withstand Macedonian conquest. The apparent exception of the Greeks to the general *dilemma of civilization* is, in fact, a resounding illustration of it.

The Western world has been slowly and intermittently creating new physical and social technology since the eleventh century, which has produced a slow and intermittent growth in wealth, first for the élites, but increasingly for the great majority of people. By the eighteenth century, this technology and its accumulated wealth, capital invest-ment, had provided the average peasant of Europe or America with a standard of living many times that of even the chiefs of primitive societies, as Adam Smith pointed out in *The Wealth of Nations* in 1776.

But it was only in the nineteenth century, when *homo economicus* was temporarily able to free himself from the constraints of the imperial bureaucrats and apply his full rationality and creativity to producing wealth, that our societies began to increase their wealth at a remarkable rate, far surpassing that of any other period in human history. By the twentieth century, in spite of ruinous warfare in this century of revived big government, the average person's real standard of living was approximately twenty times that of the average person in the eighteenth century. And, very importantly, we were able to produce this wealth in about half the time it took those earlier people.

Poverty is a harsh taskmaster, second only to the insecurity that triggers anxiety over our futures. People who must work arduously most of their waking hours are sternly constrained by their practical situations. They can hardly take time to indulge the other feelings of their bodies when they must be almost continuously at work to survive. Moreover, poverty in the past was associated with very unhygienic living conditions, which made life considerably more perilous and painful. (It was most perilous for the very young, so that in most societies far more than half the children never reached adulthood.) These conditions, especially those that produced anxiety and dread, all conspired to create other-worldly religions, which sternly enforced the civilized repression of many body feelings, including almost all of those which were most pleasurable, but which diverted attention from the necessities of civilization's work to preparation of the soul for its imminent departure from this "vale of tears." For better or worse, we in the Western world inherited the most other-worldly, most repressive religious tradition of all the great religions of civilization.

Affluence frees us from many of the harsh constraints and allows us to become creative in dealing with our world and our selves. Affluence, when long continued and, thus, secure, has always led human beings to create new, hopefully more enjoyable, more joyful lives for themselves. Men, women, and children of all societies, even the impoverished ones, generally find some time in their lives for a freer expression of their feelings.

The human body craves pleasure and the stimuli which produce pleasure. That craving for pleasure is apparently a genetic inheritance, though it varies in degree from one individual to another and can be amplified or dampened, triggered or suppressed, by a social situation. Of course, that motive is not as powerful or as low in the genetic hierarchy of motives as the motive to avoid death or to sate hunger. As long as those motives were kept dominant by the practical situation in which people lived, especially by anxiety and the dread of death, craving for the pleasures of satisfying motives higher on the hierarchy could hardly be expressed. But whenever the more demanding drives are satisfied over long periods of time by secure affluence, human beings turn their vast creative energies to creating pleasures in a vast profusion of ways.

Even in peasant societies, there were slack periods of winter months when the people could unleash their pent-up cravings for pleasure in the revels of wine, flesh, and song. The priests might howl in outrage (though most of the time they joined the revels), but the body would have its way. Thus, as soon as Western artists turned their attention to this-worldly subjects, we see drunken peasants regaling their beguiling friends with overflowing wine cups.

Whenever secure affluence frees people more, they turn their attention more to satisfying their craving for pleasure. One of the most remarkable examples of this is found in the lives of the most successful Calvinist businessmen of the seventeenth century. Social scientists were long beguiled by the historical economic theories of Max Weber (and to a lesser degree, those of Werner Sombart) into believing that these early Calvinist businessmen were inspired to capitalistic fervor by religious feelings and that they practiced a stern form of "worldly asceticism," as was obviously demanded by their faith. Hugh Trevor-Roper and other historians have shown more recently that this was not at all true, and we must suspect the earlier theorists were merely taken in by the front work these Calvinists used to hide their sinfulness. The fact was that the most successful of them soon turned to a vast consumption and display of wealth by purchasing huge chateaux and other worldly goods that would have sent a Thorsten Veblen into a moralistic rage of prudery. While there may have been some "overdriven" striving inspired by religious anxieties in these men, their hard work and intelligent investment seems to have been inspired by the usual greed for wealth and all the worldly pleasures it can buy; and, as soon as they had the affluence, they did just that. This example is all the more remarkable because there is usually a lag-effect in such human phenomena, a period when habitual responses (customary action) carries on in spite of changed situations and feelings triggered by them.

As economists find, people who get rich quick (get windfalls) commonly save a much higher portion of their new wealth than those who have long had such wealth; only later do they adjust their consumption upward. This would be especially common when there has been severe repression and, thus, neurotic feelings of anxiety aroused by luxurious living (sin). But those early Calvinists who were vastly successful did not waste much time before plunging into luxuries. As Cotton Mather was to lament in the American colonies of the eighteenth century, the same thing proved true of the American Puritans as soon as their hard work and capitalistic investment made them rich.

Unfortunately for Max Weber, as for almost all early social scientists who forgot how cunning human beings are, his historical records simply did not reveal all the "sinful" things such people were into because they hid them so well. Weber made a great deal of use of Benjamin Franklin's *Poor Richard's Almanac* and his *Autobiography* as ultimate examples of Calvinistic worldly asceticism. What he did not realize, but what more investigative modern historians have exposed, was that cunning works like that made Franklin rich and his wealth allowed him to become a very modern "dirty old man"—but all meticulously hidden. The wise rich man in a Puritanical world of still relatively poor people is a public (worldly) ascetic, but a private debauché. Regardless of how sinful or unwise that might be, his body cannot resist the temptation of pleasure once his more basic, more urgent drives are fulfilled. Just as power corrupts, so does affluence "corrupt." And it does so for the same "reasons"—genetic drives.

The vast wealth of the Western world today has unleashed our cravings for pleasure on a wider scale than in any other era known in human history. Though lifestyles are so different as almost to bar comparisons, the average middle- to upper-class person in the richer Western societies today has a standard of living more or less like that of Roman Senators, except for the relative absence of servants.

Given the same bodily inheritance, it is not surprising that people today are turning to the same kinds of bodily pleasures—"sybaritic" pleasures—as the rich of Athens, Rome, Europe, America, and everywhere else have always done—though often after a lag period when the habits that made them rich have not been changed by creative deviance. It is not surprising, from this perspective, to see our centuries-long dread of public nudity and of the public sexual expression closely associated with it rapidly giving way to more relaxed and enjoyable practices and feelings. For the first time in the Western world since Roman days, we now have *widespread* public expression of the pleasures of sex and rapidly spreading public nudity. If our affluence continues, and we are able to avoid all of the cultural catastrophes that normally befall a people dedicated to leisure and pleasure, we can expect to see more and more of both, though there will always be situational perturbations that obscure general trends.

CREATIVE DEVIANCE AND CONFLICTS
OVER THE NUDE BEACH

Basic changes in important social rules, especially those rules against forms of behavior which so threaten us that they have been stigmatized and those who break those rules ostracized or imprisoned, do not change overnight or without great individual and social conflict. All so-called "revolutions" in society, especially in the vastly complex social orders we call civilization, come about over long periods of time. Even when there is a sudden breaking in forms of political life, such as came with the executions of the royal families of France or Russia, these have been preceded by many years of growing conflicts, resentment, and anger; and the social forms that succeed the breaks almost always reestablished, generally behind symbolic masks or deceits, modified forms of the old behavior. (The main difference between Napoleon and Louis XVI, and between Lenin and Nicholas II, was that the dictators were more efficient at doing what the rulers would have liked to do.)

Moreover, all basic changes are accompanied by perturbations, or slight and/or accidental ups and downs in the development of basic social directions. Anyone who looks at the history of clothes and fashion in the Western world, as Alfred Kroeber and other researchers have done, knows that there has been a slow, progressive, but intermittent increase in body-freedom over the past century. That is, there has been a slow movement toward greater freedom in wearing what you wish, including that of wearing less and less.

But that history also reveals that there have been many fits and starts in the trend, including some regression to earlier times and some dead-ends. For example, in the 1920s, there was a relative burst of body-freedom as seen in the shorter skirts and dresses, more revealing swimsuits of the "flappers," bare breasts in some movies, and a spread of nudist camps and literature. The worldwide depression of the 1930s and the slow build-up of the terrifying threat of World War II in an age of industrial power partially reversed this development. In some societies, especially in rigid Nazi Germany, there was a reversion to Puritanical stigmatization of all such body- and sex-freedom. German society had been profoundly threatened by one great shock after another—loss of World War I, imposition of an alien form of government seen by many middle- and upper-class people as illegitimate, the shame of reparation payments, the most terrible inflation in the history of mankind, and then the depression. Profound threats to one's being, especially those immediately at hand, produce a feeling of dread which leads to stigmatization of pleasure-seeking behavior, glorification of practical activities like work and procreation, and attack of the evils felt to be the threat—which are often paranoid beliefs inspired by the anxiety and dread in the face of the unknown.

The German situation after World War I, especially that of the middle classes, was very much like that of the ancient Romans, also in particular the middle-classes (coloni), in the early centuries of the Christian era. It was in these early centuries that Christian asceticism, with all of its fanatical hatred of the "sins of the body" (above all, sex) replaced the earlier, more "human" morality of early Christianity. (As with all matters of ancient history, this one is subject to some controversy, but not too much. Probably the most interesting description and analysis of this fanatical asceticism is that by W. E. H. Lecky in his classic study, *History of European Morals.*)

Nazis stigmatized all sex other than "healthy procreation of the Master Race." Nudism was summarily repressed, and the books about it were banned. The Nazis probably felt especially threatened by nudism and the various forms of sexual freedom, such as homosexuality, precisely because Germany had seen these grow far more rapidly than had other nations of the Western world. Indeed, Germany was the cradle of nudism, and by the early 1930s there had been extensive "nude swimming" by teenagers (called *Wanderwögel*—"wandering birds"), and nude programs on stage in Berlin.

But the long period of affluence since the end of the World War II has seen a reasonably steady progression to ever greater body- and sex-freedom, including decreased feelings of threat from nudity and sex and, hence, more tolerance of body- and sex-freedom in public settings. As always in the early stages of creative deviant subcultures and social movements, this slow progression has been accompanied by a vast amount of public conflict. Every day throughout this whole period, there have been endless private anguish and conflict, public discussions and arguments, committee debates, marches by demonstrators and police, and judicial and political action over nudity and sex. When we remember that these new forms of freedom are basic violations of age-old rules associated with emotional threat and consequent stigmas, it is not hard to see why. Feeling threatened in basic ways, people attack the threat; that is, they invoke the stigmas and try to ostracize or imprison the deviants. But, as we saw, especially in considering how people join the nude beach, these feelings of threat are also commonly felt by the people who go through the transition from traditional conformity to new forms of behavior in violation of basic traditional rules—creative deviance.

Deviance is any form of behavior (or sometimes of feeling or thought) believed by most members of society to violate a rule they feel to be right. The most basic rules, such as those against public nudity, are almost universally shared; they are rarely violated. In fact, such rules are so basic, so universally shared, that they are almost never talked about, except in socializing young savages (infants) who do not yet understand them into conformity with them. In almost all other situations, as long as they are not challenged, they are merely taken-for-granted, thus unseen. (This led a sociologist, Thomas Sheff, to argue that they are "residual rules," or rules left over after all other rules are listed, and that anyone who violates them is thought to be insane—not knowing the most obvious things about social reality.)

Just think of how many times you have seen a nude person, or even merely a revealed primary sex organ, in a truly public setting (as opposed to in the movies or in a night club). Such things are so rare, even today, that people generally experience shock when confronted by them. (That's why "streaking" in a public setting was such a fine way of shocking people and getting attention.) Anyone who violates such rules is likely to be shamed intensely by the majority of the society, and it is precisely the fear of such shaming, and of ostracism or imprisonment, that leads almost everyone to religiously avoid the rule-breaking.

Violating such rules is a *creative act*, generally painful and difficult. By saying it is creative, I do not mean that it is something that is good. I am not here passing moral judgment. I mean simply that such an act of deviance involves the same searching and creating of new ways of doing things, for the purpose of solving some problem or making life better that any creative act does. All important creative acts are deviant acts, whether we are considering physics, art, or public morality. The history of music is littered with instances of public shaming—hissing and booing—of composers for violating established rules of music. An important creative act in physics, such as the assertion of the truth of the uncertainty principle, violates an earlier "law of nature" and tends to produce a sense of shock. It is strongly resisted. Even Einstein sternly denounced the uncertainty principle because it violated his basic sense of what reality is like. Conceptions of reality are rule-governed, just as any other public behavior is.

Just as I do not mean to show approval for deviance by calling it creative, neither do I mean to say that it will prove useful in the way the individuals doing it think it will—that is, in solving a problem or creating more pleasure in life. Most forms of deviance do not even "work" for the people who attempt them. Most people who go to a nude beach, or commit any other serious rule violation, do not find that it works for them. They discover they are too ashamed of themselves or that the risk of shaming by others is too great, so they do not continue. Other people find it hurts them more (or threatens them) or, at the very least, does not do anything good for them. So most forms of deviance do not spread.

Most forms of deviance are intermittent acts by individuals who return to traditional behavior. An individual does it and stops. Another individual does it and stops. Maybe millions do it, but only intermittently and independently of each other. A very few forms, such as masturbation, may be almost universally shared in certain situations, but, because they would lead to severe shaming, are kept universal *social secrets* and do not become part of publicly visible social life. As long as that is true, they cannot become consciously shared, or recognized as shared, so they cannot become the basis of group action to change the social rules against them.

But some forms of rule violations by individuals do lead to cooperative social deviance, to consciously sharing in the rule violation. Some of these, such as illicit sex, normally involve only two people, so they come to form only minimal new, shared feelings, ideas, and rules—what we call a deviant subculture. If such forms of behavior are, in fact, widespread, as most forms of illicit sex are, then we see a very interesting form of *indirect sharing of deviance*. People talk about such things and write about them, partly on the basis of experience, so that all the adult members of the society actually wind up with certain workable ideas and behavior patterns that they can use to do such things without having direct, knowing communication with anyone else doing the same things.

But there are many forms of deviance which become the basis of a larger group life, cut off from the bigger group, a deviant subculture that may even be purposefully walled off from the bigger society by secrecy which deliberately protects the deviant life from public scrutiny. (In a general way, any private space, or space partially walled off from public scrutiny, becomes a space where deviance from public rules takes place. One's home is where one "lets one's hair down"—where one does not have to be so chary of rules as in public settings. As Norman Denzin and others have argued, families and groups of friends always allow each other a wide range in *social variation* from the public rules, without defining as deviant what would be so defined in public situations.)

If the deviant behavior spreads further, if more and more people join, then they can begin to form a *social movement* to try to protect themselves better from the bigger society and, if they become big enough or powerful enough, to try to change the general rules of the society (such as laws) so that their form of behavior is first accepted and then possibly the new morality—in which case the traditionalists will now become the oppressed (shamed) deviants. (In the early days of a movement, deviants will cry for equality of treatment [all we want is the right to live our own way], but if they become dominant they almost always try to enforce their own rules by shaming the erstwhile shamers.)

The normal situation of any particular group in our society is much more complex than this simple process reveals. Our society is today in a state of what social scientists like Raymond Aron call *multipolar pluralism and conflict.* That means that there are many (multiple) groups with different kinds of rules or different constructions of the meanings of the same rules. In the case of basic rules, like those governing public nudity, the violators are still a distinct minority and, since no civilization has had widespread public nudity (not even Greece), it seems likely they will remain a minority. But even on a basic rule like this there are many different social groups in conflict over exactly how the rule should be applied in concrete situations. As we shall see in the study of the nude beach, there are quite a number of groups with different perspectives of feelings, rules (rule constructions), and ideas about the nude beach. We find that, in order to understand what is happening to this kind of behavior and what is likely to happen to it in the future, we have to determine how these many different groups look at it and act toward it. We must, as we say, study it *multiperspectively,* from the many different perspectives involved in the social conflict over deviance.

One very quickly sees that the meanings of the rules and rule violations (deviance) are multiperspectival. What is evil for one group is seen as necessary for another; and a third sees both above groups as evil; a fourth refuses to think about it; and so on. In a society as fragmented into conflicting groups as America and almost all other Western societies to a lesser degree are today, we must always expect that *a study of deviance will actually be a study in multiperspectival conflict over what is the right rule, both in general and in concrete situations; what it means in a concrete situation; and what should be done about those labelled as violators (deviants).* Moreover, we almost inevitably find that the conflicts over these definitions and actions toward deviance become highly political and are fought out with all the usual devices of politics today—lies, frontwork, mass media public relations (involving massive frontwork and considerable lying), demogoguery, reactionary stigmatization by those who come to feel deeply threatened, and so on. We saw that all of these devices are swirling around the nude beach. Our study of the nude beach is, then, a study in *the politics of rule conflicts as well as it is a study of human nature in the human social condition.* That is why we see it as a microcosm of our bigger social world—it is a direct observation study of the total human being, from the most primitive feelings, communications, and actions of the human animals interacting with each other up to the more abstract world of mass media politics, legislation, police work, and adjudication and punishment by the imperial bureaucratic state.

Contrary to what one might expect, there is almost no major realm of human life not involved in our study of the nude beach. International investment? Nuclear energy? Environmental politics? Gold markets? Medicare? Racial conflict? Sexual conflict? Eastern religions? Milking unemployment programs? Marriage and divorce? Massage parlors? All of those and far more. We have learned immense amounts about things going on all over the world from our talks with people on the nude beach. These things have been of great importance to us in our own lives and in our other studies. It should be kept in mind that all of those things that concern Americans and other people today are part of the whole experience, the total situation, of the nude beach. But, of course, they are not dealt with much in this work. Here we are concerned with getting at the fundamentals, the beginnings, the foundations of human life on which all of those more abstract and complex forms of cultural and individual life are constructed. Here we are concerned primarily with the primal feelings, situated perceptions, rule uses, communications, thoughts, and actions of the naked human animal.

These particular human animals have, of course, been trained in the rules of modern civilization, but we believe we have been able to analyze human beings in this particular microcosm through their body communications and actions, and then to compare those with all else we know about primates through socio-biology, about human beings in other cultures, and about people in other situations in our own society to arrive at a reasonably clear picture of some crucial parts of the *foundation* of human life. By relying primarily on primal body communications and acts, and then using comparative analyses to control for cultural effects, we have been able to partially peel off that which is cultural to get at important parts of what is universal about the human being in human society—what we called *human nature in the human social condition.* We have done only part of that here, leaving more for other, more theoretical works. But this is the beginning.

About the Authors

JACK D. DOUGLAS is the author or editor of more than a dozen books on social conflict, problems, meanings, and research, especially in the field of deviance. All of his work is embedded in his own personal experiences. His mother was a barmaid, and as a child he moved among many of the subcultures of society. In reaction against them, he became a serious scholar, preferring books to people. Slowly, however, the unavoidable truths of the "real world" reasserted themselves in his life. Douglas believes now that deviance is an area in which one can get behind public fronts and see what's really going on in human nature. A professor of sociology at the University of California at San Diego, Douglas is married and the father of four children. Among his better-known books are *The Social Meanings of Suicide* (Princeton, 1971), *Investigative Social Research* (Sage, 1976), *Understanding Everyday Life* (Aldine, 1970), *Observations of Deviance* (1970) and *Research on Deviance* (1972, both Random House), and *American Social Order* (Free Press, 1970).

PAUL K. RASMUSSEN began an academic career because his family—all of whom had Master's Degrees or higher—expected him to do so. He began college as a pre-med student, but dropped out from boredom several years later to join the Peace Corps. When his Peace Corps hitch was up, Rasmussen turned to sociology in the hope that he would learn things which he could use to help other people, however several years of study convinced him that altruism was useless and if he could help anyone, it would be himself. Thus, he turned to the study of sexuality. *The Nude Beach* is his first book, and he is presently working on a study of massage parlor prostitution in fulfillment of a doctoral requirement at the University of California, San Diego. He has published a number of articles in the areas of marriage and family life, prostitution, and the news media.

CAROL ANN FLANAGAN was born and raised in El Sobrante, California, and in her entire life she has never lived more than twenty miles from the ocean. From the ages of 4-13, she took tap and ballet dancing lessons, but her athletic interests later shifted to modern dance, go-go dancing, belly dancing, then stripping. From 1968 to 1972 she attended the University of California at San Diego, graduating with a B.A. in cultural anthropology. When she wanted a career (at least temporarily), the choice between anthropology and exotic dancing held no dilemmas for her. She has danced in places as varied as Guam and Alaska, working a 9:00 p.m. to 5:00 a.m. day. Flanagan began regularly going to the nude beach in the summer of 1972, and when the beach was fairly isolated, she would use it to practice her dance exercises. She is presently thinking of returning to college to pursue an advanced degree, though she has not yet decided what her area of study will be.